Black Jews, Jews, and Other Heroes

How Grassroots Activism Led to the Rescue of the Ethiopian Jews

Howard M. Lenhoff

gefen
publishing house
JERUSALEM ◆ NEW YORK

Typesetting: Jerusalem Typesetting
Cover Design: S. Kim Glassman

ISBN 978-965-229-365-7

1   3   5   7   9   8   6   4   2

Gefen Publishing House, Ltd.
6 Hatzvi Street, Jerusalem 94386, Israel
972-2-538-0247
orders@gefenpublishing.com

Gefen Books
600 Broadway, Lynbrook, NY 11563, USA
516-593-1234
orders@gefenpublishing.com

www.israelbooks.com

Printed in Israel

Send for our free catalogue

CONTENTS

DEDICATION

1 dedicate this book to my mother-in-law, Dora Grossman (1892–1969). My wife, children, and I came to Israel for the first time in 1968 so that Dora could visit with her four cousins, Holocaust survivors from Poland. One sister had followed Dora to America. But in Europe my mother-in-law had lost her parents, all her other siblings, and the rest of her extended family.

Had she not decided to go to Israel, I doubt I would have gone there for a nine-month sabbatical at that stage of my career and of rearing my young family. But I did go and came to love the State of Israel and what it stood for. As a consequence of that first visit, I returned often and in the spring of 1974 became involved with the grassroots effort to save the Jews of Ethiopia.

Dora died a few months after we returned from our first stay in Israel. Powerless to help her family in the Holocaust, I think my mother-in-law would have taken some consolation had she known that she would lead her son-in-law and daughter to contribute to the preservation of Jewish lives.

PREFACE

This memoir focuses primarily on the grassroots efforts initiated by the American Association for Ethiopian Jews (AAEJ) from the time of its incorporation in 1974 until May 21, 1991, when in one day Israel flew fourteen thousand Ethiopian Jews out of Addis Ababa and brought them to Israel. Although there had been sporadic efforts to promote the immigration of the Ethiopian Jews to Israel since the turn of the century, there had never been a sustained campaign until the AAEJ became involved.

As a member of the board of directors of the fledging AAEJ, I saw my role as that of helping to develop a solid national infrastructure for the organization so that the immigration of the Ethiopian Jews would be inevitable once the world political climate was favorable. I always trusted that the Jews of Ethiopia would eventually reach Israel. Why? Because of the people of the Jewish State. They sacrifice much to live out the principle that Israel is the homeland for the Jewish people, especially for those from endangered Jewish communities.

Although this book highlights the accomplishments of trailblazers and heroes who took great personal physical risk to see the Ethiopian Jews join their brethren in Israel, it also describes actions and attributes of the movement's elected leaders whose responsibility it was to build the framework to back those working in the field.

The AAEJ was fortunate to have had three diverse presidents, each suited for a new phase in the development of the organization. We shared several characteristics, however. Unlike presidents of many Jewish organizations, the AAEJ trio could not be co-opted.

None cared about the typical community honors and awards. All were "hands-on" active presidents who either did not have a paid staff or did not leave decision-making to staff. None depended upon "the establishment" for a salary or monetary gain: Berger was retired, I had academic tenure, and Shapiro was financially independent.

Our differing styles of leadership, which reflected our varied professional backgrounds and environments, fit the changing times remarkably well. Graenum Berger, our "pit bull," was a sharp, tough-minded former leader and teacher in the field of Jewish social services and community centers, as well as a consultant to the giant Federation of Jewish Philanthropies of New York. He knew the establishment players, how they worked, and how to get their attention. With the help of Jeffrey Stone, he organized and incorporated the AAEJ so it would have a life of its own. He gave the AAEJ focus and was relentless in his attack. He never would let go, and the establishment knew it.

As his successor, I quickly learned from Berger where the problems lay, but my background and approach were unlike his. When I became president I knew little about the Jewish establishment or its workings. I was a professor recognized for my zeal in dealing with major issues, whether in research or education. Because students saw that I enjoyed working with them, many volunteered to join me in study, research, or service. As an academic and research administrator working with prima donna scholars, I had learned to avoid appointing "democratic" committees. Instead I found success in approaching colleagues individually, presenting alternatives for solving problems, and gaining consensus before issues were brought to a vote. In addition I enjoyed writing, and with the help of my wife, was able to publish many articles about the Ethiopian Jews and the need to rescue them. These were skills I used to expand the base and support of the AAEJ.

At that stage of organizational growth, Nate Shapiro took over. Nate is extremely bright, dedicated, and modest. But on top of that, he knew how to make and raise money. That gave him special clout with the establishment and with politicians. Because the AAEJ had been growing exponentially and because he could not abandon his business, he developed an excellent staff, led first by LaDena Schnapper and later by Dr. Will Recant. Nate did what Graenum and I could not do, and he did it, I think in part, because of his background as an investor. A venture capitalist never knows which investment is going to pay off, but if one out of ten does, it may be enough to achieve success.

During Nate's years as president, many groups and individuals came to the AAEJ for money. To some I would not have given a nickel, while others I would have supported had I felt comfortable that they could truly help. Nate, however, was more daring. He was determined to have the AAEJ reach its objective regardless of the costs. Some of the projects he approved I thought were flops, but when it came to such decisions as providing medical aid to the Ethiopian Jews in the Sudan, and allowing Susan Pollack to facilitate the movement of eighteen thousand Ethiopian Jews to Addis Ababa – a decision that made Operation Solomon possible – he was on target. In fact, so much on target, that with our goal of rescue having been reached, we closed shop and dissolved the AAEJ in 1993.

Did we quit too soon?

ACKNOWLEDGMENTS

Over the years and during the writing of this book, many individuals have shared with me their firsthand experiences and documents: Baruch Tegegne, Rahamim Elazar, Avraham Yerday, Zecharias Yona, Aklum Feredeh, Zimna Berhane, Rahamim Yitzchak, Ben Baruch Ishaiahu, Yitzchak Yieyas, David Seyum, LaDena Schnapper, Barry Weise, Dr. Will Recant, Nate Shapiro, Edith Everett, Henry Rosenberg, Barbi Weinberg, Jeffrey Stone, Sandy Leeder, Eli Halpern, Sidney Weiner, Jane Fellman, Moshe Bar Yuda, Dawn Calabia, Yehuda Shapiro, Rabbi Jeffrey Kaye, Miriam Goldberg, Phil Blazer, Martin Levin, Gabriel Cohen, Rabbi Yitz Greenberg, Congressman Stephen Solarz, Chanan Lehman, and Professor Haggai Erlich.

Sadly, some of my colleagues are deceased. These include Bill Halpern, Mildred Rosenberg, Henry Everett, Professor Menachem Rahat, Ambassador Hanan Aynor, Murray Narell, Haim Halachmi, Mordechai Paran, Herb Brin, Jack Fishbein, Rabbi Robert Bergman, Eleanor Kahn, and the patriarchs of the movement: Yona Bogale, Professor Aryeh Tartakower, and Graenum Berger with his wife Emma.

I also thank my academic colleagues, Dr. Stephen Spector and Dr. Mitchell Bard, for their encouragement and suggestions. There are many others who are referred to in this volume, especially rabbis and editors of the independent Jewish press. I apologize to those whose names I may have omitted; I look forward to hearing from you and will be happy to acknowledge you should there be a second edition.

My thanks to Murray, Hana, Ilan, and the late Dror Greenfield for urging me to write *Black Jews, Jews, and Other Heroes*. As publishers of Gefen Publishing House, their commitment to the Beta Yisrael is evident; they already have published three other books dealing with the Ethiopian Jews, as well as additional books and pamphlets specifically prepared by them to assist the Ethiopian Jews in Israel. Without their support and encouragement, I probably would not even have attempted to present this material. I thank Dorit Raviv for her overall assistance, Kezia Raffel Pride for her help in the final editing of the typescript, Rachel Trager and Liat Tal for proofreading the galleys, cover artist Kim Glassman, and Smadar Belilty for tying together the multiple components necessary to produce the final volume.

Thanks to Barry Hannah, writer and professor, for his encouragement, and his model of elegant prose. Because he allowed my wife and me the privilege of participating in his classes at "Ole Miss," this book had fewer adverbs and more action.

At first the book was evolving as a series of relevant anecdotes, and it was not until I showed a draft to Jerry Weaver, the unheralded hero of Operation Moses, that it took sharp focus. Because Jerry Weaver is also a trained scholar with much experience working with U.S. and international governmental agencies, he has been an invaluable resource in helping me stay close to my main theme: to show how a grassroots organization evolved to become an effective political entity. Lastly – but in reality, firstly – I thank once again my wife, Sylvia, who has been my collaborator in another book and in a half-dozen papers in the history of science, for her invaluable editing and for tolerating my obsession to complete this work on the AAEJ and the rescue of the Jews of Ethiopia.

PART I

ABOUT THIS BOOK

CHAPTER 1

We've Won:
An Opening Epilogue

"Howard, I want you to be the first to know. The Israelis pulled it off. They took over fourteen thousand Falashas from Addis to Israel in the past day. The last two airplanes of immigrants have just left the ground. LaDena is with them. You can relax now. We've won!"

That call, with additional details, came about 5 A.M., Sunday morning, May 26, 1991. It was from Will Recant, our young, dependable executive director of the American Association for Ethiopian Jews (AAEJ) in Washington, D.C. Picking up the phone, I sensed that the message dealt with the Ethiopian Jews. Calls from Israel or Africa seemed always to come before sunrise.

My emotion at the news was overwhelming. We had known something was up but didn't know when the rescue would be completed. Since the beginning of 1991, Israeli planes had been secretly transporting about a thousand Ethiopian Jews to Israel per month. Yet many more remained in Addis Ababa waiting to leave. The window of opportunity through which the Ethiopian Jews were escaping seemed about to slam shut.

The government of Israel had made a deal with the Marxist regime of Ethiopia to take out all of the Ethiopian Jews. But in the spring of 1991, a decade-long civil war seemed about to end with the overthrow of the Marxist government. By May, the rebels were at the gates of Addis. We had no idea what would happen if the rebels took over the city before the rest of the Ethiopian Jews

1

there could leave for Israel. To learn from Will Recant that most of the Ethiopian Jews who had been waiting in Addis were now safely in Israel brought on an overpowering sense of thankfulness and relief.

That call brought closure to an eighteen-year saga which had affected my family, my friends, my health, and my career. We simply had not been able to live a normal life until my obsession with the rescue of the Jews of Ethiopia was over, until most all were living in Israel. I had become, as author Meyer Levin put it, another "*meshugah la'davar*" (one crazed with a goal), that of rescuing the black Jews of Ethiopia.

*   *   *

The call ended. As I sat quietly in the dark, images tumbled in my mind going back to the beginnings of the struggle to save the Ethiopian Jews. There was the joy in 1980 of watching the first group of four hundred Ethiopian Jewish immigrants celebrate their arrival in Israel with drums and primitive string instruments they had just made, dancing with their backs undulating at a feverish pace while the children sat around in a circle and clapped, and the old women emitted repetitive yodel-like shrieks with their tongues wagging from side to side.

Then I saw myself later racing down the halls of the Great Synagogue in Jerusalem, acting as the liaison between the two feuding chief rabbis of Israel regarding the "conversion" of new male immigrants. Scenes surfaced of rabbis, businessmen, and college students carrying signs as we marched outside the plush Israeli consulate on Wilshire Boulevard in Los Angeles to protest Israeli inaction, and, following that demonstration, being invited to join the Israeli junior staff members of the consulate for tea and cookies!

An image flashed of a visit with the aging bearded chief *kes* (priest) of the Ethiopian Jews who had recently arrived in Israel and was living in the port city of Ashdod. It was my fiftieth birthday, and, in *Ge'ez*, the holy language of both the Jews and Christians of Ethiopia, he blessed my bowed figure.

Memories came of my first meeting with Prime Minister Menachem Begin in his shabby office building across the way from the splendid architecture of the Israeli Knesset (parliament building). He seemed genuinely moved when presented with a petition signed by fifty thousand American Jews asking for the rescue of the Ethiopian Jews.

The flashbacks continued: sitting in a café in the desert town of Beersheba, teeming with Bedouins and immigrants from India, Morocco, and the Middle East, listening to an Israeli soldier, an Ethiopian Jew, as he suggested an escape route from Africa modeled after the one he had used. Then in a surprising juxtaposition, the anger in the face of an incensed millionaire when he grabbed me by the tie and shirt collar and told me to stop interfering with organized Jewish fund-raising in Los Angeles.

My mind shifted to a raucous meeting in Tel Aviv of concerned Israeli citizens and government bureaucrats clashing over issues of rescuing Ethiopian Jews. There, in the winter of 1978, I first witnessed the guts and commitment of Murray Greenfield storming out of the session when a senior government official demanded secrecy on all issues regarding the Ethiopian Jews.

The end of Operation Solomon brought thoughts of comrades who did not live to enjoy the moment: Berkeley graduate student Bill Halpern, who went to Africa in 1978 and 1979 for the AAEJ to prove that we could rescue Ethiopian Jews from the Sudan. He was killed in Kenya a few years later while trying to get one of his friends out of Ethiopia. Yona Bogale, an aristocratic-looking, goateed, educated Ethiopian Jewish elder who remained in Ethiopia to lead his people just before Operation Moses. He died in Israel. Murray Narell, a social worker always concerned about the underdog and the oppressed. He went to Africa in 1983 to help the AAEJ in its rescue program and died of cancer soon afterwards.

When I did not return to bed after Will's early-morning phone call, my wife came to inquire about the call. Blurting out the news, I choked and sobbed uncontrollably. She smiled and embraced me. She knew that, acting as relentless gadflies, the AAEJ had been important in spearheading this magnificent rescue of the Jews of Ethiopia. It had been our good fortune to participate in the greatest *mitzvah* of all, *pikuach nefashot*, "saving souls."

Who would have thought in 1974, when we first met Rahamim Elazar, a scrawny Ethiopian Jewish teenager, at a youth *aliyah* high school in Alonei Yitzchak, near the coastal wine-producing town of Zichron Yaakov, Israel, that my life as a university research scientist would be turned topsy-turvy, that we would become part of a grassroots movement which eventually saw major public policies change, sometimes 180 degrees, and finally that Rahamim's extended family of over ninety thousand souls would be citizens of Israel? But this is exactly what happened.

*   *   *

As you read this book, may you share the drama, the challenges and the heartaches we experienced along the way, and our sheer ecstasy when we learned that we had saved lives, sometimes one at a time and sometimes by the thousands. There is no thrill like it.

The younger reader may find in this book a paradigm for progressive activism. There is hardly a time when the survival of a population, Jewish or non-Jewish, is not in danger. Described here is how a small group of political activists working in a democracy, like the United States, can convince another democracy, such as Israel, to use its resources and risk its personnel to rescue an endangered population. Rabbi Hillel wrote: "To save a soul is to save a nation." That is a good start. What Israel did with the loving coaxing of the AAEJ activists was literally to save a nation.

CHAPTER 2

Meet the AAEJ

Contrary to the popular folk wisdom that no Jewish organization ever goes out of existence voluntarily, ...in June [1993] the
board of the American Association for Ethiopian Jews voted
to cease its operations at the end of the year. The executive
director [Dr. Will Recant] explained that "all of the Jews are
out of Ethiopia, that any stragglers are free to come and go
as they please. Rather than metamorphose into something
else, we decided to stick to our original guns [to preserve the
ancient Jewish community of Ethiopia and to help get them
to Israel]."

– American Jewish Year Book 1995, p. 178

History of the American Association for Ethiopian Jews (AAEJ)

Seldom has a small grassroots organization polarized American
Jewry as did the American Association for Ethiopian Jews (AAEJ)
from 1974 through 1991, and seldom has a grassroots organization
been so successful. It started with a group of activists determined
to help the threatened Beta Yisrael (Ethiopian Jews, Falashas) fulfill the dream of rejoining their brethren in the Jewish melting pot
of Israel. The AAEJ members soon were joined by college students,
American rabbis, editors of the independent Jewish press, and other
believers in Zionism. Often opposing them were leaders and executive directors of powerful Jewish organizations claiming to speak
for American Jewry and asking for our unwavering trust in their
judgment and that of functionaries of the Jewish Agency and of
the government of Israel.

Soon after the creation of Israel in 1948, and before the AAEJ was incorporated in 1974, a number of individuals, mostly Israelis, had advocated for the *aliyah* (immigration to Israel) of the Beta Yisrael community. But those noble sporadic and individual efforts were insufficient to provide the sustained pressure needed to convince key bureaucrats in the government of Israel to act.

By incorporating the AAEJ in 1974, Graenum Berger established an organization that made it possible for growth and change over the years not dependent upon only current individual activists. In addition, he knew the Jewish establishment and how it operated. He was informed and articulate both in speech and in his writings. He made certain we stayed focused.

What was my role in this memorable saga? Not as a swashbuckling hero who secretly goes to Africa and rescues Ethiopian Jews under the most dangerous conditions. But some of my colleagues are heroes who did just that. Not as a wealthy, well-connected figure able to secure major funds from associates for our projects. Nor was I experienced in working with politicians, an essential skill for convincing governments to back controversial activities. Fortunately the AAEJ had leaders, staff, and activists who could handle those important tasks.

In hindsight, my role was to do those things which professors do best, or should do best: As researchers we get our facts straight to establish our credibility with our peers, and write accurately and clearly in order to convince granting agencies to fund us. As teachers, we try to inspire others to understand and learn, and even to follow our example. Finally, to improve the university, some of us take leadership roles and become adept in getting people to work together for a common cause, whether to win a research project, promote faculty harmony, or achieve some university goal.

My primary objective was to develop and strengthen the infrastructure of the AAEJ so that it would grow, attract committed and talented people, and be recognized as a significant force among Jewish organizations.

Second, we needed to gain the confidence of the Ethiopian

Jews living in Israel. Not only did they provide us with information about conditions in Ethiopia, but our working directly with them helped us win allies in our efforts to press the government of Israel to facilitate family reunification. Through our association with Ethiopian residents of Israel, we also provided resources and techniques assisting them to press their case for bringing their families to Israel. Up until the winter of 1977, Graenum Berger made most of the AAEJ's contacts with the Israeli Ethiopian Jews; there were about 170 of them then. I took on a greater role in this work after Prime Minister Begin brought to Israel a total of 122 new immigrants in August and December 1977. Once hundreds started to come to Israel from the Sudan, Murray Greenfield and Rahamim Elazar became indispensable as the AAEJ's liaisons to the Ethiopian Jewish community in Israel.

To bring about recognition of the AAEJ as a significant force among Jewish organizations, we needed to enlist the help of American rabbis, the editors of the few hundred regional Jewish newspapers in North America, and the editors of key Israeli newspapers as well. We labored to convince the membership of major American Jewish organizations that they too must participate in this struggle. To achieve these objectives, we needed to take extreme care that we did not attack the governments of either Israel or Ethiopia directly. If we were too harsh in our criticisms, our efforts might backfire, possibly endanger lives, and deter us from achieving the rescue which was our ultimate goal. Those were difficult agendas to juggle; we needed to be constantly on our toes and fully informed.

Once the AAEJ had built a solid infrastructure encompassing a wide support network of American Jews to carry out a long-term effort pressing for the rescue of the Ethiopian Jews, and once the world political climate was favorable, I believed it inevitable that the Ethiopian Jews eventually would reach Israel. The people of the Jewish State give their blood in the belief that their country is the homeland for the Jewish people, especially for endangered communities.

Its immigration objectives having been achieved, the board of directors of the AAEJ in 1993 voted to disband.

Problems of Getting an Accurate Picture of History

Professional research scientists recognize the importance of primary evidence in getting to the truth. That is easier to do in my field of "hard" science than it is in recapturing history where truth about the past can be elusive, difficult to entangle from differing subjective recollections. In researching recent history, the firsthand primary experiences and data of those who were involved are essential, but bring with them the concern best exemplified by the time-worn analogy of five blind men describing an elephant. Which single part of the elephant did they happen to touch and assume to be the whole animal: an ear, trunk, tusk, foot, or tail? Individuals who participated in certain parts of the saga of the rescue of the Ethiopian Jews, but who were not aware of other parts, tell limited, even biased accounts because of their circumscribed experiences.

Then there are the "experts" who played no active role, but derive their views from interviews. Although this journalistic approach, if done carefully, may be objective, such treatments rely on the selective memories and veracity of those chosen to be interviewed.

Let's switch from the riddle of the elephant to a culinary metaphor. To fully describe a cake, one needs to present the entire confection: the layers, the vertical slices, the components, the frosting.

In my slice of the cake, there are many layers, starting at the bottom with "Layer 1974" and ending with the top frosting of "Layer 1991," the final rescue. That slice incorporates evaluations of how various individuals of the AAEJ and other agencies interacted during the nearly eighteen years of my involvement. Thin vertical slices or thin layers of historical analyses, no matter how carefully they have been cut, are troublesome.

Up until now, the AAEJ leadership has presented only a few of its own in-depth accounts. One consists of the memoir of Graenum Berger, the founding president of the AAEJ, and his papers in the American Jewish Historical Society (AJHS). My narrative, as presented in this volume, overlaps somewhat with Berger's; my papers and documents will also be placed in the AJHS. Nate Shapiro, the last of the three AAEJ presidents, has already given his papers to the AJHS, but has not yet written a memoir. If he, Henry Rosenberg (the member of the AAEJ board who was deeply involved in a number of our rescue efforts), and Murray Greenfield (the AAEJ's key volunteer in Israel) write someday about their important work on behalf of the Beta Yisrael, we will get a fuller understanding of the part played by these key activists.

Some of Shapiro's contributions have been discussed in the following two recommended books. One is Professor Stephen Spector's *Operation Solomon: The Daring Rescue of the Ethiopian Jews* (Oxford University Press, 2005). The other is Dr. Mitchell Bard's *From Tragedy to Triumph: The Politics Behind the Rescue of Ethiopian Jewry* (Praeger, 2002). Much of Bard's material is based primarily on documents from my archives and from interviews he conducted while he was my research associate. We disagree a bit in our interpretations, but Bard presents the most accurate report of the earlier years of the struggle compared to books written on the subject by some journalists and revisionists.

Will we ever learn the full role, whether limited or extensive, of Israel's CIA, the Mossad? Probably not, and we probably never will have its entire story because of the Mossad's inherent secretive nature. The same may be said for the Jewish Agency for Israel and for the U.S. State Department. All these chronicles would be important elements in an accurate and complete slice of history.

None of the authors who have written on the rescue of the Ethiopian Jews knew the details of the critical role in Operation Moses played by Jerry Weaver of the U.S. government. In 2004 it was my good fortune to have Weaver tell me his complete story, including how his entry in 1982 into the rescue mission was a role catalyzed by an unexpected visit to the American embassy in Khartoum by AAEJ board member Henry Rosenberg.

Two Ways of Reading This Book

Initially the intention of *Black Jews, Jews, and Other Heroes* was to describe how a small grassroots organization, the AAEJ, achieved its objective: how it was able to convince five governments (Israel, the United States, the Sudan, Ethiopia, and the coalition which overthrew the Ethiopian Marxist government) that our goal of rescuing the Ethiopian Jews and getting them to Israel also would serve their political interests.

As the research and writing proceeded, however, it became apparent that this inspiring episode in modern Jewish history teaches us much about another major issue, the frailties of organized American Jewry and of Jews living elsewhere in the Diaspora, particularly in their relationship to Israel. The stream of events also helps to give us a better understanding of the difference between the State of Israel and the Government of Israel. After you read this book, you too may gain added insight into this important difference and how it plays out both domestically and internationally.

PART II

EVOLUTION OF AN AMERICAN ACTIVIST IN ISRAEL

CHAPTER 3

The Israeli Psyche

"OK, ha'ikar lazuz (the important thing is to keep moving)*."*
– Israeli soldier to Howard Lenhoff, December 1973

Zionism was not part of my vocabulary while growing up in the small factory town of North Adams, Massachusetts. Both of my parents were born in the United States. My grandparents were Orthodox Jews who came to this country from Latvia and Lithuania before the turn of the century. As far as we know, we had lost no primary relatives in the Holocaust.

For Sylvia, my wife, it was different. Her parents were ardent Zionists coming to the United States from the disputed lands between Poland and Russia. In World War I, her father volunteered and served as a member of the Jewish Brigade in Egypt and Palestine under England's General Allenby. Her mother, who was active in the Pioneer Women and other Zionist organizations in the United States, lost her parents and all but a handful of her extended family in the Holocaust. As a child, Sylvia attended *Talmud Torah* after school and on Sundays, and she studied at the Baltimore Hebrew College as a teenager.

In 1968, Sylvia's mother, who had never been able to visit Israel, was invited to attend the wedding of an Israeli-born child of one of her surviving cousins. At that time the National Institutes of Health awarded me a Career Development fellowship, which would provide salary while I carried out research at any major institution. We could join up with my mother-in-law as I took the opportunity to work in the laboratories of the two world-renowned Katzir brothers at the Weizmann Institute of Science in Rehovot, Israel.

13

During our nine-month visit in 1968–1969, we studied Hebrew and traveled throughout the country from the Golan Heights to the Sinai. Sharing our Sabbath afternoons with Jews of diverse cultures and homelands was a special joy. Like many other professional, assimilated American Jewish visitors before and after, I became emotionally committed to Israel.

Steeped in my newly gained Zionism, we returned to the United States where a new job was to begin at the University of California, Irvine. Within a few months, I was becoming an impassioned spokesman for Israel, sharing my newfound understanding of Israel's central role in preserving the sacred heritage of the Jewish people and of its unique place as a haven for any Jew, oppressed or not, wishing to live there. As my interest in Israel grew, I returned there in 1970 and 1971 to teach two special courses, one at the marine station in Eilat, and the other at the Hebrew University in Jerusalem.

Prickly and Sweet

During those years in Israel as a visiting scientist, it did not take me long to realize that most Israelis share a unique psyche shaped by their past, present, and outlook for the future. Some are Holocaust survivors, and some are transplants from other countries where they experienced varying degrees of anti-Semitism. They and their *sabra* (native-born Israeli) children are surrounded by authoritarian Arab states set on destroying the small Israeli democracy. The Israelis know that should they lose just one war, there would be no more Jewish state. Daily life is tough in general; most everyone's ears are glued to the hourly newscasts.

Israelis not only had to fend for themselves in war, we observed, but also needed "elbows" to deal with daily peacetime life in this unexpectedly bureaucratic state. Those same testy Israelis nevertheless would be the first to help a neighbor in need. As a minor, though typical example, during our first week in Israel, my wife was surprised by the way young people would often cut in front of her and others in the long lines in the bank; yet when she had finished her business there, and was trying to find her way to the electric company office, one of the same "rude" young men who had cut in near the front of her line, came to her and not only told her where the office was, but walked with her three blocks to that spot. That was the first of many instances which helped us understand another part of the Israeli psyche, the combination of "prickly" and "sweet." For those unfamiliar with the significance of *sabra*, an affectionate name signifying an Israeli native, it refers to the fruit of the prickly pear cactus, "prickly on the outside, sweet on the inside."

It is difficult to appreciate the Israeli psyche unless one has some understanding of Hebrew. Fortunately I learned a useful smattering of the language by attending a short Hebrew language class (*ulpan*) in Israel. It did not hurt that my wife and son were relatively fluent in the language. It was customary that Israelis give rides to soldiers who are hitchhiking. Once while we were out driving our cousin's beat-up 1955 Peugeot, a soldier approached the window of the car while we were at a stoplight and asked for a lift. We told him that we were just going two blocks before turning off the highway. He said, "*OK, ha'ikar lazuz*" (the important thing is to keep moving). He opened the back door and jumped in – Uzi and all – for the two-block lift. We will never forget his words, for they captured something special of the spirit of the typical Israeli. Nothing was impossible, if you had the will to reach your goal.

Sidestepping Terrorism

To get a deeper insight into Israeli attitudes, one may need to have a close call with the seemingly constant acts of terrorism that the Israelis face, never knowing when, whom, or where they will strike. Once when we were preparing for a trip to Jerusalem from Rehovot, my mother-in-law delayed our departure for about fifteen minutes. After we got on our way, we found the traffic stopped by a road block; we were told that just about a quarter hour earlier, a car of civilian travelers on the same road had been destroyed by terrorists.

When living in a student dormitory apartment in Jerusalem, we usually rode on bus #19 to destinations around the city. Not long after we returned to the United States, a #19 bus was destroyed by hidden explosives. Also in Jerusalem, we shopped a number of times at the colorful Mahane Yehuda market, a frequent target of terrorists, especially on Friday as shoppers prepared for the Sabbath.

An especially chilling and heartbreaking event occurred during our stay in 1974. I had just returned from attending a scientific conference near the small Israeli town of Maalot when the local high school was captured by terrorists who held about forty high school students as hostages. The terrorists with machine guns killed over a score of the teenagers as the Israelis tried to rescue them.

A few days before we were to take an El Al flight to Israel, security agents at the El Al transfer airport in Europe found a girl who had been duped by her Palestinian fiancée to bring a suitcase of presents to his parents in Israel; the suitcase had a hidden compartment with a bomb that would have destroyed both her and the rest of the travelers. We can read about these incidents in the newspapers as we have our morning coffee in the U.S., but the emotional impact is different if you live for an extended period under the threat of attack, death, and maiming.

Still there is a joyousness and richness to daily life in the land, and for many it is the dream of a lifetime to be there.

CHAPTER 4
Finding Rahamim

"Dear Father Howard," the short letter began. "I came to Israel a few days ago and am so happy here and with my job at the KOOR chemical plant in Beersheba. My brother told me that your gift made this move possible, and I give you my thanks. Can you help me bring my wife and two young daughters to Israel? They are still in Ethiopia and I worry about them day and night."

– *Telahun*

*T*o name the single Israeli who changed my life most dramatically would not be a difficult choice; that person was one of the dreamers, the Ethiopian Jew, Rahamim Elazar. The chain of events leading to our finding Rahamim began with an abbreviated sabbatical granted me in 1973 by the University of California. The Department of Chemical Engineering of the Israel Institute of Technology (the Technion) in Haifa accepted my request to spend that time as a visiting professor. Because my leave was for only six months, we decided to arrive on December 15, 1973, rather than in September. That decision was based on our prior experience at the Weizmann Institute. There we had found that most Israelis, including academics, were preoccupied for over a month with celebrating the autumn religious holidays, and that sustained serious work at the universities began once the holidays ended.

Aftermath of War
October of 1973 was different and tragic. On Yom Kippur day, while most Jews were in synagogues praying, Arab armies attacked

Israel. Our family arrived in December, soon after the major fighting had stopped. Most of the students and faculty of the Technion, however, were still at the fronts. There were no classes, the laboratories were virtually empty, and the Technion was "manned" by a skeleton staff of secretaries and a few older faculty. They greeted me with shocked but pleased expressions on their faces. "Why did you come to Israel now?" they asked. "Most of the other American professors who planned sabbaticals postponed or canceled theirs because of the war."

Early 1974 was not an easy time to be in Israel. The *matzav ruach* (morale) was at its lowest ebb as the people learned of large numbers of soldiers killed. We were surrounded by the personal loss and sadness. The war's full impact did not fully hit home with us until we took two trips, one to the Golan and the other as far as the new UN line in the Sinai. In the Sinai we saw over ten thousand damaged and abandoned tanks and other vehicles. Unexploded hand grenades and shells lay about on the Golan. We witnessed groups of Orthodox Jews preparing newly found corpses to be sent home for burial.

A number of questions stirred in me. Was this loss of life necessary? If it was necessary, was it worth it? Would it ever end? For several troubled months, such questions haunted me. Soon I found my answer, and it was one that spoke to me with new fervor: Israel *must* exist because it is the only country whose *raison d'être* is to be a haven for Jews.

Bring in all the Jews who want to come, I thought; the more the better for Israel. We considered taking out dual citizenship with the intent of probably moving to Israel at some point. We looked at property near a community of Yemenites who had befriended us. We explored a kibbutz, only to be told that a man of forty was too old to join.

My Path to the Beta Yisrael: Louis Rapoport and Hezi Ovadia
As that sad winter turned to spring, a well-researched article in the April 12, 1974, *Jerusalem Post* by feature writer Louis Rapo-

port caught my attention. It seemed that government bureaucrats responsible for implementing Israel's policy of open doors held it much wider for some Jews than for others.

Author Rapoport, an immigrant from California to Israel, pointed out that although the Jews of Ethiopia were living in extreme poverty and were suffering pogroms which resulted in destruction and death because they were Jews, fewer than two hundred Ethiopian Jews had been admitted to Israel. Could it be, as Rapoport suggested, that Israel's open door policy for Jews of the world, the "Law of Return," did not include the Jews of Ethiopia?

Just who were these people from Africa who were denied admittance to Israel under its Law of Return? We felt compelled to meet some. I wrote to Rapoport, asking him for the addresses and phone numbers of Ethiopian Jews living in Israel. It did not occur to me that most Ethiopian Jews living in Israel were too poor to own telephones, but Louis did send me a few names, addresses, and phone numbers. One having a telephone was Hezi Ovadia, a Jew who had immigrated to Israel from Aden. Hezi was not an Ethiopian Jew, but he once had lived in Ethiopia and he identified with the Beta Yisrael. At the time that Rapoport wrote his article, Hezi Ovadia was the head of the small community of 168 Ethiopian Jews living in Israel. In response to our call he invited us to meet him at his office in Tel Aviv.

Hezi was a towering figure, over six feet tall, with a trademark long black handlebar mustache. We later learned that he was viewed as an institution in Israel. For years he had been the army sergeant major who broke in new Israeli soldiers to basic training. He gave Sylvia and me a short history of the Ethiopian Jews, touching on their past and current problems. He focused especially on the controversy regarding whether they were true Jews or not. Hezi's contribution *vis-à-vis* the Sephardic chief rabbi, Ovadia Yosef, in this regard was a matter of special pride. He had gotten the Rabbi to state in writing a reaffirmation of the Jewishness of the Beta Yisrael (chapter 6). But mostly Hezi stressed the urgency of getting them out of Ethiopia and bringing them to Israel.

We asked him for the name and address of an Ethiopian Jew living closer to the home we were renting in Haifa. He told us of Rahamim Elazar, a young student living in a youth village not too distant. If we called the village office, they would arrange for us to meet him. Rahamim had managed to arrive in Israel a year and a half ago with the help of Arnold Sherman, an employee of El Al Airlines. Sherman, who later authored a book on Rahamim, had met him by chance on a trip he had taken to Ethiopia.

As we were preparing to leave, Hezi challenged us. "I have met many well-intentioned American Jews who wished to learn more about the Ethiopian Jews so they could help them. All but one fell by the wayside and never did anything. That one," he said, "was Mr. Graenum Berger of New York. You, Professor, I think will be the second." We smiled, thanked him for his kindness and trust, and headed back to Haifa.

Meeting Rahamim: The Professor Hooked
Maybe because some of my childhood playmates were African American, or because my first teaching position was at Howard University when serving in the Air Force in Washington, D.C., or maybe because in the '60s I had been involved in sit-ins in Miami, Florida, to force the county hospital to integrate its cafeterias, we acted at once on Hezi's suggestion that we meet Rahamim.

The next Sabbath afternoon we got into the 1955 balky blue Peugeot, which we called the "Sus" (horse), and made our way along the Mediterranean coast to Alonei Yitzchak to meet Rahamim. He was a scrawny nineteen-year-old who had arrived in Israel just over a year and a half ago. In our limited Hebrew, we started to introduce ourselves and tell him of the reason for our visit. Within a few minutes, he interrupted us and politely asked if we would prefer speaking English. We sensed right then that he was bright and courteous, and that we were going to have an enduring relationship.

Rahamim told us that he came from a traditional peasant family of ten, and that as a child he was the family sheepherder. He had learned to read and write English in the local school through a teacher from India. He learned Hebrew from a relative who had learned it in Israel. For a while he attended a missionary school, but had to pretend that he would convert to Christianity. Determined to further his education, he would walk five miles from his tiny village to a senior secondary school in Gondar. He said he had come to Israel to fulfill the dream of the Beta Yisrael to go to Jerusalem. Now that he had arrived, he wanted to get more education, find work, and earn enough money to bring his family out of Ethiopia to Israel.

His story made me imagine that my grandfather Lenhoff might have had similar thoughts when he arrived in the U.S. alone in 1895 (coincidentally on a ship named *Ethiopia!*), and then in 1897 earned enough money to bring over from Latvia my grandmother and their three children. My father was born in the U.S. a year later.

That was the first of three meetings we had with Rahamim in the spring of 1974. For the last one, in early June, he hitchhiked to Haifa to see us just before we were to return to California. When we asked him if there was anything we could do to help his people, we expected him to say that we should tell American Jews about thirty thousand Beta Yisrael suffering in Ethiopia and the need for Israel to bring them out. Not Rahamim. He had a specific and readily achievable goal. Could we get $1,000 and give it to Hezi Ovadia? Hezi would use the money to arrange for Rahamim's older brother, Telahun, to come to Israel. Telahun already had a passport and the necessary papers and could be one of a group of seven young Ethiopian men who were given permission by the Ethiopian government to work for the KOOR Industries of Israel. We promised him that we would send the money. We hugged and kissed four times, Ethiopian style, and he left to return to his school.

Back in California, I could not shake from my mind thoughts of this remarkably determined student, alone in Israel, his parents and seven brothers and sisters still trapped in Ethiopia. A month after we were back in the United States, we took $1,000 that we usually would have given to the United Jewish Appeal and other

Jewish charities and sent it to Hezi. In December 1974, we were elated to receive a letter and photograph from Rahamim's brother, Telahun, thanking us for saving his life and bringing him to Israel. My face dropped however, when I read that we had also contributed to separating a father from his family, for Telahun was asking for help to bring his wife and two daughters to Israel.

Thus began the commitment which consumed our lives for nearly two decades. Frequently when asked why I took on such an arduous task, about the only answer that rings true is *ki ani Yehudi*, "because I am a Jew."

Postscript

In August of 1977, three and a half years after our initial meeting with Rahamim, his parents, sisters and brothers, and Telahun's wife and daughters, arrived in Israel. At last Telahun's family was united, and a year later he had a son, whom they named Yisrael. In hindsight, I could have quit then, but it was too late! Hezi's prediction was on target. I was already past the point of no return.

CHAPTER 5

Learning from Israeli
Activists and Scholars

It would have been possible to bring all of the Falashas to Israel
in the days of Emperor Haile Silasse (sic). But nothing was done
to save them and bring them here. In the Department of Aliyah
of the Jewish Agency they knew where the winds were blowing.
They knew that the religious ministers in the government do not
see the Falashas as real Jews, while ministers from the secular
parties saw in the Falashas primitive types who would not succeed to be absorbed in a progressive, technological Israel.

– Remarks attributed to former Israeli
ambassador to Ethiopia, Hanan S. Aynor,
December 17, 1982, in the Israeli daily Haaretz

During my many visits to Israel in the years 1975 to 1982, most of
my time was spent with individuals representing virtually every
aspect of Israeli society. Countless hours were spent getting the
resident Ethiopian Jews to unite and speak with one voice. To understand their needs required my visiting Ethiopian Jews in their
homes and in the absorption centers. To learn about problems
faced by other immigrants from non-Western countries, I sought
the advice of Israelis from Yemen and India. Teachers and social
workers were particularly helpful. There were numerous meetings with Israeli pro-Beta Yisrael organizations, comparable to
the AAEJ. To establish possible contact with Ethiopian officials,
Rahamim arranged meetings with the clergy of the two Ethiopic
churches in Jerusalem.

To try to crack the censorship imposed by the Government of Israel regarding the *aliyah* of the Ethiopian Jews, I held press conferences and met individually with members of the Israeli press to tell them how Americans thought about the issues. I sought the help of Israeli organizations, such as WIZO, and of Israeli academics to start social programs and to carry out surveys. When leaders of American delegations came to Israel for major meetings, I met with many of them to urge their support for hastening and increasing the *aliyah*. And whenever the opportunity arose, I would chat with Israelis on buses, in stores, and at family gatherings to get a sense of their concerns.

What I did not expect was the accessibility of high-ranking officials to non-establishment visitors like me. No significant problems were encountered arranging meetings with members of the Knesset, officials of the Jewish Agency, ministers of the prime minister's cabinet, and the deputy prime minister. There were sessions with each of the two chief rabbis to try to resolve problems of the token circumcision. Most important were opportunities to speak directly with Prime Minister Begin and his military advisor, General Poran, about plans for rescue from the Sudan.

Throughout this book, I present details of many of these interactions with Israelis, both man-in-the-street and prominent. This chapter, however, focuses on one special group. They are Israeli scholars and activists who provided me with important background information and helped to clarify the problems I would face in my quest to achieve the goals of the AAEJ. The first of these figures may surprise you. He is my scientific colleague, who also then happened to be the president of Israel.

The Professor President Tells It as It Is

Little could I have guessed in 1968 on my arrival in Israel as a scientific guest of Professor Ephraim Katchalski-Katzir, that in ten years we would be meeting in a quite different capacity while he was president of Israel. But that is exactly what happened on January 5, 1978, at the president's residence. Professor Aryeh Tartakower, chair of the Israel Committee for Ethiopian Jews (ICEJ), responding to my request, accompanied me. The president was warm and welcoming. When we began to discuss the Ethiopian Jews, he stated the official stance of the government of Israel, that Israel no longer had relations with Ethiopia. He recommended that the AAEJ lobby such countries as Poland and Romania to influence the Ethiopians. "They have relations with Ethiopia and are guilty for the way their people treated the Jews during World War II."

He also suggested that the AAEJ should focus on helping with absorption of the Ethiopian Jews into Israeli society. Responding that the AAEJ was small and had little funds, I asked him to influence the Jewish Agency to increase its funding for absorption of the Ethiopian Jews, because American Jews give so much money to the UJA for the Jewish Agency to spend on absorption. He said, "Are you telling the Jewish Agency how to allocate its funds? Why should the *sochnut* (Jewish Agency) give its funding to the Ethiopians rather than to the settlers of Yamit in the Sinai?" [Those settlers had been evicted from their homes in order for Israel to fulfill its part of the Egyptian-Israeli peace agreement.]

Like most politicians, he asked for our trust. That seemed an odd response from a scientist whose arguments are based on facts. The facts showed that since 1975 few Ethiopian Jews had arrived in Israel. Jews were dying in Ethiopia and not in Russia and Syria. Would he use his good influence?

Then came the telling moment of that meeting. President Katzir asked me, "If you were president of Israel, what would you do? What would be more important? Protecting the lives of millions of Jews in Israel, or endangering those millions in order to rescue twenty-five thousand other Jews?" He said it straight. Ephraim Katzir was more scientist than politician. He told me what others implied: the rescue of the Ethiopian Jews was of low priority because of the government's view, which I believe was in error, that it was more important to Israel not to rock the boat of its relationship with Ethiopia by pushing for the release of the Ethiopian Jews. It was simple geopolitics, probably mixed in with the biases of some powerful Israeli politicians. Such flawed geopolitics is hardly unique to Israel; analogous would be appeasement of dictatorial regimes promoted by the Arabists in the U.S. State Department based on concern about oil with the admixture of elements from Christian missionary views.

Our meeting ended on a friendly note. As I was getting my coat, Katzir and Tartakower were chatting in Hebrew, assuming that like many American guests of the president I knew little, if any, Hebrew. I overheard the president say, *"Aval yesh lo lev tov,"* meaning literally "But he has a good heart." Or idiomatically, "He means well, but he does not know what he is talking about."

I needed to speak with people who knew more about Israel's past relationship with Ethiopia than did the scientists Katzir and Lenhoff.

Moshe Bar Yuda

In my search for such individuals, Rahamim insisted that I meet with Israeli pro-Beta Yisrael activist author, Moshe Bar Yuda. I did and so did my research associate, Dr. Mitchell Bard.

A former lieutenant paratrooper and yeshiva student, Moshe Bar Yuda had been recruited to work for the Jewish Agency in Ethiopia to further educate the Beta Yisrael teachers who had been trained at Kfar Batya in Israel. The Jewish Agency began that program in 1954 when it opened a teacher training school in Asmara. The school, which had nearly sixty students, was supervised by Yehuda Sivan. In 1955, the agency had sent twenty-seven Beta Yisrael youngsters, male and female, to study at Kfar Batya, an Israeli community supported by the American Mizrachi Women.

The policy of the Jewish Agency, however, was a bit inconsistent and varied depending on the convictions, prejudices, and whims of its changing leadership (See Bard, *From Tragedy to Triumph,* 2002). Bar Yuda was recruited by Professor Haim Gevaryahu who had been a driving force in the agency behind the effort to educate the Beta Yisrael. There were problems with the program in Ethiopia, and the professor searched for an educated, religiously observant Israeli who was willing to work under the relatively primitive conditions in Ethiopia. Bar Yuda, though not well informed about the Ethiopian Jews, thought that it would be a romantic adventure and told Professor Gevaryahu that he would give him an answer after he had consulted with the chief rabbis to make certain he would not be breaking any Jewish laws by taking on that responsibility.

Ashkenazic Chief Rabbi Yitzhak Herzog told him it would be a *mitzvah* (moral duty), and if he were younger, he himself would go. The Sephardic chief rabbi, Yitzhak Nissim, on the other hand, would not agree and said, "Who needs these blacks?" Perplexed, Bar Yuda reported this mixed reaction of the chief rabbis to the head of his yeshiva, the son of former Chief Rabbi Avraham Kook who in 1921 wrote: "Brethren, please rescue our brothers, the Falashas, from extinction…. Rescue fifty thousand souls of the house of Israel, and thus strengthen our people." The yeshiva principal showed his father's letter to Bar Yuda and gave the former paratrooper his blessing. Bar Yuda soon smelled trouble when his supervisor, Tzvi Asael, said, "If it were up to me, I wouldn't send anyone to Ethiopia."

Arriving in Ethiopia, Bar Yuda found a mixed bag. On the one hand, he met Yona Bogale, a former student of the scholar and pro-Beta Yisrael activist Jacques Faitlovitch. Bogale was employed by the Jewish Agency in Addis Ababa and had distributed Hebrew educational materials as well as a book of Jewish holidays which he had translated into the Ethiopian tongue of Amharic.

But Bar Yuda found that the simple religious educational needs of the Beta Yisrael teachers were underfunded. He was particularly disturbed when he learned that the agency would not fund the printing of the Jewish calendar in Amharic. "They 'didn't have money,'" he said, "because of their ambivalent attitude toward the Ethiopian Jews."

When Bar Yuda started his job in Ethiopia late in 1957, he went to Asmara to meet with Yehuda Sivan. He was shocked when Sivan told him that the agency had decided to close the school. Nonetheless, he stuck it out, tried his best, and after four months was dismayed even more when he learned that Professor Gevaryahu was no longer with the Jewish Agency. Not only had the agency's policy in regard to the Beta Yisrael in Ethiopia changed, but Moshe Bar Yuda did not receive his salary for five months. In addition, the Jewish Agency refused to fund a school budget he had submitted that was based on a survey of needs he had completed, nor did they pay the salaries of nine teachers who had been taken to Israel, educated in Kfar Batya, and sent back to Ethiopia to teach. Those Beta Yisrael teachers were stuck once again without jobs in the impoverished Ethiopian villages.

Bar Yuda returned to Israel after the first year of his two-year contract and sued the Jewish Agency for not fulfilling the terms of the contract. He won his settlement, but continued to be angered that the nine teachers from Kfar Batya did not get any compensation. In 1958 the Jewish Agency, because of "insufficient funds," closed all of the twenty-seven schools it had started in Ethiopia except the one in Ambober.

It was too late, however. The seeds that had been planted only increased the desire of the Beta Yisrael to immigrate to Israel. And now the Ethiopian Jews had in the ex-paratrooper a committed activist to promote their *aliyah*. Moshe Bar Yuda recently lamented that "if only Israel had acted in the earlier years, all of the Ethiopian Jews could have been brought to Israel for the fraction of the cost of Operations Moses and Solomon and without the tragic loss of lives that occurred during those years." He was not the first to make that claim.

Bar Yuda referred to the late Professor Norman Bentwich, who had gone to Ethiopia in response to an invitation from Dr. Nahum Goldmann, then president of the World Jewish Congress. Bentwich belongs in the direct line of pro-Beta Yisrael activists following Faitlovitch and Haim Ben Asher (see below). Bentwich had excellent credentials: Professor of International Relations at Hebrew University, and former Attorney General of the Mandatory Government of Palestine. Bentwich had helped prepare the constitution of Ethiopia. He got along well with key players: the Israeli Foreign Ministry, Yona Bogale, and Emperor Haile Selassie of Ethiopia. The emperor told Bentwich that he did not oppose a group of Ethiopian Jews going to Israel. When President Ben-Zvi of Israel heard of the Bentwich-Selassie agreement, he proposed that about a hundred Ethiopian Jews, including some who already lived in Israel, begin a settlement in the Negev.

According to Moshe Bar Yuda, the Ethiopian emperor had agreed to another Bentwich proposal, that Ethiopia would accept $50 per every Ethiopian Jew who wanted to leave. This was not unusual in Jewish history; many Jews have been allowed to buy their way out of a country. Years later, in 1991, President Mengistu of the Ethiopian Marxist government received $26 million to release twenty thousand Beta Yisrael. That was too much and too late.

Advice from a Scholar of Ethiopian History

Rahamim was a hard taskmaster. He also wanted me to meet a professor at Tel Aviv University's Shiloah Center specializing in modern Ethiopian history, Haggai Erlich. The professor was Rahamim's mentor while he pursued and achieved his bachelor's degree in African and Mideastern Studies with the aid of an AAEJ scholarship. Eager to get Erlich's objective and blunt opinion of the current political situation in Ethiopia and his views on whether or not the AAEJ was endangering the Beta Yisrael in Ethiopia, I questioned him with some trepidation. Although we were both academics, he was a scholar in an area where I, a professor and researcher in the biological sciences, was no scholar but rather an activist. Not wanting to push, I felt it necessary to walk the same thin line as when consulting with Professor Wolf Leslau of UCLA, one of the leading scholars on the Ethiopian Jews. Systematically, Professor Erlich gave me a better understanding of the complexities of the new Marxist government of Ethiopia.

It was at a later meeting with Professor Erlich, however, that he got to the heart of the problem when he said that Israel "could be a bridge to Ethiopia for the United States," a scenario which the

AAEJ could encourage with our ties with Congress. He was right. The U.S. made a major mistake in the mid-1970s when it dropped its long-standing ties with Ethiopia, thereby allowing the Russians and Cubans to fill the political vacuum it had created there. Israel was accustomed to playing similar roles when assisting other African governments who felt it better to get aid from Israel rather than be indebted to one of the superpowers.

Erlich then said it would be possible to get President Mengistu of Ethiopia to make a deal to release Ethiopian Jews for cash, just as he had done for arms with Begin in 1977. Doctor Erlich said the key would be to ask for "family reunification," which even the Russians allow. When could we do it? "Right now," he said. That was in 1980. In 1989, Israel reestablished its embassy in Addis Ababa, and soon afterwards a steady flow of Beta Yisrael were flown monthly directly to Israel. Only then it was much more expensive (chapter 21).

Former Ambassador to Ethiopia Speaks Out

Hanan S. Aynor was the last Israeli ambassador to Ethiopia before Haile Selassie broke relations with Israel under Arab pressure triggered at the time of the 1973 Yom Kippur War. Before that Aynor had been with Israel's Ministry of Foreign Affairs, serving in various posts, as its chargé d'affaires in Leopoldville, ambassador to Senegal and to Gambia, and delegate to the UN General Assembly. When our acquaintance began, he was a Fellow of the Truman Institute at the Hebrew University of Jerusalem.

Much of what he told me during our meetings, about half a dozen in all, has been summarized in an article published on December 17, 1982, in the Israeli daily *Haaretz*. That article, written by Mordecai Artzi'eli, does not mention Aynor by name, but refers to him as a "high-ranking Israeli diplomat who served in the Israeli embassy in Addis Ababa in the early 1970s." That diplomat could be none other than Hanan Aynor; the comments published in the article match almost word-for-word remarks made to me by Aynor, and he was the ambassador to Ethiopia during the time referred to by Artziēli. I quote from the article because, first, it is more credible than my notes, and second, Artziēli and his translator write elegantly. Regarding the missed opportunities to have the Beta Yisrael immigrate to Israel and the opposition to that immigration, see the quote by Aynor from the *Haaretz* interview printed in italics at the head of this chapter.

In a dialogue regarding an agreement between the governments of Israel and Ethiopia to release Ethiopian Jews in exchange for arms, which allowed 120 Beta Yisrael to immigrate to Israel in 1977, Aynor commented: "That *aliyah* was intended to throw sand in the eyes of good American Jews who pressured the government of Israel to act to save the Falashas, and also to quiet the conscience of Israel itself."

In response "to the Jewish Agency's claim that the Emperor Haile Silasse [sic] opposed the immigration of the Falashas to Israel and therefore it was not possible [for Israel] to bring them out," Aynor responded:

> And if he [the emperor] opposed it, did we try to change his position on the subject? On other subjects which were important to us he changed his attitude. When in the course of time, it will be possible to open the protected files of the Foreign Ministry concerning our relations with Ethiopia, it will become clear how and in what circumstances the Emperor changed his views and attitudes many times in our favor. But why must I respond to your question? Greater ones than I have answered it. When Foreign Minister Abba Eban was asked why Israel didn't encourage the immigration of the Falashas, he answered that the subject was never significant and never posed a difficulty in our relations with Ethiopia. You can examine his words. They were published in the *Jerusalem Post* and never denied.

Aynor concluded the interview with his views regarding the government of Israel's policy of "silent diplomacy" regarding the immigration of the Ethiopian Jews:

The Falasha problem, even today, does not stand high in the list of priorities of the government. Governments of Israel, in the past and in the present, when they wanted, knew how to make difficult decisions and also knew how to carry them out. The decision to liberate the Entebbe captives was not easy. The decision to bomb the nuclear reactors in Iraq was not simple. There were still other difficult endeavors the execution of which was complicated, projects about which Israel has not publicized one word, and rightfully. [On the question of the immigration of the Falashas, the] government simply needs to decide.

The *Haaretz* interviews were fascinating, revealing, and in agreement with my conversations with Ambassador Aynor. Apparently the United States Department of State also found them of interest because my copy, thanks to the U.S. Freedom of Information Act, came from a declassified document in the State Department's archives!

Aynor's advice to me in our frequent meetings was in line with the *Haaretz* article. The ambassador was not simply letting off steam from his disappointment about the results of his years in Addis Ababa. He was genuinely concerned about the fate of the Ethiopian Jews and had thoughtful ideas on many aspects of the problem. Like Professor Erlich, Aynor believed that Ethiopia would like to use Israel as its intermediary to reach the Western powers; Ethiopians were wary of their relationship with Russia, but would not "beg" the United States for aid. There was a role for Israel to play. Aynor said that if Prime Minister Begin had given his backing, then he would have approached the Ethiopian leadership.

Regarding the illegal immigration of the Ethiopian Jews, Aynor felt that the Mossad was not structured for such activities and did not want to undertake them. The Mossad, he said, operates with a few at the top making the decisions, then passing down jobs to people in the field; some were their experienced operatives and others were recruited for the specific program. Planning for the *aliyah* of large numbers of people, on the other hand, said Aynor, required the coordination of many ministries of the government and at the highest level before the overall plan would be approved.

Pressing this interdisciplinary approach, Aynor said that it also would be needed for the absorption of the proposed new immigrants. He recommended that the AAEJ push the government of Israel for the formation of an "Authority" (*Reshut*) equivalent to a "Port Authority" or "Broadcasting Authority" that involved many wings of the government. A similar authority had been formed for Russian Jewry. Why not for the Ethiopian Jews?

I agreed with nearly all of Hanan Aynor's remarks to me, with the exception of those calling "the strident and critical remarks made by the AAEJ, especially by Graenum Berger," harmful because they "turned off" certain governmental and Jewish Agency officials. To accept that assertion, I replied, would mean that those irritated Jewish officials would sacrifice Jewish lives because of pride. That could not be so. Aynor had to be wrong.

Professor Aryeh Tartakower

At the time of my first involvement with the rescue of the Ethiopian Jews, Professor Tartakower was the head of the Israel Committee to help the Ethiopian Jews. He had been on the committee since the mid-1960s and knew most everyone who was active at that time, including Norman Bentwich and Moshe Bar Yuda. A prominent academic scholar in the social sciences, after he retired he was the head of the Jerusalem branch of the World Jewish Congress. When we first met he was close to eighty years old. White-haired and a short, humped old man, he was the ultimate gentleman.

Much of my time in Israel after 1974, I was the guest of my good friend Professor Menachem Rahat of Hebrew University, both at his home and in his laboratory where we collaborated under a grant awarded to us by the National Science Foundation U.S. – Israel Bi-national Fund. During those years Menachem's laboratory was in the Russian Quarter next to the Jerusalem police station and in walking distance of the Old City, Professor Tartakower's office, and the major Ethiopian Church. Hence, I made many a visit to

Professor Tartakower's office. He always treated me with warmth and hospitality.

A few years before Tartakower retired from his position with the World Jewish Congress, he phoned me at Professor Rahat's laboratory and asked me to come over to his office. I was startled when he confided in me his plans to retire as chair of the Israeli committee, and gave me a relatively large bundle which contained his personal papers and letters concerning the Ethiopian Jews. Then he gave me a draft of a book that he was writing regarding his work and views of the efforts to rescue the Ethiopian Jews. He said that he felt those pages would be in safe hands with me, and that I was free to use any of the materials with his blessings. Those papers will eventually go to the large archives now being collected by the American Jewish Historical Society.

The selection that follows presents some of his views of the years before the Beta Yisrael were declared Jews according to *halachah* and eligible under Israel's Law of Return. In those years, according to Bar Yuda and Aynor, the entire community of Beta Yisrael could have been brought to Israel legally and with little, if any, loss of life. Professor Tartakower wrote:

> After Bentwitch's death…new difficulties arose, caused this time, strangely enough, not by outside factors, but by bodies in charge of Jewish interests…. It soon appeared that important factors in Jewish life, including the Government of Israel and the Jewish Agency, not only did not support the idea of the Falasha aliyah, but actually opposed it. The issue seemingly was of a religious character, although some other factors may have played a role, too. Doubts were raised on the part of the religious Jewry, including the Chief Rabbinate of Israel, whether the Falashas can be considered as part of the Jewish people…. [T]hose doubts were shared…by several other Jewish bodies, including in the first place, the Government of Israel. So it happened that people who for centuries were struggling desperately for their Judaism, paying for it with hundreds of

thousands of lives, and being discriminated against both by the authorities and the majority population of their country, not only were not included among those authorized to come over to Israel in accordance with the existing Law of Return but were expressly excluded from it. They were to be considered as "Aliens" like other people of this category, to be admitted as tourists only for a short period of time upon deposit of a rather considerable amount of money as guarantee of their leaving the country afterwards and upon producing their return ticket to Ethiopia. Things went so far, that certain overzealous Israeli officials threatened to deport those Falashas who would be tempted to come over illegally. This policy was adopted by the Jewish Agency which refused any assistance to Falashas desirous to go to Israel.

Rabbi Yosef Adani

After 1974 during my visits in Israel, about half of my time was spent with Ethiopian Jews. Most were leaders and long-term Israeli residents. My major preoccupation was with helping them organize and speak with one strong unified voice. That was not easy. Also I met with new Beta Yisrael immigrants. What were the problems we could help them with? What information could they provide us that would be useful in stimulating the rescue of more Ethiopian Jews? There was one individual whose counsel, frequently sought, was valuable to us. That was Rabbi Yosef Adani, the first Ethiopian Jew to be ordained officially as a rabbi in Israel. The son of a Beta Yisrael *kes* (priest), Yosef Adani went to Italy to study for the rabbinate, completed his studies in Israel, and received his *smichah* (certification as a rabbi) from Sephardic Chief Rabbi Ovadia Yosef. He was employed as a religious teacher in a school in Israel.

Like any veteran Beta Yisrael citizen of Israel, Rabbi Adani's first concern was to rescue his people from Africa. But as a rabbi, he also was concerned for their spiritual lives and for their integration into the social milieu of Israel while preserving and sharing with the rest of Israel their distinct religious and social customs. This would be a difficult balance to achieve. In his words, he yearned that "the *olim chadashim* (new immigrants) become good citizens of Israel."

> Our people came to Israel because they feel it is their land and want to rejoin the rest of the people of Israel. But yet they come here and suffer because those responsible for helping them to absorb successfully into Israeli society do not understand the culture and needs.... We cannot bring the Beta Yisrael to Israel and change them into bad citizens. That is not our way.

He told me of case after case of mismanagement by Jewish Agency officials who had little knowledge of the culture of the Ethiopian Jews, and who applied to them policies similar to those used for the absorption of the Jews of Morocco. In one instance, which I assume was an extreme of mismanagement, the rabbi described 280 Ethiopian new immigrants being crowded into six one-room apartments at Arbinel near Beersheba. "Their treatment by the Jewish Agency officialdom borders on being criminal," he said.

Besides the crowded conditions, with people sleeping on the floor and lack of cribs for the infants, agency officials denied the residents of Arbinel the usual allotment of funds due new immigrants to pay for food, heat, and electricity. "In the meantime, the clerks take the *olim's Te'udat Oleh* (passbook for new residents) and write in it that they have been paid. I saw it myself with my own eyes." The rabbi had good things to say about other Israelis helping with the absorption, especially the young soldiers. But in general he was discouraged and feared for the future.

Rabbi Adani appeared to have assessed the problem correctly, but how difficult would it be to get the Jewish Agency to change the views of their entrenched employees? The problem would only continue to grow as more immigrants arrived. The AAEJ was able to help in a limited number of ways (chapter 15). Hanan Aynor also foresaw the problems and recommended a special interministerial "Authority" at the highest governmental levels to prepare for the absorption. Israel had too much at stake to botch up the absorption of its new black immigrants, who had been models of good behavior in Ethiopia.

It took a scholar in sociology who understood the customs both of Israel and of the Beta Yisrael to come up with a workable proposal. That was Professor Tartakower, who wrote:

> It still remains to be seen, whether…the problem of absorption of the Falashas will find a satisfactory solution. It is as shown by the experience of the first years of the State of Israel, when scores of groups had to be admitted and absorbed, a problem not only of bread and homes and of a decent standard of life, but also of making the immigrants part and parcel of the Israeli society and partners in its development, at the same time preserving their own cultural values as an important asset in the life of Israel.…
>
> The Falasha immigration is not an immigration of paupers, certainly not from the cultural point of view. They are, most of them, poor people struggling hard for their daily bread, but at the same time they managed to preserve their customs, their literature and their rather considerable inner culture, mostly much higher than the culture of the surrounding population [in Ethiopia].… What matters in the first place, is preserving their community life. They are not to be dispersed, but possibly kept together, while at the same time acquiring the social and cultural values of Israel. Within the limits of the expected policy of this kind arose among others the idea of special settlements/moshavim to be established for them, which is important not only in preserving their occupational structure, again very welcome in Israel, but also in preserving their way of life and their customs which best can be made in such settlements; but also those who may find positions in urban settlements, again should possibly be kept together and enabled to continue their cultural life, in addition to the general cultural life of the country. It is an important task, not less important than in the

case of similar groups of immigrants, especially those who arrived or may be expected from the countries of the Near East and also others. A proper policy of absorption on the part of the competent organs of the Government of Israel and the Jewish Agency may pave the road toward the desired solution of such problems for the benefit of the Falashas themselves and the entire Jewish people....

Rabbi Adin Steinsaltz

Although I had no training in religious scholarship, my wife did. When she read in the *Jerusalem Post* that Rabbi Adin Steinsaltz, one of Israel's highly respected religious scholars, was giving a public lecture at the Van Leer Institute auditorium in Jerusalem, she pulled me along to accompany her. My mind was on other things. But the man was brilliant. I do not remember the subject of his lecture, but only recall admiring his presentation, his logical development of his themes, and the way he captivated his audience. Determined to meet Rabbi Steinsaltz, I called him the next day, and we set a time to meet in his office. After introductions, I told him of my concern for the Ethiopian Jews and found that he had already given the subject much thought. He called my attention to a key Israeli figure in the movement, a man whom I had overlooked completely, former member of the Knesset, scholar, author, and publisher Haim Ben Asher.

Ben Asher, Rabbi Steinsaltz said, was active in creating a literary movement among the *kibbutzim* (plural of *kibbutz*, a communal village) and was a member of Kibbutz Netzer Sereni. Things started to click. My wife's cousin, Ahuva Shulman, was a teacher at that kibbutz and had introduced us to two families who were residents there; in both families there were Ethiopian Jews. One, the Etgar couple, had twin *sabra* daughters. The other family consisted of Elias Mati, his Polish wife, and their two daughters. Both the men and Mrs. Etgar, as teenagers, had been brought to Kfar Batya in Israel as part of the Jewish Agency's plan to train teachers for the Beta Yisrael. They were the only ones to become members of a kibbutz, likely through the influence of Ben Asher.

Ben Asher first got to know the Beta Yisrael in the 1950s when he visited Ethiopia. Steinsaltz told me that Ben Asher's wife at that time was dying of cancer and they wanted a "last honeymoon." As the story goes, Ben Asher, meeting some Jews in Ethiopia, asked an elder if the Beta Yisrael were descended from Abraham or from converts to Judaism. The elder replied, "Wasn't Abraham a convert? What's the difference between his descendants and us?" Ben Asher was troubled by their suffering, "caught between politics and religious problems" in Ethiopia. The non-Jews believed the Jews could turn themselves into "werewolves" and eat Christian children.

On his return to Israel, Ben Asher could not get help for the Beta Yisrael from government officials. He next approached the religious leaders who refused to deal with the question. Ben Asher then made a report of his experience in Ethiopia and gave a copy to Zalman Shazar, at that time head of the Education Department of the Jewish Agency and later president of Israel. Shazar took action; he was instrumental in starting the Jewish Agency's education program in Israel to train Ethiopian Jews as teachers. With that beginning, the World Jewish Congress arranged for Professor Norman Bentwich to visit Ethiopia, and links of the chain continued to be added.

At my request, Elias Mati of Netzer Sereni found Ben Asher, who, after his wife had died, was living in Eilat. On March 1, 1979, Elias spoke with Ben Asher. In their discussion, Ben Asher told Mati that Moshe Sharett (prime minister, 1954–1955; chairman of the Jewish Agency, 1956–1960) had not been interested in the Ethiopian Jews. Ben Asher also said that all his documents were in the Zionist Archives, and he promised to write a letter to the archives director to allow Mati to see those papers. After that I heard nothing more, though I tried unsuccessfully to find Ben Asher to get the rest of his story.

Rabbi Steinsaltz, beyond introducing me to Ben Asher's past

importance, gave new impetus to my growing activism. He said that Israel is a small country besieged by problems, and that Israel cannot handle all of its problems alone. He was not certain of which route we should take to achieve significant rescue, such as working through a third country. Rabbi Steinsaltz gave the analogy of the movement to save Russian Jewry and said, "Israel did little for the Russian Jews until American Jews and the Refuseniks themselves [Russian Jews who were refused visas to Israel] started protesting." It had to be the same with the Ethiopian Jews. "We need people like you to take the leadership."

Our mission would have been different had the government of Israel heeded the requests of wise patriots in the past. Jacques Faitlovitch, Haim Ben Asher, Norman Bentwich, Moshe Bar Yuda, Hanan Aynor, Aryeh Tartakower, Haggai Erlich, and Graenum Berger had urged that the government of Israel bring the Beta Yisrael from Ethiopia in exchange for cash or goods. The Ethiopian Jews rescued from Africa would have had more time to become better adapted in Israel, fewer Jewish lives would have been lost in the rescue attempts, the cost of the rescue and absorption would have been so much less, and Israel would have emerged as a model among nations for successfully building a "multicultural" society. That would be a feat that few if any nations have yet achieved. And this was the task the rabbi was telling us that we Jews in the *Galut* (Diaspora) must now help Israel to accomplish. Rabbi Steinsaltz had spoken clearly, and we knew what had to be done. But how?

CHAPTER 6

Politics of Religion and the Law of Return

> I am turning to you...to come and help our brothers, the Fala-
> shas...to come out of Ethiopia...to make aliyah to Eretz Yis-
> rael.... Blessed be all who undertake this holy work to bring
> freedom to prisoners, to call out to those who are captives,
> and to save those who are in darkness.
> – *Sephardic Chief Rabbi Ovadia Yosef in a responsa*
> *to Bernard Alpert, vice president of AAEJ, November 1973*

*F*or the government of Israel to initiate the mass *aliyah* of the
Ethiopian Jews, it was imperative that both the Ashkenazic and
Sephardic chief rabbis of Israel proclaim the Beta Yisrael as Jews
according to *halachah* (Jewish Law). That would give the Beta Yisrael a strong case to qualify for immigration under Israel's Law of
Return, the policy that grants Israeli citizenship and benefits to any
Jew who wishes to live in Israel. If the Beta Yisrael were admissible
under the Law of Return, then the government of Israel would be
obliged to receive them.

As the AAEJ saw it, having the Beta Yisrael declared Jews
would also gain the grassroots support of American Jews and of
the Israeli man-in-the-street. Western Jews could connect readily with the plight of Jews in Russia and protest for their freedom
to go to Israel. On the other hand, most of world Jewry could not
so easily identify with black Africans living in straw huts. Once
the Beta Yisrael were declared to be Jews and welcome in Israel,
however, it would be easier for the Jewish public to feel a spiritual

kinship with them, and to realize that they were Jews in distress who needed help.

Despite the positive declaration by Sephardic Chief Rabbi Ovadia Yosef, the issue of the Jewishness of the Beta Yisrael was clouded because there was no similar declaration by the Ashkenazic chief rabbi. Also there was confusion about who was responsible for administering the *chidush ha-brit* for the Beta Yisrael men. This was a token circumcision by removal of a drop of blood from the penis. Both chief rabbis required that ceremony, normally applied to converts, for the male immigrants brought to Israel from Ethiopia in December 1977. By January of 1978 a religious crisis about who was in charge was fermenting.

Rabbi Ovadia Yosef Recognizes the Beta Yisrael as Jews

On February 9, 1973, Sephardic Chief Rabbi Ovadia Yosef had ruled that the Beta Yisrael are Jews according to *halachah*. His statement came in a letter to Hezi Ovadia, the spokesperson at that time for the Ethiopian Jews living in Israel. Hezi was the same impressive sergeant major who led me to Rahamim in 1974.

Rabbi Yosef quoted numerous eminent religious authorities, including the Radbaz, Rabbi Azriel Hildesheimer, and two former Ashkenazic chief rabbis of Israel, Abraham Isaac Kook and Isaac Halevi Herzog. The Sephardic chief rabbi wrote:

> I have therefore come to the conclusion that the Falashas are descendants of the Tribe of Israel who went southward to Ethiopia, and there is no doubt that the above sages established that they [the Falashas] are of the Tribe of Dan…and [have] reached the conclusion on the basis of the most reliable witnesses and evidence.
>
> I, too, have investigated and inquired well into…[these matters]…and have decided that in my humble opinion, the Falashas are Jews, whom it is our duty to redeem from assimilation, to hasten their immigration to Israel, to educate them

in the spirit of our holy Torah and to make them partners in
the building of our sacred land....

I am certain that the government institutions and the Jewish Agency, as well as organizations in Israel and the Diaspora,
will help us to the best of our ability in this holy task..., the
mitzvah of redeeming the souls of our people...for everyone
who saves one soul in Israel, it is as though he had saved the
whole world.

In his letter to Hezi, Rabbi Ovadia Yosef wrote that help should
come from "organizations...in the Diaspora." He had stated that
responsibility even more strongly in a letter of November 7, 1973
(see the italicized paragraph at the beginning of this chapter), to Mr.
Bernard Alpert of Chicago, then a vice president of the fledgling
AAEJ, who later in 1978 became a citizen of Israel. These actions
by Rabbi Ovadia Yosef were to prove important in getting the government of Israel to recognize the Beta Yisrael as Jews. Although
pro-Beta Yisrael activists saw Ovadia Yosef's pronouncements as
a major milestone, some were skeptical, wondering if there was an
alternative self-serving motive, such as persuading a future mass
group of immigrants to declare themselves Sephardic Jews.

In an ironic twist, the immediate impetus for Hezi Ovadia to
seek a statement verifying that the Beta Yisrael were Jews came
when Dr. Yosef Burg, Israel's powerful minister of the interior, attempted to deport four Ethiopian Jews, claiming that the Law of
Return did not apply to the Beta Yisrael. Hezi hid the four to prevent their banishment and went to Rabbi Ovadia Yosef who then
wrote his historic letter.

Getting Rabbi Goren Involved: The Circumcision Caper

Despite the statement by Rabbi Ovadia Yosef in 1973, there was
no clamor to apply the Law of Return to the Beta Yisrael. What
besides the letter from Rabbi Ovadia Yosef could encourage the
government of Israel to bring the Beta Yisrael to Israel? Would a

similar statement from the Ashkenazic chief rabbi, Shlomo Goren, help?

My involvement with Rabbi Goren and the "religious question" began late one Sunday morning in January of 1978 when I was working in the laboratory of my Hebrew University colleague, Professor Menachem Rahat. He called me from my microscope for "an important phone call." The stern look on Menachem's face foreboded trouble.

The voice on the line was frantic. Zimna Berhane was beside himself. "The men are confused and frightened," he shouted. "Most have fled from the absorption center. Rabbi Ovadia Yosef's people just arrived and want to circumcise them!"

To put into perspective the following story about the "Circumcision Caper," it is important to know some events of the year that had just passed. Menachem Begin had been sworn in as prime minister of Israel on June 20, 1977. In August 1977, a group of sixty-two Beta Yisrael were flown to Israel directly from Ethiopia, through a deal that first Yitzchak Rabin, and then Menachem Begin, worked out with President Mengistu Haile Mariam of Ethiopia. The key negotiator for Israel was Haim Halachmi, an employee of HIAS who was "on loan" to the Jewish Agency.

Those new immigrants, the largest group brought to Israel thus far, were taken to an absorption center in Tiberias near the Sea of Gallilee (Lake Kinneret). A few months later, in December 1977, another fifty-eight immigrants came to Israel through the same agreement; they went to an absorption center in Afula, a small town near Nazareth in northern Israel. The circumcision caper involved the Ethiopian men in that group of fifty-eight in the Afula absorption center.

Zimna was one of the Ethiopian Jews who had come to Israel in 1955 to be trained as a teacher. He was acting as a resident translator-intermediary between the Jewish Agency social workers and those new Beta Yisrael immigrants in the Afula absorption center, just as he done a few months earlier in Tiberias. The AAEJ, not the Jewish Agency, was paying his salary for both those stints.

He knew that my wife and I had a special feeling for the new immigrants at Afula. We had visited their absorption center a few days after they arrived in December 1977. We had slept at the center (probably illegally), ate and chatted with them, did magic tricks for the children, took their pictures, and joined them as they attended their first *ulpan* (Hebrew language class). Zimna's phone call on their behalf was to involve me ever more deeply into one of the strangest roles of my life.

Little had I imagined for myself a role as liaison between the two chief rabbis of Israel on matters concerning the Jews from Ethiopia. But that is exactly how events played out that January. The Sephardic chief rabbi and the Ashkenazic chief rabbi had offices on opposite ends of the same floor of the *Hechal Shlomo*, the great synagogue in Jerusalem. For a hectic two weeks, I would go from office to office carrying messages between the two rabbis who usually would not talk with each other. Those messages concerned this group of new Ethiopian immigrants that Prime Minister Menachem Begin had brought to Israel that December through a deal made with President Mengistu Haile Mariam of Ethiopia in exchange for Israeli arms and supplies.

The new immigrants at Afula were still talking about a visit from Chief Rabbi Shlomo Goren, and about his promise to return that week to supervise personally the men's *chidush ha-brit*, their "symbolic circumcision" as they were to "rejoin the Jewish people." What had aroused Zimna that morning was the unannounced and unexpected arrival of two buses carrying Sephardic rabbis. These rabbis had been sent by Sephardic Chief Rabbi Ovadia Yosef, who had learned from one of his confidants of Goren's planned visit and decided to act first.

Ovadia Yosef's rabbis ordered the Ethiopian newcomers, twenty men, to enter the buses one by one for the ritual. The rabbis told them that this procedure would be according to Jewish custom and the instructions of Chief Rabbi Ovadia Yosef. Only then would those men be recognized in Israel as full-fledged Jews.

The Beta Yisrael men, said Zimna, were expecting Chief Rabbi

Shlomo Goren in a few days to perform the ceremony. At that time they had never heard of Rabbi Ovadia Yosef. Confused, the men fled in many directions, trying to escape from the Sephardic rabbis. That is when Zimna phoned.

After calming Zimna a bit, I called Rabbi Goren's office for advice. Rabbi Charles Weinberg, the American assistant to Goren, answered the phone. Rabbi Weinberg, who had known my grandfather in Boston, tried to reassure me that this controversy regarding which of the two chief rabbis was to apply the token conversion to the Beta Yisrael would be resolved, but there was nothing Rabbi Goren could do at this time. Zimna called again and told me that the men had been found, and the ceremonies had been performed.

Later I learned that because of that incident, Rabbi Goren had obtained some concessions from Prime Minister Begin regarding the handling of the *chidush ha-brit* ritual for future immigrants from Ethiopia.

Why were the two chief rabbis of Israel so contentious on issues of making the Beta Yisrael "kosher," that is, acceptable as Jews?

Rabbi Goren and Recognizing the Beta Yisrael as Jews

Goren's visit to the Afula group in January 1978, which sparked the Sephardic caper, had much significance. That visit marked the first time in modern Israel that the Ashkenazic chief rabbi indicated he recognized the black Beta Yisrael of Ethiopia as true Jews.

Zimna offered me a fascinating account of that historic meeting: When Rabbi Goren arrived, he gave some sweets and cookies to the Ethiopian children and blessed them. Then the older men gathered around the chief rabbi, and they too requested his blessing. One elderly man, a *kes* (priest) who knew the *Tanach* (Five Books of Moses) by heart in *Ge'ez*, asked Rabbi Goren, "Please tell us, Great Rabbi, what has happened to the Jewish people in those two thousand years we were in the Diaspora?" Goren was impressed with the *kes*. He was particularly astounded after hearing the *kes* describe the strict biblical customs of the Ethiopian Jews, especially those about isolating women during the menstrual period and after pregnancy.

Rabbi Goren told the new immigrants: "You are our brothers; you are our blood and our flesh. You are true Jews. Rabbi Kook said so. You have returned to your homeland." At the end of his visit, he posed for a picture with the new immigrants and said that he would return to personally carry out the *chidush ha-brit* on the men, the promise which led to the "circumcision caper."

Later that week, I visited Rabbis Goren and Weinberg once more. They showed me the picture taken at Afula, and I asked for a copy for my archives. To my surprise, they gave me the original negative and said that it could be reproduced and published at any time without their permission.

In effect, Goren was handing me a "trial balloon." He knew that the AAEJ would publish it in the United States. Did he expect that the photograph and my accompanying story would affect his image as a positive supporter of the Ethiopian Jews? If he did, he was right. The photograph was published in many Jewish newspapers together with an accompanying story regarding how the two chief rabbis supported the Ethiopian Jews. Later I published the story of his visit in an entry I wrote for the *Encyclopedia Judaica* (*Decennial Book*, 1973–1982).

Instead of issuing an official document over his own name declaring the Beta Yisrael to be Jews as did Rabbi Ovadia Yosef in 1973, Rabbi Goren continued to equivocate. When asked why, he replied that he, representing Ashkenazi Jews, did not need to make such a proclamation. Rabbi Abraham Isaac Kook, a revered chief rabbi of pre-Israel Palestine, Goren said, had asked world Jewry in a letter dated December 4, 1921, "to save our Falasha brethren from extinction and contamination…and to rescue fifty thousand holy souls of the House of Israel from oblivion. A holy obligation rests upon our entire nation to raise funds with a generous hand to improve the lot of the Falashas in Ethiopia and to bring their young children to Jewish centers in Palestine and the Diaspora…"

Rabbi Goren let American activists carry the torch for the Ethiopian Jews without his having to put his views into writing. Even a few years earlier at a meeting in Jerusalem during August 1975, he had said that he believed the Beta Yisrael to be Jews. Attending that meeting were Graenum Berger and Professor Aryeh Tartakower. Following the meeting, they wrote a letter to Goren confirming the contents of their discussion, which included Rabbi Goren's approval of the Ethiopian Jews. Rabbi Goren never replied, and this letter was not widely circulated. His statements, however, reached the *Jerusalem Post*, which reported in August 1975 that "Chief Rabbi Shlomo Goren has expressed the view that the Falashas are part of the Jewish people. Moreover, he has for a long time had a 'messianic vision' of their redemption by returning to Israel."

Goren repeated this sentiment in February 1978, when he told me of his great concern for the Jews of Ethiopia. "Although there is no need for me to make another statement [after the one made by Rabbi Abraham Kook]," he said, "nevertheless, I have been working on one." Rabbi Goren promised to send me a copy when he completed it. I never received that or any document from him. To the best of my knowledge, it was never written. I should note, however, that in response to a letter from Sol Goldberg of Seattle, Rabbi Goren sent a cable to him stating: "The Falashas are Jews. Rabbi Kook said so."

I never spoke with the rabbi again. But I was pleased to learn that in December 1981, in Jerusalem at the unique Beta Yisrael holiday of the Sig'd, Rabbi Goren wrote and read a poem he had written for the occasion. The poem in essence recognized the Beta Yisrael as Jews and prayed for their rescue to Israel. Taking advantage of this opportunity to print a statement by Rabbi Goren, Rabbi Robert Bergman, a fellow California activist and former translator for the *Jerusalem Post*, rendered that poem into English for the AAEJ. We saw to it that it was published in numerous newspapers. Rabbi Goren had written:

May He who blessed our fathers —
Abraham, Isaac and Jacob,
Moses, Aaron, David and Solomon —
Bless, redeem and save our brothers,
The Israelites in Ethiopian exile,
Them and their wives,
Their sons and their daughters,
And all their kin
Who are subject to difficulty and distress
Who are oppressed and severely persecuted.
Wherefore we pray for their lives,
Their welfare
And their freedom.
May the Holy One, blessed be He, preserve them
And save them from their enemies and pursuers;
May the Rock of Israel bring them
From the darkness of their exile
To great light;
From their subjugation
To redemption.

Had Rabbi Goren set me up again? I wondered.

Beta Yisrael Recognized as Jews under Law of Return

With the religion question apparently settled, the government of Israel in the spring of 1975 finally recognized the Beta Yisrael as Jews entitled to automatic citizenship and full benefits as prescribed under the 1950 Law of Return. This action was taken by a blue ribbon committee made up of members drawn from the Ministries of Justice, Immigrant Absorption, Religion, and Interior. In the wake of this announcement, the *Jerusalem Post* quoted an expert on the Ethiopian Jews as saying that the Ethiopian government "will not oppose Falasha immigration."

Is it coincidental that the Law of Return was first applied to the Beta Yisrael during a short six-month interval when Yosef Burg was not minister of the interior? Dr. Burg held that post for over thirty years under both the Labor and Likud governments, presumably because the National Religious Party (NRP) was required in political coalitions needed to form a majority government in the Knesset, the Israeli parliament.

Shlomo Hillel, who had served in such positions as Speaker of the Knesset and head of Israel's police, and who earlier had been a key player in the rescue of Iraqi Jews, was acting minister of the interior during Burg's six-month absence. He told me once, when I was visiting his home in Jerusalem, that he had found papers regarding the Beta Yisrael in the ministry office. They included a copy of Rabbi Ovadia Yosef's letter to Sergeant Major Hezi. They were compelling, and he had decided that it was time to act.

This monumental decision, however, was overturned by the returning minister of the interior, Dr. Burg. His deputy director general, Judith Huebner, released a statement in July of 1975 to Israel radio notifying the public that "the officials of the Ministry of the Interior changed their minds with respect to the Falashas and are not of the opinion that they are Jews, for whom the Law of Return is applicable."

This reversal was attacked from many quarters including correspondents in the Israeli newspapers *Davar* and the *Jerusalem Post* and Knesset Member Shulamit Aloni. The travesty was squelched on Friday, July 25, 1975, when over Israeli radio it was announced that "the government's interministerial committee has reaffirmed the right of the Falashas to come to Israel under the Law of Return..."

American Rabbi Steve Kaplan Meets a *Kes* in Ethiopia

The approval of the chief rabbis was crucial, as was the applicability of the Law of Return, if there was going to be a significant immigration of Ethiopian Jews to Israel. The average American Jew, however, does not follow the internal Israeli political and rabbinical battles over issues such as these.

They are moved by real life experiences that they can relate to.

It is one of these experiences, a conversation between Rabbi Steve Kaplan of Fremont, California, and a Beta Yisrael priest in Ethiopia in the summer of 1981, which influenced many American Jews to identify with the Beta Yisrael and be concerned for their welfare.

That encounter occurred when Rabbi Kaplan participated in a mission to Ethiopia. During the visit, the group came across an isolated village inhabited by Beta Yisrael. Through the help of a translator, Brett Goldberg, members of the group talked with residents of the village. Rabbi Kaplan asked if there was a *kes*. There was, and later in the day, after the *kes* returned from working in the fields, the two religious leaders had a lively conversation.

Rabbi Kaplan was astounded when the *kes* told him that the *parsha* (portion of the Bible) that he was going to read in his synagogue that Sabbath, was exactly the same *parsha* that was being read that Sabbath in Rabbi Kaplan's synagogue and in all of the other synagogues around the world. Imagine, after being isolated for centuries, the Beta Yisrael priests in the plateaus deep in Ethiopia were in sync with the rest of world Jewry!

This remarkable and moving story had to be told. At our request, Rabbi Kaplan wrote an article so that the AAEJ could distribute it through our mailing list of Jewish newspapers and magazines. This report of a conversation between a contemporary American rabbi and a Beta Yisrael *kes* in the high plateaus of Ethiopia was simple, clear and compelling. It probably did more to help American Jews identify with the Ethiopian Jews than all of the pronouncements by the chief rabbis.

The only other equally simple, clear, and unambiguous statement was made by former president of Israel Zalman Shazar. He told Shalom Rosenfeld, editor of the Israeli newspaper *Maariv*, "If the Falashas observe as Jews, believe they are Jews, and suffer as Jews, then in my mind they are Jews."

Postscript

Religious infighting, especially about the *chidush ha-brit* ceremony, continued until after Operation Moses. Much of it seemed to use the Beta Yisrael as political footballs. Secular Israelis were battling the powerful Israeli Orthodox organizations. Some Sephardic Jews were trying to increase their voting base by luring the Beta Yisrael as members. A few groups of the Beta Yisrael themselves were opportunists who used religious issues to build a political constituency. Among the Ashkenazi Orthodox were those who did not want to appear too lenient in accepting the definition of "Who is a Jew," always a divisive issue in Israeli and Diaspora circles. The AAEJ could not become diverted by the ongoing religious controversies. It needed to focus on rescue.

PART III

BROADENING THE BASE

CHAPTER 7

Nine Months of Gestation, 1974–1975

"Do you mean to tell me that there are fifty thousand American Jews who are concerned about the Ethiopian Jews?'
– *Prime Minister Menachem Begin*

"No, Mr. Prime Minister. These are only the names of fifty thousand American Jews who signed this petition. The number of American Jews who are concerned about the fate of the Jews of Ethiopia is more like twenty times that number."
– *Howard Lenhoff*

Back in California from war-torn Israel in June 1974, I sensed that to become an effective activist on behalf of the Beta Yisrael would be a formidable task. A perusal of Jewish newspapers indicated that the few handfuls of knowledgeable activists working on behalf of the *aliyah* of the Ethiopian Jews were in New York and Chicago; two were in New Orleans. I called Graenum Berger, founding president of the AAEJ, whose phone number had been given to me by Louis Rapoport. Berger, who had been an advocate for the Ethiopian Jews since 1956, seemed pleased to hear from me, encouraged me to become involved, and promised to send some background literature.

His packet arrived in less than a week. Most of the articles were written by him. He had a clear, logical, and forceful style. It was comforting to know that there was a ready and reliable source of information. Berger was on the East Coast three thousand miles away, however, and it appeared that I would be starting out in California working alone.

Fortunately for my impending mini-career as an activist for the Ethiopian Jews, the southern California Jewish community held Sylvia and me in some regard because of our broad experiences in Israel. It had not taken long for local rabbis and leaders of Jewish organizations, such as the enlightened Ken Levin of the Orange County Jewish Federation, to find us, and within a few months, we became regular lecturers on Israel at synagogues and at meetings of Jewish organizations from San Diego to Los Angeles.

In addition, I'd been active in raising funds for Israel and served for a while as national faculty chairman for Israel Bonds. Sylvia, working as a university extension specialist, programmed courses in Hebrew and a lecture series on the Mideast conflict; as a member of the university's speakers bureau, she gave talks on women in Israel. On the campus, I helped start the one-hour radio program "Hatikvah," run by Jewish students on Sunday mornings.

My credibility as a committed Zionist continued to grow. The next four years saw me serving for various periods at three more Israeli academic institutions: the Hebrew University near the Old City in Jerusalem, the Marine Biology Laboratory in Eilat and the Israeli Institute of Technology (the Technion) in Haifa. In subsequent years I was also to be a fellow of the Hubert Humphrey Institute of Ben-Gurion University, and to help start a program training Beta Yisrael social workers at Bar-Ilan University.

I did not guess it at the time, but a visitor to our apartment near Haifa just before we returned to California from our "Yom Kippur War sabbatical" also was to figure importantly in my pro-Beta Yisrael activism. In June 1974, a Dr. Noah Orian of the Jewish Agency in Jerusalem, working with Jewish academics who were guests in Israel, came to see us. The good doctor's message was clear. "Israel," he said, "will be in big trouble in a few years unless American youth, especially those in college, get involved in some sort of Judaica curriculum which has courses such as on the Holocaust, the Mideast conflict, and the study of contemporary Hebrew." He looked squarely into my eyes and said, "You could help the people of Israel by encouraging your university in California to implement a program in Judaic studies."

That was my charge. Little did we know that this Judaica activity would inaugurate my training in California as an activist for the Ethiopian Jews. To start a Judaica program at a public university would be a formidable challenge, especially in Orange County, known then (and even now) as politically conservative and "WASPish." The first task would be to win the support of Jewish students attending the University of California, Irvine (UCI).

Hebrew: A Catalyst for Jewish Activism

My first opportunity to get student support at UCI came in August 1974. Leaving the campus parking lot near my laboratory, I noticed a messy pile of Hebrew books in the back seat of a car. The owner of the car and books turned out to be David Paskil, an undergraduate student. The bespectacled David, mustached with a receding hairline, who looked much older than his nineteen years, was a third year pre-med student with a deep commitment to Judaism. Though not fluent in Hebrew, he was more advanced than I was. We began meeting once a week during the remainder of the summer to practice our Hebrew. Soon we were joined by co-ed Gila Keithen, a recent convert to Judaism who had lived in Israel for a year.

In the fall of 1974, twenty students, mostly Jewish, were enrolled in a newly established Hebrew course. David and I went to the class and told the students that we were meeting once a week to read a relatively elementary Hebrew magazine, *Mishpacha* ("Family"), and that those who wished were welcome to participate. About six of the students took up our offer, and that reading group proved to be the nucleus of a new student organization. Within a month they formed a "Jewish Student Union." Thanks to this organization, many more Irvine students came to identify with Judaism and Israel. Within a few months, the newly created Jewish Student Union (JSU) started to sponsor regular Friday evening

Sabbath suppers at a university dining hall, with attendance ranging between 100 to 120 people. Some of these students eventually
became the initial participants in the UCI Judaic Studies Program
inaugurated two years later.

Students Open Opportunities for Activism

My service as advisor to the JSU opened new doors to increase
interest in the Beta Yisrael among California Jews. Many of the
Jewish students at UCI came from the Los Angeles area, home to
a large number of synagogues, and they convinced their rabbis to
invite me to address their congregants, usually by offering a short
sermon about the Ethiopian Jews at the Friday evening Sabbath
services. Others arranged special hour-long lectures.

For those congregational talks we found that showing colored
slides of the Beta Yisrael in Ethiopia and in Israel made a powerful impression on the viewers. At first my slides were provided by
Graenum Berger, but eventually others were added to my collec-
tion. Some came from Los Angeles Jews who had visited Ethiopia.
Journalist Donna Rosenthal, author of the recent book *The Israelis*
(2004), gave us some of her professional photographs. The most
effective visual aid we had was a movie made in 1968 by author
Meyer Levin. It was particularly moving as it focused on the life
of one Beta Yisrael family in Ethiopia and again after they moved
to Israel.

These brief appearances stirred many people who clamored
for reading material and for information about how they could
help. To meet these requests we prepared a one-page newsletter,
"Falashas – Black Jews of Ethiopia." It began with a call for action
to save the Ethiopian Jews and contained stories about their history, about the Ethiopian Jews already in Israel, and about living
conditions in Ethiopia. It suggested ways American Jews could
participate as well as obtain sources of more information. Word
about the Ethiopian Jews began to spread.

There seemed to be no shortage of events to attend where we
could publicize the need to rescue the Jews of Ethiopia. Two events

in particular stand out as indicators of how "student power" can be harnessed to achieve important goals. One was the Student Leadership Training Institute held at the Camp JCA in Malibu, November 1–3, 1974, and the other was the Western Regional Leadership meeting held in Palm Springs in mid-December 1974. Both were sponsored by the UJA and the Los Angeles Jewish Federation.

The student camp was an experience! Apart from the singing and dancing, this weekend offered the opportunity to meet and influence dedicated Jewish students from other southern California colleges and universities. But perhaps more importantly, at the camp I met a number of "establishment" notables, and my presence made them aware for the first time of the growing concern of American Jewry for the welfare of the Ethiopian Jews. Among those attending was Irwin Field, a young entrepreneur who later became national president of the UJA. In subsequent years, we often crossed paths; and although we sometimes disagreed on policies or programs, he always was a gentleman.

Saturday afternoon at the Malibu camp I spoke at a workshop on the Ethiopian Jews. The response of many of the students was encouraging. One informed me of a major community lecture in Los Angeles to be given in January by Abba Eban, former Israeli ambassador to the UN. "It would be an excellent chance to reach a large number of influential Jews," he said; "All the *machers* ('big shots') will be there." He wanted me to attend and offered to arrange for a group of his friends to distribute literature on the Ethiopian Jews.

An unexpected payoff came out of this weekend. Since my name was now on the local UJA mailing list, my mailbox overflowed with voluminous mailings from establishment organizations. One of the letters told of a UJA leadership meeting to be held in Palm Springs that December, where the deputy prime minister of Israel, Yigal Allon, was scheduled to be the featured speaker. If we were going to make our presence known at an event featuring Abba Eban, I thought, why not do the same at an event featuring Yigal Allon? It did not take long for me to recruit two carloads of students from the JSU. This Palm Springs venture marked the origin of the Student Pro-Falasha Committee, with the dynamic, personable Sylvia Haas (Burlin) as its first chairperson.

Whereas Sylvia Haas was a fully committed student activist, not all of this early cadre were like her. Students can be effective activists as long as the activism does not interfere with their studies. They have endless energy and can come up with creative ideas. They are in tune with their generation and have a good instinct for what works. They are especially receptive to participating when the event has an element of adventure, free food, and a chance to socialize. Add a short trip to an exotic location, and we have a winner. Never plan an activity involving them, however, just before mid-term or final examinations.

Meeting the Press in Palm Springs

Fortunately, the Palm Springs meeting was scheduled to take place during the winter break after finals. The students were ready for adventure. At our organizational meeting at UCI, we agreed to be polite and not confrontational when speaking with UJA delegates. Men would wear a shirt, tie, and sport coat. We made signs that were informative and not accusatory. We took some of the "We Are One" posters that the UJA office in Los Angeles had previously sent to the JSU and modified them so that the Ethiopian Jews should be part of the "One." The students had a stack of one-page information flyers to distribute, but were told in no uncertain terms never to force a delegate to take one and not to embarrass them if they declined. If they could not answer a question, they should ask my assistance.

Our two-car caravan left Irvine early and arrived in Palm Springs just after the leadership breakfast. With a friendly smile, each student stood at a prescribed place in the hotel where the delegates would pass on their way to the various sessions. This was the first public demonstration I had participated in since the early sixties, and I was not sure what to expect. How would fellow Jews take to our public campaign?

To our surprise and pleasure, there was no open hostility to us or to the message we presented. Many of the delegates stopped and asked questions. Most seemed satisfied with our responses; they may have been impressed because the students knew the facts and presented their case powerfully. Some of the delegates came back afterwards and invited students to join them as their guests for lunch. More important to our long-range campaign, we met men and women of the Jewish press. For example, Herb Brin, the publisher and editor of four editions of southern California's *Heritage* newspaper, and Miriam Goldberg, publisher and editor of the *Intermountain Jewish News* of Denver, published articles on our protest in Palm Springs. Herb Brin gave us a front-page spot with an excellent photo of the student activists holding their signs. Herb called them "the beautiful University of California students."

Our maiden voyage was not entirely smooth, however. Sylvia Haas said that she was "horrified when one lady, beautifully dressed and wearing fancy jewelry, walked toward me and said, 'Listen, honey, those blacks are not Jews. Don't you have something better to do with your time?' " Mindy Sher, another volunteer, told of a delegate chiding her for "crashing" the meeting. If anything, these mild rebukes seemed to strengthen the students' commitment.

Another activity involving students was the Abba Eban lecture, a major event in Jewish Los Angeles attended by many community leaders. We were there to publicize the plight of the Jews in Ethiopia, not to criticize Abba Eban. A negative approach would be counterproductive, because American Jews had given celebrity status to that former Israeli ambassador to the UN, primarily for his scholarship and eloquence. As the guests came in we distributed a one-page flyer headed in large print, "WELCOME ABBA EBAN!" We had no problem distributing the flyer because people believed that they were getting a program for the evening's event. The remainder of the flyer contained background information about the Ethiopian Jews and the urgency of getting them to Israel. We believed the flyer provided interesting reading for the guests while they were waiting for the program to begin. That belief was confirmed by students who went inside to hear the lecture.

While Eban spoke, some of our entourage remained in the parking lot holding "Save Falasha Jewry" signs. As the crowd was leaving to go to their cars, many stopped to talk and said that they appreciated what we were doing. Two contacts made that night became important to us. One was Al Gillen, the director of the UJA in Los Angeles; he was relaxed and friendly. We talked about the Ethiopian Jews and about the University of California at Irvine and whether it was the right place to send his son. I sensed a rapport which was helpful in the following years when we established a "desk" of the AAEJ not too far from his office in the prestigious Los Angeles Jewish Federation building on 6505 Wilshire Boulevard.

One of the most important connections made that evening was with Eleanor Kahn, president of the local Hadassah. Unbeknown to me, she was the local expert on the Ethiopian Jews at that time. It was like finding a lost relative; she felt the same because she too was working alone. Eleanor invited me to come to her home and to bring along some student activists.

She told us how she and her husband, Otto, a Holocaust survivor, first became involved with the Jews of Ethiopia. In the early 1970s they had thought of visiting Africa. Before finalizing their plans, they attended a bat mitzvah at the Wilshire Boulevard Temple in Los Angeles where they met Rabbi Alfred Wolfe. When he overheard the Kahns discuss their plans to visit Africa, the rabbi said, "You must go to Ethiopia and visit the Jews there." Eleanor and Otto were startled by his suggestion because they had never heard about Ethiopian Jews. The rabbi not only knew of them, but he himself had visited their villages in Ethiopia in 1955.

In 1973, just before the Marxist revolution, the Kahns journeyed to the Beta Yisrael in their villages in Ethiopia. The poverty and sorry state of the Jewish community appalled them. Shortly after their return, word of their adventure spread in the Jewish community of Los Angeles, and Eleanor was invited to lecture to clubs and synagogues about the Ethiopian Jews, their culture, and dire straits.

At last we had an informed colleague in Los Angeles. We

shared information and photographs. She was familiar with conditions in the Ethiopian villages, whereas my expertise was the political situation in Israel. Together with Graenum Berger in New York and Lester and Sylvia Gerson in New Orleans, we were the seeds of a national speakers bureau. We had much work to do if we were to get the support of American Jewry.

Faitlovitch and Reines Attract International Attention
It started just after publicity had appeared about the students' demonstration held at the UJA leadership meeting in Palm Springs. One day while I was walking on the campus, a student stopped me. He introduced himself as Emil Faithe, the new co-host of the university radio station's Sunday Hatikvah hour. He mentioned that he had learned about my interest in the black Jews of Ethiopia and asked if I knew about his father's deceased Israeli cousin, once a leader in the movement to help the Jews of Ethiopia. His question startled me. Who was he talking about? Then it hit me; that relative might have been Dr. Jacques Faitlovitch, the scholar who went to Ethiopia at the beginning of the twentieth century and started schools for the Beta Yisrael there. Was the name "Faithe" an abbreviated Anglicized form of Faitlovitch?

Emil concurred. Faitlovitch was the name. He told me that his father was going to visit relatives in Israel in a few weeks. I called Emil's father and asked him if he had ever visited the former Tel Aviv home of his deceased cousin. He had not. Thinking that he might like to see the homestead, called Beit Faitlovitch, I arranged for him to meet Hezi Ovadia. After Emil's father toured the home, Hezi gave him a family memento, a wooden convex ink blotter from the desk once used by the late Jacques Faitlovitch.

That was it. Continuing my busy schedule, I gave the incident little further thought. A Young Judea club of high school students from Anaheim asked me to speak at one of their meetings. The kids were alert and seemed genuinely interested. They wanted specific suggestions as to how they could help the Ethiopian Jews; they were not too favorably impressed with my answers. One fifteen-year-old female student suggested that we start a petition campaign to "Save the Falashas." Agreeing with her that it was a good idea, I promised to consider implementing it. Frankly, it sounded like a lot of work, and mentally I tossed the idea into my "to do later if time" folder.

Not long after, I read that in 1906 Jacques Faitlovitch had crafted a letter to the Jews of Ethiopia addressed as "our brethren, sons of Abraham, Isaac, and Jacob, who dwell in Abyssinia," assuring them help in religious education and expressing hope that G-d "will gather us from the four corners of the earth and bring us to Zion." Faitlovitch got forty-four leading rabbis from Europe, America, and Egypt to sign the letter. Among them were a number of great rabbis including Jacob Reines of Russia, the first head of the Mizrachi movement.

The name Reines struck me because on our campus there was a prominent physicist – who twenty years later was to be awarded a Nobel Prize – named Frederick Reines. He and I had been active together soliciting funds among the Jewish faculty to assist Israel during the Yom Kippur War.

Now the suggestion of a petition by the Young Judea student took on a new and interesting shape. I called Reines and he told me that he was a grandnephew of the Rabbi Jacob Reines who had signed Faitlovitch's letter. Why not commemorate the signing of the famous 1906 letter by initiating a petition on behalf of the Ethiopian Jewish community and having Professor Reines be the first to sign? The second to sign would be Emil Faithe, a Faitlovitch relative. To add a little color to the ceremony, after both signed the petition, they would dry the ink from their signatures with the wooden blotter originally owned by Jacques Faitlovitch.

They both agreed, and the signing was set to take place in Professor Reines' office. Herb Brin, editor of the *Heritage*, sent a photographer to record the event and assigned his star reporter, Tom Tugend, to describe the ceremony. The story also ran in the *Jewish Chronicle* in England and the *Jerusalem Post* in Israel, because

Tugend served as California correspondent for those newspapers. In short order, the story was picked up by numerous Jewish community newspapers all over the country. In Israel, the story reached Hebrew readers when it was published in the popular newspaper *Maariv*. It was such a good story that it was published as a feature article in the *Los Angeles Times*. The pro-Beta Yisrael movement was getting on the map.

Petition Presented to Prime Minister Begin

It took three years to gather fifty thousand signatures, but then the petition was to provide the opportunity to acquaint Prime Minister Begin with the AAEJ. We requested a meeting, and he received AAEJ board member Henry Rosenberg and me in early March 1978. Also present were Yehuda Avner, a bureaucrat holdover from the Rabin regime, and Begin's military advisor, General Ephraim Poran. Dressed in a stuffy suit and tie, I presented Begin, who was wearing his usual short-sleeve, open-collar, tie-less shirt, a petition signed by fifty thousand Americans calling for the rescue of the Ethiopian Jews. This was the petition first signed by physicist Fred Reines.

Begin's response to the petition is in italics at the top of this chapter. He appeared touched that so many American Jews cared. This became the first of a number of meetings the AAEJ leadership subsequently had with Mr. Begin. Did he recognize that the AAEJ was an up-and-coming force in American Jewish organizations to be watched?

Incorporation of the AAEJ as an Institution

The publicity of early 1975 began to feed on itself and generated more coverage in the Jewish and secular press. Because of the publicity and response to the petition campaign, at the end of our lectures at synagogues and clubs, we made it a habit to have a volunteer pass around two clipboards. One held petition sheets for people to sign; we supplied extra petition forms with our return address for those who wanted to get friends to sign. The other clipboard held a yellow pad with room for the names, addresses, and phone numbers of those who wanted to be on our mailing list and perhaps also volunteer.

By the end of 1975, we had over a thousand names of interested people. Fortunately, one of the student volunteers, Vicki Toback, told me that her husband, Bruce, was expert in making computer databases and they would volunteer to organize our mailing list. From that humble beginning, we began one of the most effective mailing lists in the Jewish community, a list that by 1982 would help raise about $250,000 yearly.

The 1974–1975 academic year saw the building of a grassroots organization of dedicated, committed people across southern California. In this early vanguard, college students played a seminal role. Beginning largely on one campus, each month saw interest and participation spread to other campuses. It seems strange in hindsight that in an era when student activism in civil rights and the anti-war movement alienated so many in conservative southern California, the movement on behalf of the Ethiopian Jews constantly gained momentum. While the students could be liberal Democrats or conservative Republicans, they were united in their dedication to solving the plight of the Ethiopian Jews.

Yet students' time is segmented and limited, and for all their emotional commitment and energy, they cannot be the only source of volunteers. Eventually most graduate, leave campus for jobs, get married, and start families. Adult responsibilities bring new issues that crowd out youthful ones.

The normal turnover of activists, whether students or elders, demands that there be an incorporated organization that has a lifetime of its own and can sustain continued advocacy. Such an organization could adapt with time to new situations, and recruit, train, and keep new members over the years. That is why it was so important and fortuitous that a handful of activists, working independently of each other, joined forces and incorporated the AAEJ in February of 1974. Up until then, there had been three separate small groups of activists. The story of their union into the AAEJ can best be summarized by the words of the AAEJ's first secretary, Jeffrey Stone:

In 1969 I was a young [law] associate at Willkie Farr & Gallagher. Another young associate, and a friend, was Jed Abraham, an observant Jew who had served in the Peace Corps in Ethiopia, where he developed an interest in the Falasha and an intense desire to help them. Being a lawyer, his first instinct was to establish a tax-exempt corporation; it was called Friends of the Beta-Israel (Falasha) Community in Ethiopia – a catchy name. The corporation was essentially a one-man operation. Jed would make the rounds of synagogues…raising money through small contributions. Once a year, he'd tally up the receipts and would then arrange to buy something useful…, which would be duly shipped off to the Falasha.

Although Jed did all the work, NY law required the corporation to have at least two officers and three directors. Jed [eventually]…asked if I would fill in as the third director. I was assured that nothing at all would be required of me, other than to sign off on the annual report. Over the next couple of years, Jed and the other director moved. So much for the promise that I'd have no responsibilities.

[Before he left,] Jed had met Graenum [Berger] and Ted [Norman of the Baron deHirsch Fund] and they'd discussed joining forces. If I remember correctly, Graenum more or less headed two organizations, one called the American Pro-Falasha Committee [actually headed by Mrs. A. Kavey] and the other called the AAEJ. Graenum wanted to merge…[the three] organizations and asked me…[to help]. I discovered that neither the AAEJ nor the [American Pro-Falasha] Committee was then incorporated – both acted pretty informally. Merging not-for-profits is a real megillah, so I proposed a simple solution: since…two organizations were not formally organized, they could be informally dissolved without court action or IRS

approval. ...We then changed the name of the Friends [orga-
nization] to A A E J and amended its certificate of incorporation
to expand the number of officers and directors; that required
court approval but was a simple process. The final step was to
anoint Graenum as the president and Ted as the treasurer of
the corporation, and to contribute the funds in the coffers of
the other organizations to the [entity now called the] A A E J. I
was rewarded for my efforts by being named secretary, the post
I held until [1984] after Nate [Shapiro] took over as president
and moved the headquarters to Chicago.

In April 1975, just a bit over a year after Jeffrey Stone had engi-
neered the incorporation of the A A E J, my pro-Beta Yisrael activism
received a major boost from his work when the A A E J recognized
our grassroots efforts in southern California by electing me – sight
unseen – a vice president.

A UCI Postscript
The effort to initiate a Judaica program eventually was realized
over the next few years. UCI formed a cooperative program with
the University of Judaism of Los Angeles, an arrangement which
brought its star faculty (David Gordis, Elliot Dorff, and Joel Rem-
baum) to our campus. The campus pro-Beta Yisrael activities and
the campaign for a Judaica program fed on each other. The latter
effort attracted student activists, and our activism brought the distinguished author and producer of the film on the Ethiopian Jews,
Meyer Levin, to visit us when he agreed to serve as honored guest
in a community fund-raiser for the embryonic Judaica program.
Today, UCI has the Teller Family Chair of Jewish History, Professor Daniel Schroeter.

CHAPTER 8

Trailblazing Moments, 1975–1978

The board of directors of the AAEJ is a diverse rag-tag group of individualists, most who would never meet socially, united by their love of Israel and their obsession with bringing the Jews of Ethiopia there.

– Henry Rosenberg, charter
board member of the AAEJ

As the plight of the Ethiopian Jews became more widely known throughout southern California, growing numbers of young Jews came forward wishing to help. Some were drawn by the magnitude of the tragedy they saw happening in Ethiopia. Some could not accept that the rescue of their Ethiopian brethren was not a high priority of the government of Israel. Others, reflecting the civil rights and anti-war sentiment of the period, may have seen the issue as another case of an unresponsive "establishment" refusing to do the right thing. For all these and other reasons, the AAEJ seemed to provide both a cause and a vehicle for them.

At that time, however, the year-old Association was home mostly to older members who had different ideas and methods for securing goals. Add a few "children of the 60s" to this group of successful businessmen and women, professional staff members of major Jewish organizations, and retirees, and it became evident that there were to be some interesting times to come.

It was not uncommon for board members of the AAEJ to disagree, sometimes bitterly, and at times, even to work at cross-purposes. Regardless, each deserves credit for his or her part, large or small, in paving the way for the ultimate rescue of the Beta Yisrael.

Barry Weise Gets on Board

How this diversity of opinion and style worked itself out is illustrated in the story of a controversial board member, one of its youngest, Barry Weise. Though Barry was an active and creative member of the AAEJ board of directors for a time, once he started to work for the Los Angeles Jewish Federation's Community Relations Council in January 1981 – and a few years later in November 1983 became a major spokesman regarding the Ethiopian Jews for the national office of NJCRAC in New York – most of the AAEJ board labeled him a turncoat and agent of the establishment. In his defense, however, responding to a complaining board member, I wrote, "I'd rather have Barry's activism than the ignorance and/or indifference of most American Jewish leaders."

In retrospect, I still disagree with some of Barry's views and past actions. We both wanted to see the Ethiopian Jews living in Israel, but because of our different experiences, we interpreted events differently.

Weise came to the AAEJ through a circuitous route. We first met in 1975. A recent dropout from Yale, he was living in a communal residence for college-age Jewish men near UCLA. I was in Los Angeles to give a lecture about the Ethiopian Jews at the Westside Jewish Community Center. After that presentation, as became routine, a gaggle gathered around the lectern to ask questions and to offer help. Waiting in back of the group was a tall guy with a black mustache and wavy hair (considered handsome by the girls, I am told). It was Barry. We talked, he joined the movement and, as the cliché goes, the rest is history.

To call Weise a "Yale dropout" masks the man's most important character trait. Barry was a committed Zionist and champion of Israel. He quit Yale to join the Israeli army, serving as a medic from November 1971 through June 1973. For that alone, one must admire him.

Barry quickly demonstrated his activism shortly after joining the AAEJ. For example, as a native of southern California, he was familiar with events which attracted many Jewish participants and onlookers. One was the annual "Israel Fair" in Los Angeles in the spring of 1975. Preceding the fair was a "unity march," which included representatives from dozens of community organizations. Barry organized more than a dozen high school and college students to pass out literature to onlookers while other students displayed "Save the Falashas" signs. At the fair, Barry and the students constructed a realistic Ethiopian straw home called a *tukul*. Inside were displays, literature, and students who explained the plight of the Ethiopian Jews and told visitors how they could help. This "talking *tukul*" attracted much attention, both at the fair and in Jewish community newspapers.

After nearly two years of activism, in order to earn credits for a university degree, Barry enrolled at UC-Irvine for the spring quarter of 1976 and lived at our home. There we spent endless hours discussing tactics and strategies for getting the Ethiopian Jews to Israel.

Effective and Sometimes Controversial Tactics
Barry volunteered to represent the AAEJ at local and regional meetings of Jewish organizations which attracted students. His energy sometimes took him over the line. At the national meeting of the powerful General Assembly (GA) in San Francisco, he gave an impromptu impassioned speech on behalf of the Ethiopian Jews; not surprisingly, he was ejected. But his words had found a target. In that audience was Simcha Jacobovici, Israeli born and then a student in Canada. He followed Barry out of the hall, talked with him, and soon became an active advocate. In later years, Jacobovici produced a powerful and influential award-winning documentary on the Ethiopian Jews. The infectious movement to rescue the Ethiopian Jews was spreading virtually exponentially among college students.

Not only was Weise an effective speaker and organizer, he also possessed political acumen. In one instance he suggested that the AAEJ would gain community credibility if it had an "establishment" address in the Los Angeles area. This made sense, especially as I already had good relations with Ted Kanner, the executive director of the Los Angeles Jewish Federation. We had met in January 1975 after the AAEJ had leafleted Abba Eban's appearance (chapter 7). An inquiry to Graenum Berger resulted in a go-ahead to seek such an accommodation.

Murray Wood, director of the Federation's Community Relations Council (CRC) who was sympathetic to AAEJ's goals, offered us an office. Shortly, our volunteers were at work there. The AAEJ changed its stationery to reflect Los Angeles as its national office. Graenum Berger came to Los Angeles for the ribbon-cutting in 1977, and it was there that he and I met personally for the first time. All in all Weise's suggestion resulted in a positive arrangement which lasted so long as the CRC's "Oppressed Jewry" desk was administered by the outstanding Roberta Fahn. Alas, after her move to Israel, there were a few "family fights" and a downturn in our relations with the CRC.

Linking up with the CRC did increase somewhat our visibility within the U.S. Jewish community. We also, however, wanted to be noticed in Israel, the focus of our efforts. Although Graenum Berger and others had published numerous articles about the Ethiopian Jews, we never knew the degree to which this publicity influenced Israeli governmental or public opinion. We seemed to be shooting in the dark with no indications whether our missives were doing us any good. Our first clue that those articles did matter came from a story, "The Black Jews," written by Barry Weise and published in the Los Angeles biweekly Israel Today (Nov. 12–25, 1976).

Weise learned from a friend in the Los Angeles Israeli consulate that a transcript of the story had been cabled to the Israeli embassy in Washington. It is standard practice for consular offices to send to their embassy local material dealing with Jewish issues which might impinge on bilateral affairs with the U.S. State Department. Not knowing this at that time, I concluded that they really cared about our activities. So from then on we made it standard operating policy to collate copies of every article dealing with the Beta Yisrael, whether they emanated from the AAEJ or other sources, and send packets of them to Israeli consulates, major Jewish organizations and the community relations councils in every North American city with a significant Jewish population.

Later, Barry Weise led us to a productive source of information in Israel. Unknown to most American Jews, the Zionist Archives in Jerusalem are available to the public. Barry, relatively fluent in Hebrew, translated many of the documents from the archives dealing with the Ethiopian Jews. Most had not been made public, and some contained controversial material. When the AAEJ launched its massive information campaign in 1979, these documents proved powerful ammunition in arousing public support for the Association's program (chapter 11).

Soviet Jewry

My wife and I never expected to become directly involved with "Refuseniks," the Soviet Jewry dissidents, even though we empathized with them. We felt that American Jews, many of whom had family roots in Eastern Europe, would readily identify with Russian Jews and support them. That was not the case, however, with the poor, mostly illiterate black Jews of Ethiopia. Nonetheless Barry Weise sucked us into the Refusenik movement for a brief though memorable time.

It started when Barry, through his contacts with Israeli-based organizations, was recruited to visit the Soviet Union in the fall of 1976. He was joined by Sylvia Haas, the UC-Irvine student who, along with Weise, was co-president of the Student Pro-Falasha Committee. When they returned, Barry convinced my wife and me also to go to the Soviet Union under the secret sponsorship of the Israeli consulate. We would attend meetings of the Refuseniks, mostly academics who had lost their jobs after applying for visas to immigrate to Israel and being refused permission. I usually gave two lectures, one on my scientific research, and the other on the plight of the Ethiopian Jews. Sylvia spoke on women's issues in Israel and America.

We arrived in early March 1977, right after Anatoly Shcharansky (now Natan Sharansky) was arrested, and we experienced some of the stresses of coping with an authoritarian Communist government. We were surprised by the way the Refuseniks empathized with the plight of the Ethiopian Jews, and by the fact that some already knew about the pioneering work of Jacques Faitlovitch. When we returned to California, as the Jewish community learned of our Soviet experience, we were in even more demand as speakers, and our credibility regarding our concerns for the Ethiopian Jews was enhanced.

Our involvement with Soviet Jewry also was to influence AAEJ strategies on behalf of the Ethiopian Jews. Barry, for example, knew of, and argued for, various tactics used by his friends in the movement to save the Soviet Jews. Those methods worked for them; why not use them to advance the cause of the Ethiopian Jews? He urged us to have volunteers phone the Israeli consulate to tie up their lines. This did not seem appropriate, but we did agree with his suggestion to demonstrate on the sidewalk in front of the consulate. In deference to other, less aggressive Association members, we rejected Barry's call for a pride of roaring college students in favor of a flock of adults, conservatively attired, carrying "Save Falasha Jewry" signs. We distributed literature and answered questions raised by interested passersby. Among the dignified, short-haired participants were Rabbi Robert Bergman and businessmen Michael Pinto and Jerry Strauss. Our attention to details paid off when our demonstration was widely reported in the Jewish press.

As we were preparing to leave, several young Israelis working for the consulate invited us to join them for tea. We talked with them about the Ethiopian Jews and the need to bring them to Israel. They were open-minded; some may well have supported our cause, I thought.

Another tactic Barry carried over from the Soviet Jewry movement was the effective use of posters. He realized that we needed more permanent reminders of the plight of the Ethiopian Jews and got one of his artist friends to prepare a poster for distribution to synagogues in the Los Angeles area. The posters were an immediate success in increasing awareness. He later persuaded Los Angeles graphic artist Roen Salem to prepare another poster which the AAEJ distributed widely. Those were the first of a half-dozen posters from the AAEJ which eventually ended up in synagogues and Jewish community centers across the country.

"Der mahn mit der bord" Sends Barry to Ethiopia

"Der mahn mit der bord" (Yiddish for "the man with the beard") – that is how Barry's aging grandmother referred to me. In her eyes I was an ominous character who was sending her grandchild into the dangers lurking in darkest Africa. She had already survived the trauma of his serving in the Israeli army in 1971–1973 and skirting trouble in the Soviet Union in the fall of 1976. What now was in store for her grandson in Ethiopia, a venture arranged for him by *der mahn mit der bord*? No wonder Barry's grandmother was worried; he was going to live and work in one of the poorest countries in the world run by a new ruthless Marxist government. For Barry, this experience was to shape his attitude on how he was going to view activities thereafter dealing with the rescue of the Ethiopian Jews.

Weise's Ethiopian adventure originated in January 1977 when Graenum Berger learned that World ORT Union, now called Organization for Educational Resources and Technological Training, needed to find a worker for its program in Ethiopia who could speak both English and Hebrew. I suggested Barry Weise, the AAEJ board approved, Berger passed along the recommendation, and ORT offered Barry the job.

The World ORT Union was one of the largest nongovernmental training organizations in the world. Its programs focused on such basics as improving drinking water, providing medical care, building schools and furnishing them so the residents could get training in agriculture and in crafts that would help them get jobs. World

ORT received its major funding from the American and some European governments. In addition, it also received support from an outstanding volunteer group called Women's American ORT. The World ORT Union is nondenominational, although most frequently it works in countries that have some Jewish population in need. For that reason, there were problems with the ORT program in Ethiopia. Many thought that the Jewish population there – that is the Ethiopian Jews – were not getting sufficient help and sometimes were actually discriminated against by non-Jewish employees of ORT.

Barry Weise embarked on what was to be a short but informative odyssey in February 1977. His first surprise came when he reached Geneva and was advised by Gershon Levy, an Israeli heading the ORT program in Ethiopia, to remain in Geneva until the "political situation" improved in Addis Ababa. Barry finally arrived in Addis on March 3, where he promptly fell ill. He never made it into the hinterlands, but he did meet a number of Ethiopian Jews in Addis, including their venerable leader, Yona Bogale.

During that Passover Weise met Haim Halachmi, an employee of HIAS (Hebrew Immigrant Aid Society) "on loan" to the Jewish Agency. Halachmi was planning for the transfer of some Beta Yisrael from Ethiopia to Israel, an event which did transpire later that year. From that moment on, Barry was convinced that the government of Israel was serious about rescuing the Jews of Ethiopia. Weise later told me that Menachem Begin had been the person who made the difference. I found the conclusion strange because Halachmi was sent to Ethiopia to arrange for the transfer of Ethiopian Jews during the earlier Labor administration by Yitzhak Rabin, the prime minister at that time.

While recuperating, Barry spent a great deal of time with his boss, Gershon Levy, whom he came to admire. When he learned that ORT planned to fire Gershon, Weise protested. Dissatisfied with the response he received regarding Levy's dismissal, Barry quit ORT on June 23, 1977. In the winter of 1978 he resumed his education at the University of California, Berkeley, before taking a job with the Los Angeles Jewish Federation in 1981.

One-by-One Rescues

Weise's brief sojourn in Ethiopia had certain positive results. He had met several Beta Yisrael from Gondar province, and he had learned that ORT was doing little to help them. He returned committed to rescuing them. Barry suggested a "trial run" at actually bringing out one Ethiopian Jew at a time. With the board's approval, a set of fictitious papers was concocted saying that a Beta Yisrael who had worked for ORT had been granted admission to an American college's Rural Development Program. The college was the University of California, Irvine; it had no such program. The admissions papers were written by my wife, who was an administrator there; the official seal was that of an assistant registrar, my tennis buddy Richard Everman. With these documents and official ornamentation in hand, the "student," Barry's Beta Yisrael assistant in Ethiopia, was able to secure an Ethiopian passport and exit visa. He flew to Europe to subsequently end up in Israel. The AAEJ employed that method with success many times during 1985 through 1989 (chapter 20).

While with the Los Angeles Federation, Barry used his knowledge of Ethiopia to initiate a number of rescues. With the participation of Henry Rosenberg, Barry was instrumental in bringing Semu (Simcha) Desta from Ethiopia to the United States. [Semu proved to be a key contact in later rescues of Ethiopian Jews (chapter 20).] Also while with the Los Angeles Federation, Barry was instrumental in arranging for getting to Israel, via a "detour" through the United States, the wife and children of Gedalia Uria. Gedalia was a veteran Beta Yisrael teacher who had been arrested and tortured by the Ethiopian government. He was eventually brought to Israel by Henry Rosenberg.

First American Mission to Marxist Ethiopia

Graenum Berger had been touting the idea of sending a mission of American Jews to Ethiopia to evaluate the situation of the Beta Yisrael there. It was a good idea, although organizing such a mission would require an enormous amount of work. In order to learn how the establishment would react to our plans, I announced at a national NJCRAC meeting in San Diego that the AAEJ was going to organize such a mission. Barry approached me about participating, and I grabbed the chance to pass the project to him. He was working for the Los Angeles Federation and had the staff and resources, and I suggested that he arrange the mission under the Federation's auspices. It was a great project for Barry, and he followed through admirably. He wanted others to witness in Ethiopia what he had learned while there working for ORT.

Barry organized the mission, a number of AAEJ members went on the trip, and it provided the seed for some of the other members of the mission to organize the North American Conference on Ethiopian Jews (NACOEJ). AAEJ board member Henry Rosenberg was a participant and was able to smuggle a young Beta Yisrael couple on the airplane to Cairo when the mission left Ethiopia, and then they proceeded on to Israel. That mission was Barry's second trip to Ethiopia. He subsequently traveled there two more times prior to Operation Moses while he was employed by the NJCRAC national office in New York.

It was during his employment by the New York NJCRAC, an organization that tried to control and defuse the AAEJ, that Barry drew the wrath of Graenum Berger and most of the board members of the AAEJ. I knew Barry better and understood that the NJCRAC served him as a vehicle to continue his work for the Ethiopian Jews. His opinion of the leadership of NJCRAC was not very high; in fact, it seemed much the same as Graenum Berger's.

Differing Views Bring Change

No doubt Barry had creative ideas. His innate intelligence, commitment, and energy, bolstered by his experience with ORT in Ethiopia, albeit for a short time, gave him background and credibility that most of the activists, including me, did not have. Many members of the AAEJ board knew him primarily for his strong, sometimes overreaching opinions. These traits were about to place him in the eye of a storm that seemed destined to come.

It began innocently enough: Graenum Berger, president of the AAEJ, threatened to publish an advertisement in the *Jerusalem Post* on July 15, 1978, castigating the government of Israel for dragging its feet in rescuing the Ethiopian Jews. Graenum believed that such a warning would bring about action; he was not prepared, however, for the action to come from Barry Weise.

Barry was in Israel that spring, and, because of his relationship with the AAEJ and his experience in Ethiopia, he was developing good rapport with many of the Beta Yisrael leaders there. He was convinced that Menachem Begin was sincere in his pledge to rescue the Ethiopian Jews and that Haim Halachmi, whom Barry had met in Ethiopia during Passover 1977, was the man who was going to make it happen.

Weise then sent two telegrams to the AAEJ. To me, on July 6 he wrote:

> Falashas not ready for Graenum's July fifteenth action. They insist decision by vote. Stop him at all costs. I believe that Halachmi can do it if given time.
>
> – *Barry*

The next day, Barry sent Graenum this telegram:

> Have spoken with people below: following consensus of opinion, they are very upset and unhappy with your proposed action on July fifteenth. They feel this is a life and death decision of a magnitude which cannot be independent action and can only be made by the families and relatives of those in Ethiopia.
>
> They insist that you not proceed without approval.
>
> Send text of proposed action for a vote of the Falasha Community of Israel, who will send you their decision.
>
> Rahamim, Rav Yoseph Adani, Zimna and Yoseph Wube.
>
> Cable me – Barry Weise, 1 Metudela, Jerusalem. Phone 37295.

That telegram, I think, forever severed Barry's relationship with Graenum. Reacting to the telegram, Graenum on the same day sent copies to me, Ted Norman, and Henry Rosenberg, adding this startling declaration:

> In light of the above and the feelings of our own board members, I will obviously not insert any ads in any papers – Jewish or public.
>
> However, since I do not believe that our present efforts are going to bring about any substantial changes in the actions of Israel, the Jewish Agency or world Jewish leadership, I think that it is best that I step down and turn over the reins to those who have more patience and faith than I possess. I will call a meeting in September, which will present a slate of new officers and directors of the association.

What at first seemed a minor issue now had far-reaching consequences. It reflected a basic difference in approach for operating the Association. Was it a classic case of the old guard versus new blood, except that in this instance the old guard was more radical?

It was a complete surprise when Graenum called to tell me I was the ideal choice to succeed him as president of the AAEJ. He informed me, however, that "there was some opposition." Smelling trouble, I told Graenum that if my leadership was not wanted, this was fine with me; there was nothing to gain wasting our energies in internal disputes. Rather than being bogged down in a contentious environment, I would be more effective continuing to develop a grassroots effort in California, as I had been doing during the past four years. This arrangement could even be pursued independent of the AAEJ. "I am not a good politician," I said. Graenum asked for time to work things out. A few days later he called and said that the nominating committee wanted me to run for president unopposed. As Graenum was about to hang up, he chuckled and said, "Howard, you *are* a good politician."

Taking over from Graenum Berger, I was propelled from a familiar and comfortable role as teacher and mentor of students into a new and decidedly more threatening role, that of heading a grassroots organization. As Henry Rosenberg so aptly put it, the AAEJ was composed of "individualists, most who would never meet socially, united by their love of Israel and their obsession with bringing the Jews of Ethiopia there."

Was this admixture of *individualism* and *obsession* that characterized the AAEJ board members a recipe for eventual success, or for rapid combustion? There were more questions than answers.

PART IV

PRESIDENT OF THE AAEJ: 1978–1982

CHAPTER 9

From Living Room to World Stage

[Howard's] reports were masterful descriptions of work accomplished and still to be done. Perhaps one day he will write about how the AAEJ was born, developed, achieved its objectives, and closed its doors when its work was finally completed.
— *Graenum Berger,* Rescue of the
Ethiopian Jews! *Page 80, 1996*

*M*y first year as president of the AAEJ proved more formidable than expected. I took the plunge having no idea of the intricacies of the work that was to evolve. It was one thing to give lectures and publish articles. It was another to become the leader of an incorporated organization of about one thousand members with an annual budget of $15,000 – and without any paid staff.

A remarkable year ensued: clandestine rescues in the Sudan, an increased budget reaching $75,000, negotiations with the prime minister of Israel, demonstrations at the Israeli Knesset, work to resolve long-standing factionalism within the various Beta Yisrael organizations in Israel, and all while handling a quantum jump in membership and in contributions. In addition, the AAEJ, "new kid on the block" of Jewish organizations, through this newly aggressive activism was now being recognized as a force to be considered and was receiving broad coverage by the Jewish press.

Each activity was a different adventure, yet many of these adventures were going on simultaneously. This chapter describes the broad range of national and international activities of that year. Our role in initiating the rescue of the Beta Yisrael from the Sudan in the spring of 1979 and the subsequent negotiations with the government of Israel are described in chapter 10.

Situation of Ethiopian Jews Worsens

Our information about the Ethiopian crisis came from five main sources: (1) Ethiopian Jews who had recently arrived in Israel; (2) communications from the Beta Yisrael in Ethiopia; (3) individuals who had spent some time in Ethiopia and/or surrounding countries; (4) reports (some "confidential") from various agencies and governments; (5) numerous news reports.

The picture was startling. As of December 1978 about ten thousand of the Beta Yisrael could not be accounted for by the local Jewish leaders in Ethiopia. The Jewish Agency reported in January 1979 that two thousand Beta Yisrael had been killed or wounded in the past two to three years. Letters and firsthand accounts told of Ethiopian Jews being enslaved. About two thousand lived in the country's famine area. Another report told of seven thousand being dispossessed from their homes. Word also came to us that hundreds of Beta Yisrael had been languishing as refugees in the Sudan with little likelihood of getting to Israel.

Ethiopia was still in turmoil. The revolutionary government had not gained control of the country. Numerous counter-revolutionary fronts held large areas of Ethiopia including the regions in which substantial numbers of the Beta Yisrael lived. The war in the Ogaden region near Somalia wore on, generating hundreds of thousands of refugees. Insurgents were fighting the Ethiopian government in Oromo, Tigre, and Eritrea, with the conflict in the latter two provinces spreading into areas where Beta Yisrael villages were located. Repression and police-state policies reinforced traditional discrimination to further oppress the Beta Yisrael.

ORT and JDC in Ethiopia

During winter 1979 worrisome revelations surfaced about the World Organization for Rehabilitation through Training (ORT) education program in Ethiopia. Back in 1976 the World ORT Union had taken over a smaller program in Ethiopia from the England-based Falasha Welfare Association (FWA). World ORT then started its Ethiopian programs with financial aid in the millions provided by a number of foreign governments including those of Canada and the U.S. Although the AAEJ thought these programs were intended to aid the Beta Yisrael, ORT publicly claimed them to be nonsectarian.

We received firsthand reports from the two main Israeli workers for the organization and also from a major leader and educator of the Beta Yisrael in Ethiopia. Our sources told us that not only was the ORT program failing to help the Ethiopian Jews (only 10–15 percent of whom lived in areas serviced by ORT), but also those Jewish children attending the ORT schools were not getting any Jewish education. The Ethiopian Jews in Israel made their concerns about the ORT programs public, and our Association compiled a list of twenty-two specific charges. Until June 1979, the AAEJ reported those accusations only to ORT and did not make them public.

In response, ORT declared that all the charges were without foundation and that it planned to continue its program as before. Representatives of World ORT accused the Israeli workers of theft or lying. The Beta Yisrael leader was described as "senile" by the Jewish Agency. ORT did not honor AAEJ requests to make available evidence negating the accusations against the organization.

The degree to which sectarian programs were acceptable was problematic. The Ethiopian government indicated that it welcomed sectarian programs, whereas the World ORT Union, which received its funds from foreign governments and not from Jewish sources, said it could remain in Ethiopia only as a nonsectarian organization. Because of my respect for ORT's overall past record and for the good women who support it, and because we were too small an organization to divide our energies when the major battle was *aliyah*, I recommended that the AAEJ not pursue the ORT issue with vigor.

The American Joint Distribution Committee (JDC), on the other hand, is a Jewish organization funded by Jewish monies, which is supposed to help Jews in distress. According to their publicity material and the report of their December 1975 annual meeting, the JDC budgeted $100,000 toward assisting the Ethiopian Jews. Nonetheless, as 1978 merged into 1979, and the danger to the Beta Yisrael increased, the JDC failed to come to their aid. They did, however, establish a program there in the 1980s after ORT had left Ethiopia.

The Ethiopian Jews in Israel Demonstrate

After years of being told to "remain silent, trust us, and be patient," and having seen only three hundred of their brethren arrive in the thirty years of Israel's otherwise proud history of *aliyah*, the Ethiopian Jews in Israel decided to demonstrate against the government of Israel, the Jewish Agency, and the worldwide Jewish establishment. They wanted action, the reunification of their families.

Having the available names and addresses of the Beta Yisrael in Israel, the AAEJ wrote each family a letter urging them to speak out. The letter was written in Amharic for the AAEJ by student linguist Brett Goldberg. We asked Bill Halpern, who was in Israel at the time, to assist the Beta Yisrael leaders in charge. The AAEJ backed up its words with cash, transmitted with the help of Dr. Bernard Resnikoff, a friend of Graenum Berger and head of the Jerusalem office of the American Jewish Committee.

The Ethiopian leaders began their first public protest in late December 1978 with press conferences and news releases that broke the years of silence on matters regarding the Ethiopian Jews. On January 7, 1979, they demonstrated in front of the Knesset, attracting worldwide attention. News of their protest reached the pages of many foreign newspapers, including the *New York Times*, the *Los Angeles Times,* and the *San Francisco Chronicle.* Critical comments against the government and the Jewish Agency were made by Israeli reporters and commentators. The *Jerusalem Post, Davar, Maariv,* and the Sephardic *Bamaarach* were particularly incensed over the foot-dragging by the government and the Jewish Agency on the *aliyah* of the Ethiopian Jews.

This demonstration was a major factor turning the tide of Jewish public opinion in favor of the rescue of the Jews of Ethiopia. Especially noteworthy was the leadership exercised by Avram Yerday, Zimna Berhane, Zecharias Yona, and Rahamin Elazar, who put aside all partisan differences and united the Beta Yisrael community in Israel. They chose to demonstrate recognizing the possibility that the Ethiopian government might harm their relatives in Ethiopia. Fortunately there were never any reports of Beta Yisrael in Ethiopia suffering as a consequence of the demonstration in Jerusalem.

The secret was out. The Israeli Ethiopian Jews wanted their families in Ethiopia to join them in Israel. They demanded that the government of Israel and the Jewish Agency become more proactive.

Lecture Tour of Zecharias Yona

The AAEJ realized that although we had many able American speakers, it would be more effective to sponsor a tour in North America of an Ethiopian Jew who could provide firsthand information. A major advocate of such a tour was Barry Weise. The speaker was Zecharias Yona, son of the Ethiopian leader Yona Bogale, and an officer of the Association of Ethiopian Jews in Israel. Weise first tried to get the American Zionist Youth Foundation (AZYF) to sponsor the tour, but that group was ordered by the Jewish Agency, which supports the AZYF, not to do so. Then Barry got the approval of the North American Student NETWORK. He and Canadian Steve Bauman of NETWORK managed the tour, consulting often with the AAEJ. We picked up all the travel costs for Zecharias.

The lectures by Zecharias Yona generated a windfall of publicity in the Jewish press in North America. And, keeping pace with the events of the year, the AAEJ continued to send out weekly news releases. Although the AAEJ had much to do with initiating the burgeoning publicity on the plight of the Ethiopian Jews, our message was spread further by a number of well-known individuals. In August 1979, Elie Wiesel issued his first cry on behalf of the Beta Yisrael (*Present Tense*). The Jewish Defense League rabbi, Meir Kahane, added his voice. Even the Jewish Agency's own news service issued a number of releases on the Ethiopian Jews. The editor of that news service prefaced the articles with the following remarks: "The Jewish press in the world has recently made the Falashas into one of the best-covered stories in Jewish journalism."

Widening Our Influence

By June 1979, groups of pro-Beta Yisrael activists had sprung up in fourteen North American cities. To get some new blood and broaden our base, we placed representatives of these groups on our board of directors and asked that they consider setting up chapters in their respective geographical areas. Those cities and their representatives were:

> *Baltimore, MD* (Sandy Sager and Mark Rothschild); *Boston, MA* (Alan Iser); *Denver, CO* (Neal Price, Martin Zerobnick, and Murray Brilliant); *Chicago, IL* (Nate Shapiro and Gail Winston); *Eugene, OR* (Leonard Landis and Dr. Jerome Maliner); *Los Angeles, CA* (Dan Witties); *Miami, FL* (Yossi Yanich and Miriam Shulevitz); *Minneapolis, MN* (Rabbi Max Jacobs); *New Orleans, LA* (Sylvia and Lester Gerson); *New York, NY* (Yehuda Shapiro and Eli Rockowitz); *San Francisco, CA* (Murray Narell and Miriam Levy); *St. Louis, MO* (Dottie Cohen and Barry Mehler); *Washington, D.C.* (Bert Silver); *Winnipeg* (Martin Levin).

Others joined the roster of influential activists: Daniel Mann of the Washington Federation and Brant Coopersmith of the American Jewish Committee in Washington, D.C.; Robert Loup of Denver; Rabbi Shalom Singer of Highland Park, IL; and Earl Raab of the San Francisco Jewish Federation.

As part of our efforts to broaden our reach, we began to develop a nationwide speakers bureau. Although well-written and well-researched newspaper articles were important, there was nothing like listening to an informed, effective speaker with evocative visual aids, who could answer questions and suggest ways to help.

The AAEJ soon had an active and fast-growing speakers bureau of close to a hundred individuals. In addition to speakers on the AAEJ list, many communities and organizations developed their own speaker cadres. The AAEJ provided slides and a script to each group or speaker. In addition, Roberta Fahn of the Los Angeles Jewish Federation, with the support of CRC director Murray Wood and executive director Ted Kanner, produced a narrated slide show which greatly facilitated their presentations.

Mail solicitations were another avenue of spreading our message. In addition to our mailings to individuals already on our database, that year the AAEJ gambled: we purchased a mailing list from another organization and hired a commercial company, led by the able Jerry Benjamin, to handle the mailings. Not only did we recover our costs, we also received an additional $25,000 in denominations ranging from $5 to $150, with the average donation being around $25. From that one mass mailing, we added over one thousand new donors to our existing database.

New Alliances at Home and Abroad

The AAEJ information campaign, in addition to stimulating the formation of new grassroots groups in North America, also influenced numerous long established Jewish organizations. Some of them passed strong resolutions urging Israel to rescue the Ethiopian Jews; others expressed their concern. Among them were the North American Student NETWORK (both the U.S. and Canadian groups), the Zionist Organization of America, the Jewish American War Veterans, the Wiesenthal Center for Holocaust Studies, and the American Jewish Committee.

- **RABBINICAL GROUPS:** With a little coaxing by our rabbi activists, rabbis of the Conservative and Reform movements started to speak out in 1978. Forceful statements were made, for example, by Rabbi David Saperstein and Mr. Al Vorspan of the American Hebrew Congregation. Rabbi Saul Teplitz, president of the Rabbinical Assembly (Conservative), wrote a particularly compelling letter which stressed the importance of rescuing the Ethiopian Jews.

- HIGH SCHOOL STUDENT GROUPS: These young people, brimming with energy, continued to provide a core of workers. I enjoyed attending meetings of such groups as the BBYO, Young Judea, NFTY (North American Federation of Temple Youth [Reform]), USY (United Synagogue Youth [Conservative]), and Habonim.

- AMERICAN SEPHARDI FEDERATION: This organization, representing about a million American Jews, identified with the dark-skinned Jews of Ethiopia. Its staff, particularly executive director Gary Schaer, actively kept the membership of the Federation informed.

- NATIONAL JEWISH COMMUNITY RELATIONS ADVISORY COUNCIL (NJCRAC, formerly called NACRAC): This group, the major community education arm of the Jewish Federations in the U.S., at its national meeting in Cincinnati (January 1979), sponsored its first workshop on the Ethiopian Jews and had Zecharias Yona participate.

In addition to our newfound domestic alliances, we bolstered our relationships with Israeli activist groups as well.

- ASSOCIATION OF ETHIOPIAN JEWS (AEJ): We reviewed our respective activities, concerns, and plans and agreed on having better lines of communication. They indicated that amongst all of world Jewry, they depended most upon the AAEJ. To temper their expectations, I reminded them that the AAEJ was a small organization and did not have the resources that larger American organizations possessed. For the AAEJ to represent them more effectively in the U.S. and for them to have a stronger voice in Israel, I urged them to unite the various disparate organizations of the Ethiopian Jews in Israel.

After listening to the able leadership of the AEJ, I felt strongly that on matters dealing with the Ethiopian Jews, they must participate or at least be consulted by the Israeli government, Jewish Agency, and support groups such as ours. Not only were they capable, they were much closer to the problems than any other group. We discussed getting their organization legal status so that they could accept funds directly from us and run their own financial affairs without going through any intermediary organizations.

- ISRAEL COMMITTEE FOR ETHIOPIAN JEWS (ICEJ): This group consisted of a small number of dedicated Israelis, who for years had been assisting the Ethiopian Jews in Israel with business, absorption, and organizational matters. Their major funding to assist the Ethiopian Jews came from the AAEJ, with occasional reimbursements from the Jewish Agency and help from the Israel Colonization Association of England. The ICEJ had been led for years by octogenarian Professor Aryeh Tartakower who was quite ill and preparing to step down in 1979; he was to be replaced by Knesset Member (MK) Shlomo Hillel. Our meetings with them were amicable, and we settled a number of financial matters. They were dedicated people, who were doing much to help the Ethiopian Jews and the AEJ. The workhorses were Chanan Lehman and Mordechai Paran, who ran the Israeli branch of the Israel Colonization Association (ICA) and always kept their offices and facilities available to the AEJ. Despite occasional differences, I had particularly warm relationships with Professor Tartakower and Chanan Lehman.

- PUBLIC COMMITTEE FOR ETHIOPIAN JEWS: Michael Corinaldi, a lawyer in Jerusalem then, and now a professor at Haifa University, formed this new group of Israeli activists. His committee's initial goal was to organize Israeli public opinion to pressure its government to aid the Ethiopian Jews. Later that committee became more preoccupied with religious issues, such as eliminating the ceremonies required by the chief rabbis to "reconfirm" that the Beta Yisrael are Jews according to *halachah*.

Intensifying the Pressure

Once the Beta Yisrael started to leave Ethiopia for the Sudan, the AAEJ needed to reflect upon our new role. How, for example, was our small volunteer organization going to handle all of the new responsibilities we had taken upon ourselves and still give rescue the attention and resources required? We decided that it was not the time to hire a professional staff. We could better achieve our objectives by reorganizing. The AAEJ's executive committee would assume a greater number of responsibilities, and the board of directors would be broadened to include grassroots activists from across the country.

The rescue of the Ethiopian Jews would not be achieved overnight. If large-scale rescues were to start, would Israel be prepared to assist the new refugees by using workers who could speak the Ethiopian languages and by providing appropriate absorption facilities? How would help get to the Beta Yisrael still remaining in Marxist Ethiopia or in the Sudan? Because those responsibilities were those of the government of Israel and the world Jewish community, not the AAEJ, what were effective ways to get them to carry out those missions?

We needed to proceed with care. Israel was then facing difficult times; U.S. foreign policy was changing, and American Jewish organizations were stirring the pot by alienating the African American community. Were the AAEJ to criticize Israel for neglecting its black brothers, our words could backfire. Our opponents would label us as either misguided or anti-Zionist or self-hating. We had to think this one through, although we had heard all this before.

Despite some AAEJ successes in getting support from a number of Jewish organizations in 1978–1979, most of the large establishment organizations continued to be passive and ignore the plight of the Ethiopian Jews. It became apparent that if we could not convince them to participate and inform their membership, we had to speak their language – *money*, attacking their lifeline by asking our supporters to withhold their contributions to the UJA.

At the time of our annual meeting in late September 1979, there were no signs that the Jewish Agency was going to resume rescue efforts, even token ones. We needed to decide if the AAEJ were going to start again to rescue Ethiopian Jews from Africa. To do so would require the AAEJ to raise our fund-raising activities to new levels.

Perhaps now was the time to seek the help of American politicians, of African Americans, and of other countries. We needed to proceed with care and discretion. There would be no turning back.

Although risky, expanding our efforts in the public policy arena might well prove our most effective path for reaching our goals. We certainly could not achieve it solely through our own rescue activities. The history of the Soviet Jewry movement suggested that we could win. The exodus of Russian Jews was not encouraged at first by the government of Israel, for it was trying to maintain good relations with the Soviet Union. It took the protests of the Soviet dissidents themselves with the help of Jewish grassroots support groups in America, England, and elsewhere to jump-start the movement; then world Jewry and the government of Israel joined. The more we could help the Ethiopian Jews to speak out for themselves, the faster American Jewry and Israel would take the cause of the Beta Yisrael seriously.

In 1979 there was no comparison between the plight of the Beta Yisrael and the horrors suffered by the Jews in the Holocaust. Yet there was a parallel. Just as the world had ignored the warnings coming out of Germany in the early 1930s when the Jews of Europe could have escaped, too many Jews in the 1970s ignored the warning signals coming from Mengistu's Ethiopia about a looming tragedy about to hit the Beta Yisrael. In the 1930s there had been no Israel to harbor oppressed Jews from Europe. Since 1948, however, there was a safe harbor: Israel. If "never again" was to be more than an empty fund-raising slogan, it was vital that people of good will be mobilized.

The AAEJ had to plan carefully to woo Israel and world Jewry to modify their priorities so that when geopolitical events presented opportunities to rescue the Beta Yisrael, they would be prepared.

CHAPTER 10

Operation Elijah: The Secret Rescues from the Sudan, 1979–1980

I cannot find the words to express the extremely terrible situation of the [Jews here].... They are at death's end and do not know how to escape the situation.... There was a belief in their heart that with troubles like there are now, the nation of Israel and the Jews of the world will arrive to help them. They are waiting for this to happen every day. But now they despair and lack hope. Against their will they are enslaved by their neighbors. Those who flee their homes to save their lives are without food or clothing.

Lost is the nation of Jews who kept the Laws of the Torah and the Jewish traditions. And this is so sad that it happens precisely now, when the State of Israel exists.

– Letter from a Beta Yisrael in Ethiopia, translated from the Amharic, August 1978

As the number of AAEJ volunteers grew, voices were raised demanding more aggressive measures be taken to rescue the Ethiopian Jews. We were hopeful during the latter half of 1977 when newly elected Prime Minister Menachem Begin brought in 120 Beta Yisrael, and it appeared that, as part of a deal with the Ethiopian government, he was going to bring more Ethiopian Jews to Israel on a regular basis. But then came Moshe Dayan's ill-considered admission of the arms-for-Jews deal with Ethiopia at a press conference in Zurich in February 1978. Addis aborted the exodus.

By fall 1978 we were getting a stream of firsthand reports about the worsening situation of the Beta Yisrael in Ethiopia. The Marxist government was arresting and killing students, bandits were raiding the Jewish villages, and Ethiopia was experiencing one of its many famines. Because of the growing violence and hardship in their home districts, the Beta Yisrael were reported to be heading to refugee camps in the Sudan.

In light of these deteriorating circumstances, some AAEJ board members began calling for direct action. Others urged caution: After all, none of us had any firsthand operational experience, and only one – Henry Rosenberg – was familiar with the Ethiopian countryside. We weighed the hazards and advantages, but could not come up with a viable rescue plan.

Sudan Rescue: Bill Halpern Comes on the Scene

Just at that juncture someone appeared with the knowledge, experience, and commitment to break through our impasse: William P. Halpern. While a graduate student at the University of California, Berkeley, Bill Halpern came to Israel in 1973 to conduct research at the Rehovot Institute, an agricultural branch of Hebrew University. In Rehovot, he met two non-Jewish visiting Ethiopian scholars who encouraged him to carry out his research in Ethiopia. Bill agreed, and during 1974–1975 he went to work in Ethiopia for the Haile Selassie Foundation. While traveling there to see firsthand the health and social problems of the country, he was startled to find a number of primitive synagogues and the Beta Yisrael. He was dismayed by their living conditions and the dangers they faced.

In Addis Ababa, Bill met Yona Bogale, a distinguished-looking Ethiopian Jew in his mid-fifties who had been a student of Jacques Faitlovitch and had studied in Israel. Bogale administered the village schools of the Ethiopian Jews, schools started first by Dr. Faitlovitch and later supported by the Jewish Agency for a while, and then by other Jewish organizations. Yona's role as titular head of the Beta Yisrael in Ethiopia brought a constant stream of visitors to his home. Halpern soon became acquainted with a number of the Beta Yisrael activists including Baruch Tegegne and his younger cousin, Semu Desta, soon to become Halpern's good friend. But then the Marxist coup took place, Haile Selassie was dethroned, and the new government cancelled Bill's stay permit.

Halpern returned to Berkeley to continue his studies, but he could not get the Ethiopian Jews out of his mind. Over the next few years, he returned to Ethiopia several times; to do so he received help from a congregant of his temple in Minneapolis: Rudy Boschwitz, a Republican member of the United States Senate. Through Bill, Boschwitz became committed to the rescue of the Ethiopian Jews. First the senator raised funds to help Bill get to Ethiopia. Later, he founded a congressional caucus for the Ethiopian Jews. In 1991, Boschwitz was a key player in winning President George H.W. Bush's support for Operation Solomon (chapter 21).

While commuting between Berkeley and Ethiopia, Bill came across articles written by Graenum Berger. He approached Berger with an idea for bringing Beta Yisrael from Ethiopia to the Sudan. There they would become refugees, a status which might make it easier for them to be taken out of the Sudan, either clandestinely or through recognized international resettlement groups. Bill already had contacted the International Rescue Committee, an organization created after World War II to bring displaced persons and Holocaust survivors out of Europe. Once the Beta Yisrael were in Europe, he proposed, they could be taken to Israel.

In fall 1978 I met Halpern and was impressed with his knowledge of Ethiopia and his commitment to rescuing the Beta Yisrael, but most of all with his well thought out plan. "You do not know these people. They are strong," he told me. "They can walk for days on end. Many know the countryside and the terrain along the Sudanese border."

Can-Do People: Tegegne, Shapiro, Weinberg

Apart from his own experience and zeal, Halpern had another resource vital to a successful rescue operation: a man who could go undetected inside the Beta Yisrael community, who had credibility with his kinsmen, and – most important of all – was willing to risk his life to lead them to safety. This person was Baruch Tegegne.

Tegegne had come to Israel in 1955 along with twenty-five other Ethiopian youths to study at Kfar Batya, a cooperative village (*moshav*) run by the American Mizrachi Women. They were trained so they could become teachers in Ethiopia in the Beta Yisrael village schools. Tegegne returned to Ethiopia and eventually worked for an Israeli company there. As the situation deteriorated, he fled to the Sudan to start his own incredible trek back to Israel. Once there, in 1977, and quite by chance, Baruch was spotted by Halpern at a Tel Aviv bus stop!

Over a cup of coffee at a street-side cafe, Halpern was intrigued by Tegegne's story of his escape from Ethiopia. Most important was that Baruch had walked to Sudan along a route similar to the escape plan Halpern was proposing. Tegegne had made friends along the way in the Sudan and learned how to evade capture at the many Sudanese checkpoints.

Recognizing Tegegne's potential value to his rescue plan, Halpern told him that Graenum Berger was giving an important lecture in Jerusalem on the need to save the Ethiopian Jews, and that he should attend, meet Berger, and tell him how he had escaped via the Sudan. Tegegne did, and the seeds of a possible rescue by the AAEJ were planted.

As fate would have it, soon after my inauguration in the fall of 1978, I received a call from Nate Shapiro, a stockbroker in Chicago. He had been told to call me by his friend, veteran AAEJ board member Bernie Alpert. Nate's first words to me, spoken in a low, almost hoarse, voice, were: "I want to save Jewish lives." When I mentioned possible projects and our lack of funds, he said: "Money is not a problem." I told him about Bill Halpern and what I knew of his proposal and suggested that he speak with Halpern. That was it. Nate joined the AAEJ. Together, Nate and Bill, working with Graenum Berger, undertook to develop a rescue plan to be implemented by spring 1979.

In voluntary organizations, there often are a few "can-do" individuals who by personality, resources, or sheer force of commitment get things done. Once Shapiro and Berger had bought into Halpern's rescue scheme, the next step would be to gain the support of key board members. In the Los Angeles area, such a "can-do" pivotal person was Barbi Weinberg.

Barbi was special. In addition to serving on the AAEJ executive committee, she was president of the powerful Los Angeles Jewish Federation. Barbi was not the typical token president who signed policy papers written by a highly paid executive director. She was smart and active. Her husband, Larry, was president of AIPAC (American Israel Public Affairs Committee), a powerful pro-Israel lobby in Washington. I arranged for Halpern to meet her and describe his plans. Our meeting went well; Halpern made a clear and persuasive case for implementing his rescue plan. We had gained the support of a key member of the AAEJ board.

Before approaching the board, it was important to gather convincing evidence that there were Ethiopian Jews in the Sudan who needed help. We obtained that information from various sources. Graenum Berger received a letter from Aklum Feredeh who had reached the Sudan by himself in 1979. Henry Rosenberg, by peeking at the cluttered desk in the office of Haim Halachmi of HIAS (Hebrew Immigrant Aid Society), saw a letter from an Israeli relief worker in Ethiopia telling of eighteen Beta Yisrael who had reached the Sudan and had requested assistance to get to Israel. Professor Tartakower of the AAEJ counterpart organization in Israel sent a letter to me indicating that fifteen Beta Yisrael were in the Sudan. He wrote again, this time stating that there were twenty in the Sudan and that he expected more. Halachmi denied those claims, as also did Israel's foreign ministry in a letter to me written February 9, 1978.

With our own evidence and Halpern's experience to draw on,

and with the backing of Nate Shapiro, Graenum Berger, and Barbi Weinberg, a conference call was made convening the executive committee. We asked ourselves a number of questions and considered the possible outcomes. Could Halpern do it alone, or if not, who could help? Who was this Tegegne fellow? Most of us had not met him. Should the AAEJ stay only with advocacy and wait for the Israelis to initiate the rescues from the Sudan? Or does the Association want to initiate its own rescue missions there? If we do, will we be prepared for the consequences of a possible failure of our mission? How would we handle the consequences of success?

Would we, for example, be able to gather the resources and personnel to continue more rescues? Would a success backfire, with the AAEJ being perceived as "amateurs" who could endanger the lives of the Ethiopian Jews and Israeli operatives by getting involved in what should be the proper role of the Israeli authorities? After a spirited exchange of views, the executive committee decided that despite the risks, we must try; we had witnessed no significant action by Israel since December 1977.

Tegegne Plan, General Poran, and the Mossad

In February 1978, while addressing a group of Ethiopian Jews in Jerusalem, I noticed one of them staring at me, albeit with a pleasant smile. After the meeting ended, this smiley guy came up to me and said, "Professor Howard, I am Baruch Tegegne."

We went to my apartment, and Tegegne began talking about rescue. He was full of ideas. Most of all he wanted to tell me of his master plan for bringing over large numbers of Beta Yisrael from the Sudan. He had obviously given his plan much thought. The essence of it was as follows:

Tegegne and his friends would bring Beta Yisrael across the frontier and outfit them with clothing commonly worn by the Sudanese. Then they would take them past the many Sudanese checkpoints and spread around *baksheesh* as needed to grease the wheels. They would take buses or freight lorries to the outskirts of Port Sudan on the Red Sea. After locating and bribing the captain of a suitable small ship, Tegegne would gather groups of Beta Yisrael in small boats and take them to the ship. The steamer would sail up the Red Sea to an Israeli port where the new immigrants would be presented to the Israeli authorities.

I took prolific notes, went over the details, and made suggestions for an alternate plan should things go wrong. Satisfied that Tegegne's plan made sense, I called General Poran of the prime minister's office and requested a meeting. He seemed surprised to get my call, for we had just met a few days before, but he agreed to see me. We met later that morning. He listened intently and seemed surprised again by my message. After we discussed the Tegegne plan, I gave Poran a memorandum summarizing the details. Here is an excerpt:

> Through the cooperation of the EDU [a revolutionary group that was trying to overturn the Marxist government of Ethiopia], and with the help of five Falashas [friends of Tegegne], and through bribery, it should be possible to bring thousands of Falashas to the Sudanese border by foot in one to three days. Once there and declared political refugees (Christian or Moslem), they can be transferred by truck and/or rail to Port Sudan where a ship is better than [a] plane because going to [the] airport is too dangerous and housing Falashas [can] arouse suspicion. A ship is less obvious, more people can be saved, and [it] can be used as a hotel.

Within days of the Poran meeting, the Mossad contacted Tegegne to discuss his plan. Tegegne told them that a friend of his, an Ethiopian Jew from Tigre, Aklum Feredeh, was in the Sudan and could help. Shortly afterwards an undercover Mossad agent working as an anthropologist in Sudan, whom I will call "Dov," contacted Baruch. Dov told Baruch that he was needed. He sent Baruch to Athens, told him to get a visa for the Sudan and then to wait there for further orders. Baruch did, and after a month, Dov told Baruch that he was not needed any longer. Dov ordered him to hand over his Israeli passport, and said that, as an Israeli citizen, he was forbidden to enter the Sudan. Needless to say, when the AAEJ heard what had happened to Tegegne, we vowed to get his passport back to him, and asked him to join Halpern in the Sudan. But how could he get there without a passport? The Mossad forgot that Baruch still had a valid Ethiopian passport.

Halpern and Tegegne arrived in the Sudan in late winter and spring 1979 independently of each other. Baruch posed as an aide to an American businessman. Halpern had connections with the International Rescue Committee (IRC) and said that he was in the Sudan to get information to help the IRC build a clinic in the refugee area. While Halpern and Tegegne were finding small numbers of Ethiopian Jews in the Sudan, Aklum Feredeh, working for the Mossad, was also finding small numbers. [For more on Feredeh, and how he got to the Sudan, see chapter 12.] Sometimes they crossed paths, with each claiming credit for finding some of the same individuals.

Regardless of who found them, all were hidden and cared for in safe-houses in Khartoum. Feredeh worked alone for the Mossad; he met infrequently with Dov of the Mossad, primarily to get funds for the refugees he was assisting. There was a time that he did not see Dov for weeks and ran out of money. Feredeh asked our team if the AAEJ could loan him the money, and we did. We never thought the loan would be repaid, because if the Mossad were to repay it, they would be admitting that they had not been taking Feredeh's rescue seriously. Some of the AAEJ board thought that Dov had other missions in the Sudan and was diverted from them to find Beta Yisrael in the Sudan and get them to Israel before the "amateur" AAEJ did.

After thirty-two Beta Yisrael were placed in safe-houses by the three activists, the AAEJ needed help from Israel to get airplane tickets and entry visas to "helpful" countries in Europe and to obtain exit visas from Sudanese authorities. We also requested Israel's help to fly the Beta Yisrael refugees from Europe to Israel. At first the Israelis in charge balked, claiming that many of the refugees the AAEJ found were not Jewish, even though we had checked with the most recent census available of the Beta Yisrael in Ethiopia. As pressure mounted from influential friends of the AAEJ, Israel agreed to take the refugees out of the Sudan. After arriving safely in Europe, they were brought in two groups of sixteen to Israel, one group in May and a second in July 1979.

This initial rescue, although of small numbers, had far-reaching consequences. It showed that, contrary to what some Israeli officials said, there were Ethiopian Jews in the Sudan who wished to come to Israel, and that they could be rescued – even by "amateurs." This first operation became a template for larger future operations. We also could use it to exert leverage on the Israeli government to expand its rescue work.

Political Aftermath of the June 1979 Rescue

Rewards from the rescue operation followed quickly. Word came that Prime Minister Begin wanted me to come to Israel in June to discuss the future of the *aliyah* of the Ethiopian Jews who were in the Sudan. I am not certain who was behind this meeting. Perhaps it had much to do with our having a number of influential major contributors on our board, because Graenum Berger was not invited, while Barbi Weinberg and philanthropist Edith Everett were.

Our meeting with the prime minister was set to coincide with the annual meeting of the board of the Jewish Agency. Only later was I to learn that this is one of the major gatherings of the world Jewish establishment. We expected to be meeting with Prime Minister Begin and his advisors, Shaul Ramati (head of the Foreign Ministry), Yehuda Dominitz, and Haim Halachmi. To my surprise, a number of uninformed representatives of American Jewish organizations were invited to attend.

A few days before that session arranged by the prime minister's office, I visited with the first group of sixteen new refugees from the Sudan. We met in Beersheba, in one of the typical bare-bones apartments given to new immigrants: a few cots, a table, wooden chairs, a stove, and a refrigerator. All of those immigrants were males except one. Most were in their twenties with a few teenagers among them. Zimna Berhane was acting as social worker and translator, just as he had done for the 120 Beta Israel who came in 1977. Although Israel claimed to have been responsible for finding most of the sixteen, the A A E J was still footing the bill for Zimna's salary.

After my welcome to them, we discussed how they were being treated. No one complained about his own situation, but they were concerned about the welfare of their families, some of whom were still in Ethiopia or in Sudanese refugee camps. I wanted to hear from their own mouths about the conditions in Africa, their personal sagas, how they had been found and rescued, and their suggestions for evacuating more Ethiopian Jews from the Sudan. At the end of the meeting, when asked if any Israeli officials or employees had debriefed them, "No," they replied; I was the first non-Ethiopian to ask them such questions. They had been in Israel for three weeks.

Before the appointment with Begin, I was invited to a closed session on "Oppressed Jews in Foreign Lands," held for delegates to the Jewish Agency conference. The question of the Ethiopian Jews was raised, as were the problems said to be caused by the American amateurs. The next day, in the Knesset office of the prime minister, we met with Menachem Begin, his emissaries, and his American guests. The A A E J was represented by Barbi Weinberg, Edith Everett, and me. The meeting was tense and hostile, although Begin was always courteous and respectful. Dominitz and Haim Halachmi of the Jewish Agency, on the other hand, painted the A A E J as a group of reckless, publicity-seeking "bleeding hearts," who were doing much harm to the Ethiopian Jewish community by making its plight public.

Finally, the meeting with Prime Minister Begin started. The prime minister asked me to describe what we were doing. As soon as I mentioned that we were concerned about the Ethiopian Jews who were in the Sudan, Haim Halachmi literally jumped out of his chair and exclaimed: "See how irresponsible Lenhoff is; he is mentioning the country of the Sudan in public." Begin interjected and asked me to be more cautious. I apologized, but said: "Sir, we are all talking about sensitive issues, and I would think that if any place is safe to speak openly, it would be in the confines of the prime minister's office in the Knesset."

I told him that the AAEJ knew that Israel could do rescues better than we could, but since December 1977 we had not seen any serious evidence of ongoing commitment. Begin assured me that the Israeli government was concerned and asked that the AAEJ continue these discussions with "his man" responsible for rescuing the Jews of Ethiopia, Yehuda Dominitz of the Jewish Agency. We did not like the choice of Dominitz, a man who was affiliated with the National Religious Party and who seemed to share its opposition to the immigration of the Beta Yisrael. But we had no alternative.

Some gains were made in our negotiations. Dominitz agreed to expanded efforts to rescue Ethiopian Jews from the Sudan. This was of paramount concern to the AAEJ. As an ancillary component of this pledge, the agency promised to communicate with us regularly on all matters regarding the Jews of Ethiopia. Dominitz also agreed to hire Zimna Berhane to oversee the programs for Falasha immigrants at the absorption centers. In return for these concessions, Dominitz asked that we stop our operations in Sudan. He also asked that we stop issuing all publicity and press releases regarding the Ethiopian Jews. We agreed to both requests.

As a final token of the newly established alliance, we asked the Jewish Agency to repay us for our role in rescuing the thirty-two Ethiopian Jews. We made this request directly of Arye Dulzin, director of the Jewish Agency. He offered us much less than our costs. I convinced the board that we should take what we could get. The offer itself was evidence that the Association was rescuing Ethiopian Jews from Africa. And by paying us so little ($6,000 of an expenditure of $70,000), the agency implied that rescues were not expensive to carry out!

By July 1979, it appeared that in five years, the AAEJ had achieved some important milestones. For one, our small grassroots organization had been recognized by the powers that be in Israel and was holding formal discussions with senior governmental officials. But more importantly, Ethiopian Jews were being moved from the Sudan to Israel. By participating in the rescue, the Association had taken a giant step – from advocacy to direct action. We were hopeful that our sole mission of seeing the Ethiopian Jews become residents of Israel would be more quickly realized.

It was a heavy week. After those meetings, I packed my belongings in a small carry-on knapsack, put on my traveling jeans and denim Eisenhower jacket and grabbed a cab for Ben Gurion Airport. Before boarding the El Al airplane for New York, I walked up to the security checkpoint and expected to go through in a few minutes, as had always been my experience in the past. But this time the security agents called other agents to the table and chatted among themselves for ten to fifteen minutes, every so often looking me over out of the corner of their eyes. I was surprised, because I know some Hebrew and often had teased the airport guards, especially the female ones. Finally, they let me pass. Before leaving them, I asked in Hebrew why it had taken so long. They responded: "Look, here you are, a fifty-year-old man, dressed like a hippy with a scrubby beard, and when we asked you your occupation and what you were doing in Israel, you responded that you are a biochemistry professor and were called here to have a meeting with the prime minister. Really, sir, that is quite irregular (*Zeh lo ragil*)."

I smiled, waved, and walked away, saying, "*V'gam ani lo ragil*" (And also I am not regular). They shook their heads and said, "*Americai meshugah*" (Crazy American).

Once our crowded El Al 747 took off, I inserted my trusty beeswax earplugs to dampen the loud chatter of enthusiastic returning tourists and tried to get some sleep, but could not. My mind kept returning to two of my meetings: the one in the prime minister's office in the Knesset, and the other in Beersheba with the new immigrants, the first to arrive via the Sudan, mostly through the initiative of the AAEJ. What would happen next? Would Israel keep its promise and start rescuing larger numbers using the Sudan route?

I hoped so. Although I was pleased with the work of Halpern and Tegegne, the AAEJ had not been founded nor funded to carry out rescues. For the rescue of Jews at risk, world Jewry, including the AAEJ members, looked to Israel. Such rescues were an important reason for our support of Israel, part of its *raison d'être.*

But it was the visit with the immigrants that kept me from falling asleep. I wished I knew more about their stories. I had prepared a long questionnaire to ask each of them, but their minds were on their families in Africa, and I had decided not to probe too deeply. I was particularly haunted by the troubled looks on the faces of the three quiet teenagers of the group. It seemed that they wanted to tell me something, but could not.

IN MEMORIAM – HAIM HALACHMI

NOTE: *Even though most reports on the rescue of the Ethiopian Jews have implied that the relationships between the Israeli operatives and AAEJ activists were bitter and strained, that was far from the truth. Many of the key players on either side respected and even admired their so-called antagonists. Both wanted the same thing, but each needed to operate within a different set of restrictions. Those were my feelings regarding Benjamin Abileah and Haim Halachmi. While writing this book I learned that Halachmi had died. I did so want him to know of my warm feelings toward him. The following is what I had written.*

Ani Haim Shtaim ("I Am the Second Haim")

I use this strange title to introduce my relationship with my supposed adversary, Haim Halachmi, architect of the rescue of 120 Beta Yisrael from Ethiopia in 1977 and active behind the scenes in so many of the other rescues of the Ethiopian Jews. The last time I saw him was in 1986, about a year and a half after Operation Moses. We greeted each other like generals of two opposing armies meeting years after an armistice has been declared, each having vivid memories of the battles won and lost. Only in our case, we both felt that we had won.

When Halachmi and I first met – on January 26, 1978, at Beit Faitlovitch in north Tel Aviv – I coined the expression "Haim Shtaim"; the phrase always was to get a laugh from the Ethiopian leaders in Israel. Beit Faitlovitch ("The Faitlovitch House") was the Israeli home of Jacques Faitlovitch. He had a valuable library there and willed his home and its contents to the City of Tel Aviv supposedly to be a center for the Beta Yisrael community in Israel. Unfortunately, the City of Tel Aviv later decided to use the building for a local library and sent Faitlovitch's books and papers to the library of Tel Aviv University.

But on that January evening, the building was still the meeting place of the Beta Yisrael, and over fifty Ethiopian Jews came to listen to Haim Halachmi describe the particulars of the 1977 rescues. The only other Ashkenazi in the room aside from Halachmi and me was Ahron Hollander, husband of the Ethiopian woman Esther Wube. Halachmi, a broad-shouldered man in his early fifties, with graying wavy hair and a warm, friendly look, spoke in Hebrew and gave an hour-long detailed report. Afterwards there was a lively discussion during which he pointed to me and asked in English, "Can I see you outside afterwards?"

As we exchanged greetings I told him that my Hebrew name was also Haim, and because he was recognized for his great accomplishment, I was honored to be taking second place by calling myself "Haim Shtaim" (*shtaim* is the Hebrew word for "two"). I think he liked that, and he invited me to visit him in his office where he would tell me the whole story in English. We walked together that night to my bus stop. I said I felt he needed more help so that more Ethiopian Jews would be brought to Israel. He replied, "You talk like a Falasha," and I countered that from some of the runarounds I had been getting, I was beginning to feel like I was one. He laughed.

We set our meeting for February 3 when he was to have returned from a weekend with the army reserves. He then turned to me and said, "I think that you are trying to open a door that is already open." I replied that we just wanted to open it wider.

On February 3 we had a lively and mutually informative two-hour meeting in Halachmi's office. I noted that like me, he had a particularly messy office with piles of papers scattered all over the room. After I left I wrote him a detailed six-page, single-spaced letter telling him of the concerns of the AAEJ and of my willingness to work together with him. The letter was written on February 8, 1978. Around the same time at a Zurich press conference, Foreign Minister Moshe Dayan was revealing that Israel was giving arms to Ethiopia in exchange for Ethiopian Jews. From that moment the "open door" that Halachmi had boasted about was slammed shut; the bolt was removed only eleven years afterwards in 1989 when Israel and Ethiopia resumed diplomatic relations.

For the rest of the year Haim and I continued our constructive correspondence, but relations became strained once the AAEJ started its rescue operations in the Sudan. Haim Halachmi was a patriot who would have done more had the Jewish Agency and the government of Israel given him a staff. It was too much to expect of one man.

CHAPTER 11

Misery Worsens, AAEJ Builds Momentum: 1979–1980

Unless we convince world Jewish leadership to make the rescue of the endangered Beta Yisrael the number one Jewish priority, we are condemning our Ethiopian brothers to their death. And, G-d forbid, if this happens, the stories of Jewish racism of Jew against Jew will tarnish our children and our children's children generation after generation. We cannot relent. We cannot wait. We must act now.

> – *Howard Lenhoff, to* AAEJ *board of directors, September 1980*

The second year of my presidency was a mixture of promise, disappointments, intensive grassroots activity, an increased *aliyah,* and hope. The Association intensified its pressure on establishment organizations to recognize the plight of the Beta Yisrael. We also sought to win more members of Congress to our cause. To advance both goals, we greatly increased both the volume and scope of our public education campaign. We rejoiced that in 1980 nearly seven hundred Ethiopian Jews were brought to Israel (chapter 12), but the deteriorating conditions in Ethiopia caused growing concern about the thousands yet to be rescued.

Misery in Ethiopia

During 1979 and 1980, the situation of many Ethiopian Jews worsened still further. Many Beta Yisrael villages were attacked either by the various anti-Mengistu insurgent groups or by roving bands of *shifta*, Ethiopian bandits. If a liberation group thought that the Beta Yisrael were pro-government, they were driven from their villages, killed, kidnapped, or conscripted. Because the Beta Yisrael were able blacksmiths and potters, the insurgents wanted their assistance. Beta Yisrael who lived in areas controlled by the Marxist government were drafted into Ethiopia's army.

As rural Ethiopia became increasingly engulfed in warfare and famine, historic enmities between the Beta Yisrael and their Christian or Moslem neighbors were fanned into acts of violence. Individuals were beaten, houses burnt, and some Beta Yisrael were denounced to the government authorities as "spies" or "agents" of the CIA or Mossad. Many rural officials harbored traditional superstitions and religious prejudices and treated the Beta Yisrael cruelly. While authorities gave lip service to the free practice of religion, Ethiopian Jews were prevented from attending religious schools or receiving instruction in Hebrew.

Large numbers of the Beta Yisrael lived in areas affected by drought; many were starving. In September 1980, the *New York Times* reported that Ethiopians had one of the lowest caloric intakes of any people in the world. Because of the confiscation of their land, warfare, and indifference of government officials, the Beta Yisrael often suffered more. As their health weakened, their susceptibility to the diseases that plague Ethiopia increased. Whereas Ethiopia averaged an appalling one physician for each seventy-nine thousand inhabitants, most Beta Yisrael areas had none.

As might be expected, hundreds of Ethiopian Jews tried to escape to the refugee camps in Sudan. Some were captured by insurgents, robbed, and the men conscripted. When a government patrol caught escapees, they often were beaten, raped, and robbed, and their homes and farms confiscated. Those who made it to the Sudan received the supplies and services of the United Nations; yet unlike other Ethiopians, the Beta Yisrael had a safe, secure place awaiting them in Israel, away from the misery of the refugee settlements. Where were the efforts to rescue them? The AAEJ had no alternative but to push for increased *aliyah*.

AAEJ Efforts

By 1979, the Association had become committed to expanding its pressure on mainline American Jewish organizations that seemed hesitant to support the rescue of the Ethiopian Jews. The task was to reach their membership so that they would be informed of the plight of the Beta Yisrael. We could reach them as well as hundreds of thousands of American Jews in a number of ways. In 1979–1980 the AAEJ focused on two approaches: One was to get the issue of the Beta Yisrael placed on the program of key national meetings of those organizations. To do this we informed some key supportive members of these groups that there would be representatives of the Ethiopian Jewish community in Israel available to speak at their major meetings; it would be tough for their leadership to refuse. The second approach was to mobilize the independent American Jewish press so that the story of the Ethiopian Jews would be on the tables of most informed and caring North American Jews. The support of these good people would be crucial in getting the support of Congress and the governments of the United States and Israel.

A major step forward was taken at the November 1979 General Assembly of Jewish Federations (GA) meeting in Montreal. We knew that most policy matters concerning the North American Jewish community's relationship with Israel were decided at these annual GA conferences. Up until then, the issue of Ethiopian Jews had not been discussed publicly at the GA meetings. This year, however, the pressure on the GA organizers was mounting. They knew that famed Beta Yisrael scholar and leader Yona Bogale and his wife and daughter were brought from Ethiopia to Israel through arrangements made by the embarrassed UJA-supported Jewish Agency, while the AAEJ picked up the tab for their air travel. They also knew that the Ethiopian Jews in Israel were getting more attention when they demonstrated in Jerusalem for the second time in one year without the instigation of the AAEJ.

To further increase the pressure, the AAEJ brought Rahamim Elazar and Baruch Tegegne to the meeting. They were joined by Yona Bogale and his son, Zecharias Yona. Together with AAEJ

members, they attended a workshop on "African Jewry." GA organizers, after witnessing a standing room pro-Beta Yisrael crowd
at the workshop, invited Yona Bogale to address a plenary session of the convention. His presentation moved many previously
ill-informed delegates, who responded by passing a pro-Beta Yisrael resolution. This action marked the first time that this major
establishment organization officially recognized the need to save
the Ethiopian Jewish community.

The momentum generated in Montreal continued at three
other important meetings. In December 1979, the AAEJ prodded
the UJA to allow Baruch Tegegne to speak to its national meeting
in New York City. The organizers conceded at the last minute, but
gave him a two-minute prepared speech to read. The UJA paid for
Tegegne's expenses and published its first release in five years on
the Ethiopian Jews.

At the end of December, the AAEJ contributed $2,000 to the
North American Student NETWORK for a meeting which brought
Baruch Tegegne and Israeli Defense Minister Ezer Weizmann as
speakers. Weizmann, when asked in his session by a student to address the issue of the Ethiopian Jews, made his notorious *faux pas*,
replying: "Falasha shmalasha. Is that all you students think about?"
It was a clear, unguarded illustration of the level of concern held
by that important official who went on to become president of Israel. While serving later as president, Weizmann was to be photo-
graphed at a number of photo-ops with Ethiopian Jews. *Hoo-hah!*
But in early 1980 the AAEJ published his callous "Falasha shmalasha" remark, which energized us – especially the students – to increase the pressure.

Although the National Jewish Community Relations Advisory
Council (NJCRAC) had sponsored pro-Beta Yisrael resolutions for
years, in January 1980, Abe Bayer, a NJCRAC employee and member of the AAEJ board of directors, established a committee to deal
with the Ethiopian Jews. On it were representatives from most of
the principal groups belonging to the NJCRAC. Its importance for
us lay in the fact that it was officially recognized by the government

of Israel as representing the concerns of American Jews regarding the Ethiopian Jews. Bayer placed AAEJ executive committee members Edith Everett and Graenum Berger on the committee. After a year, however, the AAEJ recognized that the committee was only a symbolic gesture and a cover for doing nothing. Our people resigned, and we never heard from that committee again.

Rahamim's Tour
By early 1980, we were revving up our public education campaign. The appearance across North America of Rahamim Elazar produced a windfall of press coverage. Rahamim was a great choice to be our Ethiopian lecturer for the year. He was bright, articulate, and spoke in a low-key yet emotional manner that won over most listeners. He had proven himself a worthy Zionist by serving in the Israeli Defence Forces. And he was recognized in his community as an officer in the Israeli Association of Ethiopian Jews. Standing before an audience of North American Jews, he had great credibility.

Rahamim first spoke at the national NJCRAC meeting and then embarked on a whirlwind tour covering Boston, New York, Baltimore, Philadelphia, Washington, Chicago, Cleveland, Detroit, St. Louis, Miami, Los Angeles, San Francisco, Portland, and five Canadian cities. The press coverage was phenomenal, not only in the Jewish press and TV, but also in the *Washington Star, Baltimore Sun, Philadelphia Daily News, Boston Globe,* and *Miami Herald.* Rahamim also published an op-ed piece in the *Los Angeles Times.*

The AAEJ paid his travel costs, and Gary Schaer, executive director of the American Sephardi Federation, took care of most travel arrangements and much of the publicity.

While Rahamim was well received in North America, his message must have tweaked the noses of some officials back in Israel. When he returned home, he was dubbed by Jewish Agency officials "an agent of the Americans" and accused of spreading distortions about Israeli policy. As a consequence, he was barred from attending meetings with Israeli officials regarding Beta Yisrael matters –

meetings he was entitled to attend as an officer representing the Ethiopian Jews in Israel. Rahamim's treatment paralleled that experienced by Zecharias Yona after his lecture tour of 1978 and his participation in AAEJ rescue activities.

On the heels of Rahamim's successful tour came an annual meeting of the American Jewish Press Association (AJPA). This organization brought together hundreds of writers, editors, and publishers of scores of community, regional, and national community media. They invited me to speak at a plenary session. After presenting a fact-based lecture on the conditions facing the Ethiopian Jews and the need for their expedited rescue, I met my first "truth squad" apologist, Mr. Dominitz of the Jewish Agency. He gave a different picture of conditions in Ethiopia, criticized the AAEJ for spreading distortions, and asked the journalists for their trust.

Impact of Louis Rapoport's Book

The AAEJ campaign got a big boost and affirmation upon the publication of Louis Rapoport's book *The Lost Jews: The Last of the Ethiopian Falashas*. Rapoport, an American-born Israeli, was author of the April 1974 *Jerusalem Post* article on the Ethiopian Jews which had so influenced me. In his *Lost Jews* book, he covered the history of the Ethiopian Jews from Biblical times to 1980, detailed the misery and hardships facing contemporary Beta Yisrael in Ethiopia, and essentially repeated our call for their immediate rescue by Israel.

The book won well-deserved praise. Meyer Levin wrote: "Rapoport's book is journalism at its best – imbued with a cause and yet objective, fully informed, fearless." Simon Wiesenthal said: "Today the Jews of Ethiopia face the danger of [a holocaust]. It is our obligation to do everything in our power to facilitate their rescue. History will judge us if we fail them in their hour of need." Elie Wiesel wrote: "It is a disturbing document on an urgent issue. I hope it will bring to the attention of the public the tragic fate of our forgotten brothers – the Falashas."

At first Rapoport could not get financial support for writing about Ethiopian Jews. He sought unsuccessfully prepublication advances from a number of major publishers known for books dealing mostly or solely with Jewish subjects. Finally, he had approached the AAEJ for help. Although we were able to supply him with information for the book and many rare photographs of Faitlovitch and his students from my own files, the AAEJ could not offer funds from our meager coffers. One member of our board, however, was able to acquire sufficient funds to underwrite a research trip to Ethiopia and to provide a stipend that allowed Rapoport to complete the book. His compelling manuscript was published in October 1980 by Stein & Day.

In 1986, Rapoport published *Redemption Song: The Story of Operation Moses*. He died in June 1991 of a heart attack, soon after Operation Solomon. I learned of his death minutes before giving the keynote address at another meeting of the AJPA. After my address, I contributed my honorarium to the AJPA to initiate a Louis Rapoport Journalism Award, which they did and which they have awarded ever since. Nate Shapiro and other AAEJ members also donated to this memorial.

Publish or Perish

To a young professor, "publish or perish" meant that if you did not publish good peer-reviewed scholarly articles, you would not last long in the academic world. But as an academic in the arena of grassroots activism, for me that expression had a different meaning. It reflected my belief that if we did not publicize the plight of the Ethiopian Jews, then they would perish as a community. Once at an absorption center housing a group of Beta Yisrael new arrivals, a guard, a short man in his mid-fifties wearing baggy military pants, noticed that attached to my belt was a holster-like leather case for my glasses that also had two slots for my pens. Jokingly, he pointed to the holster and asked if it was for my *neshek* (weapon). Taking my ball point pen in my hand, and waving it in front of his eyes, I said in Hebrew: "Sir, this is my *neshek*."

Our publicity blitz began in January 1979 with a series of

articles published in Los Angeles' *Israel Today* and the *Jewish Post* of Canada to coincide with a UJA meeting being held in Los Angeles. Following the pro-Beta Yisrael resolution by the General Assembly of Jewish Federations, many more newspapers started to carry news items on the Ethiopian Jews. But shortly after the November 1979 meeting, there was a virtual news blackout on Ethiopian Jews in the American Jewish press. Friendly editors of Jewish newspapers and national magazines confided that they had been asked by either Israeli consulate officials or Federation leaders to refrain from publishing articles on the Ethiopian Jews. Some of these same editors later confided their regrets for following such "advice."

This effort to control the news was soon overcome, however, by the media's reaction to Rahamim's 1979–1980 lecture tour. It stimulated a surge of feature articles in most of the Jewish press in cities he visited. For the first time in the history of the AAEJ, significant numbers of journalists in the U.S. not associated with the AAEJ began writing feature articles on the Ethiopian Jews. Among them were: Rochelle Saidel Wolk (*The Jewish Veteran*), Michael Alloy (*Baltimore Jewish Times*), Tom Tugend, syndicated writer (Los Angeles *Heritage*), Aliza Abrams of the University of California, Santa Cruz, whose compelling and detailed article on Baruch Tegegne's exodus from Ethiopia via the Sudan was picked up throughout North America, and Yoav Levy, who went to Ethiopia on his own and published an excellent photographic essay in the May 1980 *Find Magazine*.

Another influential article was put together by Diane Winston, writing for *Perspectives* of the National Jewish Resource Center, which had as its director the distinguished modern Orthodox rabbi, Dr. Irving "Yitz" Greenberg, a member of our board. Winston's twenty-four-page, in-depth document, entitled "The Falashas: History and Analysis of Policy Towards a Beleaguered Community," coupled with a letter by Rabbi Greenberg, must have hit a nerve in Jerusalem, because it elicited a five page, single-spaced letter to Rabbi Greenberg from Yehuda Dominitz. In it, the Jewish Agency spokesman claimed the report was "replete with error and uses either half-truths or outright distortions…, is prejudicial…, [and] violates basic codes of secrecy…. I choose to discredit it."

Editors who were particularly strong and courageous on the issue of the Ethiopian Jews include Phil Blazer (*Israel Today*, Los Angeles), Herb Brin (*Heritage*, California), Gabriel Cohen (*Jewish Post and Opinion*), Robert Cohn (*St. Louis Jewish Light*), Jack Fishbein (*Chicago Sentinel*), Miriam Goldberg (Denver *Intermountain Jewish News*), Martin Levin (Winnipeg *Jewish Post*), and Gary Rosenblatt (*Baltimore Jewish Times*). Jack Fishbein and Gabriel Cohen deserve special recognition. Having met the Beta Yisrael in 1968 in Ethiopia, Fishbein was a major advocate. Gabriel Cohen also was an early champion, sponsoring campaigns to send tractors and other materials to the Beta Yisrael in Ethiopia.

If not for the small, independent Jewish community newspapers, the AAEJ would not have been as effective in building a widespread base of public support for rescuing the Jews of Ethiopia. Originally, Graenum Berger's articles were published in magazines of national Jewish organizations. While these stories reached a select readership, we wanted to capture a larger audience not affiliated with any particular group. Thus, my articles were directed to a number of independent Jewish newspapers in southern California. Some were reprinted in newspapers of other locales. Gradually we accumulated a national list of such Jewish newspapers in the U.S. Soon our tally grew to 140, but I wanted two hundred.

Why this arbitrary number? Simple. In order to get the reduced mass mailing postal rate for nonprofit organizations, the Association needed at least two hundred addresses. We learned that there were weekly Jewish-oriented newspapers published on fifty college campuses in the country and eventually obtained their addresses. Then by adding addresses of ten members of the AAEJ executive committee, we stepped over the threshold and tried to send out two to four news releases a month.

Many small newspapers operated with a skeleton staff, some with only one writer. They welcomed interesting, well-written articles and usually published them with no editing. They got print-ready material, and we got an accommodating forum. The AAEJ mailing address was printed at the end of our news release or story, indicating that donations were tax-deductible. Some of these papers included sidebars with excerpts of letters from Ethiopian Jews, suggestions about how readers could help, and addresses for contacting Israeli or American officials to register the need for action.

Because not all newspapers could regularly publish full-length articles, we sent out five- to six-hundred-word abridged versions of our feature pieces. We also sent an inexpensive five-cents-a-page group of photos which the newspapers could keep in their files. We noted that some papers would have an occasional blank space which they would fill in with a Jewish star or a reminder of a community event. To fill that need (and space), we sent out a number of small fill-in phrases in various sizes and fonts, such as "Save Ethiopian Jews."

The Jewish newspaper campaign was immensely successful. Soon there was an outpouring of feature articles, letters to the editor, and stories of visits with Ethiopian Jews written by individuals not associated with the AAEJ. Some even reached the secular press; we began to see op-ed pieces in major secular media such as the *New York Times*, the first being written by Grace Kraut of Rochester, NY.

Most of these articles eventually were sent to our office. We would cut and paste them so that they fit on standard 8.5 × 11-inch paper, reproduce them en masse, and send packets regularly to the Israeli embassy and consulates, to the community relations councils of all U.S. Jewish Federations, to the major Jewish organizations (such as Hadassah, B'nai B'rith, Anti-Defamation League, and American Jewish Committee), and to key members of Congress.

Our media blitz required new, relevant, and compelling material. One great store of material was the Zionist Archives in Jerusalem. There we found unpublished public opinion polls showing that the Israeli public welcomed the Ethiopian Jews, but also documents which revealed that certain Israeli agencies recommended that the government not pursue the rescue of the Beta Yisrael. Many letters and reports from Ethiopia were stored in the archives. Our core of Hebrew-speaking friends, including Louis Rapoport and Barry Weise, helped with the translations.

In addition we constructed stories out of reports from travelers witnessing conditions in the villages or in the refugee camps. Murray Greenfield and Beta Yisrael friends in Israel provided information and photographs for us to write stories about the absorption of the Ethiopian Jews in Israel, about Ethiopian immigrants succeeding in the universities, and about many hardship cases. We published a great deal about courageous acts of the Beta Yisrael and their successes and failures in attempting to get to Israel. When the situation was getting critical, we would publish obituaries of Beta Yisrael who died in Africa. In many cases we substituted fictitious names in order not to endanger families of the deceased. And there were always accounts of the deteriorating and dangerous situations of the Ethiopian Jews in Africa. We urged readers to pressure the establishment and Israel to rescue them before more lives were lost.

We knew that our readers might tire of our material if we constantly painted a dire situation. So from time to time we wrote about religious controversy, rabbinical opinions, and some non-Western differences in the customs and practices of the Beta Yisrael. And there was the occasional comical anecdote, such as the remark of Baruch Tegegne that some Jews going out of Egypt with Moses ended up in Ethiopia because they got *"farblunget,"* a Yiddish expression for getting confused and lost. We were especially happy to report when American Jewish youths raised funds creatively or donated their bar or bat mitzvah money to the AAEJ to save an Ethiopian Jew.

The *Encyclopaedia Judaica* provided a lucky break in the publicity department. The editors of Keter Press asked me for a specific photograph from the AAEJ archives for the *Encyclopaedia Judaica Decennial Book, 1973–1982*. When in Israel, I hand delivered the photo only to find that the article had yet to be written. Editor

Fern Seckbach, apparently impressed with my knowledge of the Beta Yisrael, asked me to submit an essay on the Jewishness of the Ethiopian Jews. That essay was published in the decennial volume and served as a source for numerous articles subsequently written by others about the Beta Yisrael.

Was AAEJ Publicity Harmful?

As our publicity campaign produced more and more press coverage of the Ethiopian Jews, defenders of Israel charged that we were endangering Beta Yisrael by calling attention to them. No doubt Ethiopian authorities did treat some harshly. We received well-documented eyewitness accounts of individuals who were suspected of helping those trying to escape being brutally tortured. Often they received what was known as *Wofe Lala* where the victim was tied upside down, hanging from the ceiling by the ankles. Then one interrogator would flog the prisoner's back with a leather whip while the other beat the soles of the feet with a steel bar. We knew of one Beta Yisrael teacher who worked for ORT and was denounced by a Christian ORT administrator who claimed the teacher to be a Mossad agent. The AAEJ finally secured his release. After a number of surgical operations and years of physical therapy in Israel, he was able to walk with only a slight limp.

It was different for Beta Yisrael in Sudanese refugee camps. That government, although legally at war with Israel, did not forbid Ethiopian Jews to leave the country. To the contrary. They were permitted to exit Sudan through the auspices of the International Committee for Migration (ICM). Yet the AAEJ was repeatedly instructed never to use the name of the Sudan in our news releases, because if we did, we would endanger the Beta Yisrael there.

Was this caution of not mentioning the Sudan necessary? Years later, former U.S. State Department officials said it was not. Officers who had worked for years on the movement of Ethiopian Jews out of the Sudan argued convincingly that newspaper stories had no deleterious consequences there. They point to accounts in major American newspapers such as the *New York Times* and *Washington*

Post reporting the rescue of Beta Yisrael during and after Operation Moses having caused no backlash on the Sudan's continued cooperation in taking Beta Yisrael refugees out of the Sudan.

At the time we did not know and chose to err on the side of safety; every article needed to be written with extreme care and forethought. To maintain our credibility and to show that we were responsible, we kept the word Sudan out of our publicity. In our correspondence and internal memos and even when in the prime minister's office, we referred to Sudan as "the other country" or "TOC."

Why, then, all the posturing and nay-saying by Dominitz and others? Perhaps they genuinely believed that our stories could hurt Ethiopian Jews still in Africa. Or that Sudanese authorities might be bullied by hard-line Arab states into stopping the tiny rescue operations the Mossad was attempting. Or were our critics simply trying to intimidate us into being quiet, because we were "amateurs," and worse yet, "outsiders," whose actions and words were embarrassing them? By painting us as "irresponsible," our opponents, such as the Jewish Agency in Israel and NJCRAC in the U.S., tried to cast us as unreliable, even dangerous.

The Balance Sheet: Growing Support

Even with our self-censorship, our educational efforts were paying off. Our message was spreading, and more and more editors and publishers were identifying with our cause. One example of this mounting support occurred in February 1981. Aron Hirt-Manheimer, editor of *Keeping Posted*, a magazine published by Reform Judaism's Union of American Hebrew Congregations (UAHC), prefaced an issue dedicated to the plight of Ethiopian Jews with the following words:

> We have tried to present both sides of the bitter Falasha controversy, but certain disturbing questions remain unanswered. Why has Israel been so reluctant to help Falashas reach the Jewish state? Are pro-Falasha activists helping or endangering the

Beta-Israel (as claimed by Israeli officials) by forcing the issue before the public?

What we do know is that the Falashas are an endangered Jewish community and that their most cherished hope is to reach the Promised Land. They cry out to us for deliverance from their tormented exile. We must respond before it is too late.

The sixteen-page issue of *Keeping Posted* contained a variety of outstanding photographs and articles covering the history of the Ethiopian Jews, with a two-page table listing important dates in their history (Appendix A). Also included were: a responsum on the Beta Yisrael as Jews, letters from the Beta Yisrael in Israel and in Ethiopia, statements of the activist view and the Israeli view, the odyssey of Baruch Tegegne escaping via the Sudan, an account of a visit to a Beta Yisrael Passover observance, and a guide for community action. I presented the AAEJ position, and Benjamin Abileah, deputy consul general in New York, wrote the Israeli side.

With that issue of *Keeping Posted*, for the first time we had in print virtually the same arguments long made by the AAEJ, but this time by an organ of the largest Jewish religious organization in the United States, the UAHC. We distributed copies widely, sending them to supporters in Congress, to officers of the major Jewish organizations, and to the Jewish Federations scattered over the United States wherever there was a significant population of Jews.

That year our membership doubled, reaching five thousand. A major benefit of having an expanded membership was the stronger base it gave us for getting support from key members of Congress. Such support, we believed, was prerequisite to achieving an accelerated *aliyah*. By 1980 we began to see real progress toward this goal. A few years into our press campaign, the vast majority of informed and committed American Jews knew of the plight of the Ethiopian Jews and that they were not getting to Israel fast enough. Many made their concerns known to members of Congress as well as to the national offices of such major Jewish organizations as Hadassah and the American Jewish Congress. We received hundreds of copies of their letters. One New York man, Mr. Irwin Ferber, would write three to four letters daily. Frequently the respondents who would reply included staff of the prime minister's office.

In Congress, an informal caucus on behalf of the Ethiopian Jews was forming around Senator Rudy Boschwitz. The senator from Minnesota had become a deeply committed friend of the AAEJ. We now could count on an open door to such key leaders as Richard Stone of Florida, Abraham Ribicoff of Connecticut, Howard Metzenbaum of Ohio, Carl Levin of Michigan, Alan Cranston of California, and Jacob Javits of New York. In the House of Representatives, Stephen Solarz, Barney Frank, Tom Lantos, Gary Ackerman, Ted Weiss, and Howard Wolpe were our allies.

Another successful grassroots effort was our "Chai Campaign." Calculating that it cost approximately $3,000 to rescue one Ethiopian Jew from the Sudan, we asked donors to contribute $3,000 to save one life, referring to the Talmudic proverb that if you save one life, you have saved a nation. *Chai* is the Hebrew word for life. The response was spectacular. From Denver three synagogues sent contributions: Congregation Rodef Shalom, Beth Joseph Congregation, and Beth Medrash Hagadol. Two young Denver working couples each gave $3,000 checks to be matched by their synagogues; that "matching" campaign in Denver was spearheaded by Rabbi Bernard Eisenman and AAEJ board members Neal Price and Martin Zerobnick. The $3,000 given by one of those couples, children of Holocaust survivors, represented the savings they had planned to use for their first trip to Israel.

Two other donors were Temple Beth El in Bakersfield, California, under Rabbi Steve Peskind, and the Jewish community of Eugene, Oregon, with the leadership of AAEJ board members Leonard Landis and Dr. Jerome Maliner.

The Committee on Jews in Arab Lands set up by Reform Judaism's rabbinical association (Central Conference of American Rabbis – CCAR), deserves special mention. The committee, chaired by Rabbi Stephen Goldrich of Cleveland and later by Rabbi Rifat

Sonsino of Chicago, included such pro-Beta Yisrael activists as Rabbi Judah Miller of Rochester, Rabbi Robert Gan of Los Angeles, and Rabbi Robert Bergman of Newport Beach, California. Those rabbis were influential in getting the rescue of the Ethiopian Jews high on the agenda of the UAHC.

The UAHC youths associated with NFTY (North American Federation of Temple Youth) also had a Chai Campaign. Ten chapters of a NFTY region would join to give gifts of $300 per chapter for a single Chai donation. The Chai Campaign was becoming mainstream.

More youths were inspired to participate. A growing number began to donate their bar and bat mitzvah gifts toward the AAEJ Chai Campaign to rescue an Ethiopian Jew. The first of these marvelous young people to participate and to reach that goal was Meryl Levin of Anaheim, CA. Other synagogues joined in, especially at Temple Shir HaMaalot in Newport Beach, CA, under the leadership of social activist Rabbi Bernie King.

Large gifts were welcome, but I was moved also by the hundreds of small donors who contributed far beyond their means. Numerous donors were people living on social security, a retired postman contributed checks periodically, an African American woman sent $2 to $3 postal orders almost every other week, a young couple donated all of their wedding gifts of $1,700, an elderly couple gave their fiftieth anniversary gifts, a Hebrew teacher gave one of his monthly salary checks each year, and children from classes in Jewish religious schools sent their small gifts.

From these and other sources, the AAEJ in 1979–1980 was able to spend nearly $80,000 rescuing Ethiopian Jews. Contributions for the year passed the $100,000 mark for the first time, reaching $134,000. Unlike most other private organizations, we held to our unofficial policy that "overhead" expenses were to come from the pockets of the board members. We wanted our contributors to know that every dollar they gave would go to support programs for the Ethiopian Jews in Israel and Africa and for rescuing our people.

Also, because so many of our gifts came from people who were not wealthy, I was quite stingy on how we spent our funds.

Next Year in Jerusalem

The year 1980 had its moments of frustration and satisfaction, sadness and happiness, and failure and success.

- SIX BOARD MEMBERS MAKE *ALIYAH*: In 1979–1980, six of the fifty members of the board of the AAEJ took up residence in Israel.

- DEATH OF HIGH SCHOOL STUDENT BOARD MEMBER LANNY BARASH: In August we grieved the loss of two outstanding young activists who had given every promise of becoming leaders in the Jewish community. A two-year member of our board, Lanny Barash, drowned at Yosemite while heroically trying to rescue his friend, Gordon Van Zak, who also drowned. These two were among the first student pro-Beta Yisrael activists in the U.S. They had worked with the AAEJ since 1975 and were on our speakers bureau. The Committee on Ethiopian Jews of the Los Angeles Federation established a fund in their memory to provide aid to the new Beta Yisrael immigrants.

- ISRAELI GOVERNMENT AND THE JEWISH AGENCY: We recognized that Israel could not broadcast its state secrets. When meeting in the prime minister's office in August 1980, in an attempt to cooperate, I suggested that Israel reveal information about its rescue plans to only one member of the AAEJ executive committee. Before I could finish, Yehuda Avner of the prime minister's inner circle exploded and said, "We will not let you Americans participate [in any Beta Yisrael rescue efforts]." Regarding the same suggestion, Yehuda Dominitz said, "We don't have to report to the Americans weekly how many Falashas arrive." In retrospect, my suggestion was naïve, and I am relieved that it was not accepted. If they had agreed to confide in the AAEJ, then we would have been co-opted and committed to secrecy. That would have made the AAEJ less vocal and less effective.

The AAEJ leadership believed that the foundation was being created, both in North America and in Israel, for an expanded rescue effort. We finally had gotten our toe in the door and opened it a crack. We needed to persist until that door was wide open. We were gaining confidence and would not retreat.

CHAPTER 12

Elijah Two, 1980:
Israeli Turning Point

Thank you for your wonderful cable. After all the pain caused
to me for over two years, your words are the real consolation.
We shall continue for they are our brothers and we are our
brothers' keepers.
                    – Menachem Begin, June 3, 1980, cable to H. Lenhoff

Returning home to California in the summer of 1979, my mind
was spinning from the intense and provocative meetings with the
first Beta Yisrael refugees rescued from the Sudan, and then with
the prime minister and his advisors. We could not lose our momentum. Because we had no formal written agreement between
the AAEJ and the government of Israel, I wrote a letter to Prime
Minister Begin containing my understanding of the commitments
made by the AAEJ and the Jewish Agency regarding the rescue
of the Ethiopian Jews at that meeting and in a follow-up meeting
with Yehuda Dominitz. In mid-July 1979, that letter was sent by
diplomatic pouch via the Israeli Consulate in Los Angeles to Prime
Minister Begin with a copy for Mr. Dominitz.

On August 28, a response from Yehuda Dominitz, written on
August 6, arrived through the public mail stating that there was
no such agreement. Despite the Dominitz letter, the AAEJ had no
choice but to keep our part of the agreement and to wait and see.
Later we learned that he had shared my letter to Begin with American Jewish bureaucrats to demonstrate that the upstart AAEJ was
dictating policy to the sovereign State of Israel.

Although the Association had pledged to cease publishing stories about the Ethiopian Jews, Israel was not applying the same censorship to other news organs, especially the World Zionist Press Service, a division of the Jewish Agency in Jerusalem. In early fall 1979 the service sent out three press releases about the Beta Yisrael; the releases made light of the plight of the Ethiopian Jews and denigrated the pro-Beta Yisrael movements.

More troubling, although the AAEJ held to our side of the agreement to withdraw from rescue efforts in the Sudan, our sources in Israel indicated that as far as they knew Israel had not rescued a single Ethiopian Jew from there after the original thirty-two had come. Nor had we been kept apprised, as promised, of any rescue plans or timetable. By December the AAEJ decided to resume the rescue of Beta Yisrael refugees from the Sudan.

AAEJ Rescues Resume

Baruch Tegegne seemed the right person for our Sudan rescues. He was eager to help, knew a number of escape routes, had made many friends in the Christian and Moslem communities, and was able to negotiate with some of the anti-Marxist dissidents who operated from behind the lines.

Before leaving for Khartoum, Tegegne met with Nate Shapiro in Chicago and gave him a list of Beta Yisrael he knew to be in the Sudan. Nate sent the names to Benjamin Abileah of the Israeli consulate in New York. Abileah's sources denied that those individuals were Jews. Frustrated by Abileah's response, we sent Tegegne to the Sudan in February 1980 to arrange for six Ethiopian Jews to fly to Frankfurt, Germany. The six, two families with one child each, remained in the airport for three days while the Israelis said they were trying to confirm that they were Jews, even though their identity had been vouched for by Rahamim Elazar. The six refugees became disgusted with the treatment they received from the Israeli officials and decided to claim asylum in Germany.

Not to be deterred, on February 20, 1980, Baruch brought to Frankfurt two teenagers. One was a Jew whom Baruch had known and who swore to Baruch that his seventeen-year-old companion was also Jewish. The Israeli representatives in Frankfurt met with this teenager. When they questioned him about his mother, he balked because he did not want to tell them that she had become a prostitute in the Sudan to help her family. Jewish law requires that for one to be considered a Jew, the mother must be Jewish, and the authorities refused to give him a visa to Israel without more information about his mother. Ashamed and dejected, the young man returned to Khartoum and hung himself in the airport.

We were devastated by the news. We had hoped that it was a rumor, but learned later in Israel from Abraham Sahilu, an Ethiopian Jew who was in Khartoum at the time, that the suicide did happen and that the boy was his friend and Jewish.

Steeled all the more to rescue Ethiopian Jews, Shapiro gave Tegegne permission in March 1980 to bring fourteen additional Beta Yisrael from the Sudan to Germany. Once again the Beta Yisrael refugees were met with questions about proof of their Jewishness, even though Zecharias Yona, hired by the AAEJ for this rescue, possessed a copy of the only census taken of the Jews in Ethiopia and vouched for their authenticity.

Graenum Berger was beside himself when we learned that the visas would not be forthcoming from Israel. For the first time, I agreed to join him and threaten to expose the fiasco in Frankfurt to the press. When news of our threat reached American Jewish organizations, especially the powerful National Jewish Community Relations Advisory Council (NJCRAC), they pressured Israel, and the fourteen were given their visas. Although only fifteen Beta Yisrael reached Israel through the efforts of Tegegne, Shapiro, and Berger during the winter and spring of 1980, these were pivotal rescues. Not only did they prove once again that there were Ethiopian Jews in the Sudan, but also that the AAEJ could and would rescue them as opportunities arose. Furthermore, NJCRAC and Israel took our threats seriously.

I give the name "Operation Elijah II" to those little-known rescues carried out from 1980 until Operation Moses in 1984. Some of those were undertaken by the AAEJ; the majority were carried out by the Israelis, initially in 1980 with the help of Aklum Feredeh. Like "Operation Elijah 1" in 1979 (chapter 10), those clandestine rescues were little known to the press or the public until after Operation Moses (chapter 19) was disclosed.

The year 1980 proved to be a turning point in the rescue of the Beta Yisrael from the Sudan. Not long after Tegegne's group of fourteen cleared Frankfurt, rumors began to swirl in the small Beta Yisrael community in Israel that a large contingent was about to arrive from the Sudan. Word had it that this rescue took place primarily through the efforts of Aklum Feredeh with the help of the Mossad and the Jewish Agency. This is the same Feredeh who in 1979 had been involved in the rescue of the first thirty-two refugees from the Sudan.

Feredeh's Story

To fully appreciate Feredeh's accomplishments, we need to go back to 1977 when he was one of the first Ethiopian Jews to decide to flee to the Sudan. The Ethiopian government considered Feredeh, a former school teacher, a *wombedeh* – an anti-government activist. When Feredeh learned that there was a warrant for his arrest, he fled toward the Sudanese border. En route he befriended a Christian arms trader who helped him get to Gedaref, about seventy-five miles from the Ethiopian border and the site of a large refugee camp. From there it was another 250 miles to the capital city of Khartoum.

After Feredeh reached Gedaref, he persuaded a representative of the Red Cross to send him to a village on the outskirts of Khartoum, rather than place him in a refugee camp. Feredeh told the Red Cross official he had friends in that village who had promised him a job. There were no such friends. Feredeh reached Khartoum in early spring 1979. Almost penniless, he slept in an abandoned car and begged for food. In desperation, he sold his ring to get money so that he could buy writing supplies and stamps and be able to send faxes and letters for help.

Feredeh tried to reach a number of contacts, among them his former employers at ORT in Geneva and Graenum Berger in America. In a matter of weeks, Feredeh received a letter from Haim Halachmi, the man in charge of rescuing Ethiopian Jews for the Jewish Agency. Halachmi told him that help was coming. Soon afterwards "Dov," a Mossad agent working in the Sudan, contacted Feredeh. Dov was aware of the AAEJ plans to have Halpern and Tegegne in the Sudan and asked Feredeh to find Jewish refugees for the Mossad. If Feredeh was successful in finding them, Dov promised that he would provide the resources for Feredeh to get them to Israel. Encouraged by this offer, Feredeh sent many messages to his friends in the Beta Yisrael villages in Ethiopia. He told them that if they would come to the Sudan, the Israelis would fulfill their dream and get them to Jerusalem.

Discouraged and deeply concerned for his family in Tigre, Feredeh, with money supplied by Dov, hired a Moslem trader he had befriended, and asked him to go to his mother's village in Tigre and convince her to send his two younger brothers, Le'ul and Kadashay, to the Sudan to meet with him so he could send them to Jerusalem. If the trader succeeded, Feredeh promised him even more money after his brothers arrived in Khartoum. His mother, Avrehet Worku, fearful that this request might be a ploy to get her sons for the slave market, asked the trader for proof that he had gotten that message from Feredeh. Knowing his mother and suspecting that she would want proof, Feredeh had given his Moslem friend a photograph of himself in Khartoum to show that he was safely in the Sudan and had sent the message.

Convinced by the photo, Feredeh's mother allowed her two teenage sons to set off to the Sudan with the Moslem trader. Joining them was a neighborhood friend, Negusseh. Less than a month later, in May 1979, they joined Feredeh in Khartoum. Feredeh sent the three teenagers to Israel along with thirteen other Ethiopian Jews whom he, Halpern, and Tegegne had found in the Sudan. This was the group I had debriefed in Beersheba with Zimna Berhane just before my meeting with Prime Minister Begin. Only after hearing details of this story from Feredeh did I know the identities of the three youths whose faces had haunted me after I saw them in that Beersheba encounter. They were Le'ul and Khadashay, Feredeh's younger brothers, and Negusseh, their friend.

After these young men and thirteen other Beta Yisrael refugees left for Israel, Feredeh asked his Moslem friend to visit his mother again. This time he was to give her two messages. First he was to give her a photograph of Feredeh and the three boys and tell her that the boys were now safely in Jerusalem. The second message begged her to gather her family and friends and make the trek to the Sudan. There Feredeh would find them and get them to Israel. His mother sought advice from many village elders and decided that, despite the dangers, they must leave Tigre and get to the Sudan. They did not all leave at once. Meanwhile, in July 1979, Aklum Feredeh was with the second group of sixteen from the Sudan who were brought to Israel.

In October 1979, when Mossad agent Dov asked him to go to Khartoum to find some Ethiopian Jews in the Sudan, Feredeh had no idea whether his mother and family had left their village in Tigre. He gladly accepted Dov's offer with the hope of finding his family. After a month in the Sudan, Feredeh had found no Beta Yisrael, and Dov ordered him to stop looking and return to Israel. Feredeh told Dov that he wanted to stay in Khartoum a little longer, because he had some good leads – which he did not.

Feredeh was convinced that his mother and most of his family had reached the Sudan. To get another time extension, he concocted a fictitious list of a dozen Beta Yisrael and sent it to his Israeli contacts in Geneva. Feredeh got his extension, and that December his mother and family reached the Sudan.

He found his mother through a most unusual unanticipated encounter. One December day in 1979, while on a bus in Khartoum, an old woman spotted him and asked if he was Feredeh. Flabbergasted, he said yes, and asked her how she knew. She said she recognized him because she knew his mother in Gedaref, and when his mother learned that she was going to Khartoum, she gave her a letter for Feredeh and a photograph of him. Overjoyed by this miraculous serendipitous meeting, Feredeh began to make arrangements for his mother and her companions to get to Khartoum. The Mossad provided the money, but Feredeh had to make most of the early arrangements himself. He had much to do.

Immediately he started to buy passports through the black market, taking advantage of the Sudan's policy of allowing for family passports. Feredeh told me that he removed the photographs of the previous passport holders and saved that space for group photographs of six to eight children and two parents. If a family had only four children, Feredeh would find four more kids and add them to the group. He became skilled in forging passports and eventually had enough for hundreds of the Beta Yisrael in the Sudan. By late spring 1980, there were four hundred Beta Yisrael from Tigre in the refugee camps in Gedaref, and more were coming.

Feredeh and his friends went to Gedaref where he gave his mother and her companions some money, took photographs for the passports, and obtained travel permits for them so they could go from Gedaref to Khartoum. He warned them if they were questioned at the various checkpoints along the way never to mention his name or the destination of Jerusalem. Feredeh had arranged for them to stay in a safe-house on the outskirts of Khartoum to ready them for their flight on the Dutch KLM airline to Athens. There they would be met in the airport by Jewish Agency people and would be placed on an El Al flight to Israel.

Feredeh needed to prepare these refugees from rural mountain villages to cope with flying in an airplane for the first time. To quote one of them, Shmuel Yilma, a nephew of Feredeh:

> We all changed clothes and shoes so as not to stand out in the airport as village people. For two weeks Feredeh prepared and trained us in all the things that had to be correct in the flight.... He gave everybody new names and made the ones without family into members of one of the group's extended families. He drilled us in our new names and gave minute instructions in

how to get through the airport procedures at Khartoum and the stop at Athens. [After] we were ready...we were given our vaccinations and set out for the airport. (*Shmuel Yilma*, From Falasha to Freedom [*Jerusalem: Gefen Publishing House, 1996*].)

Four Hundred Beta Yisrael Arrive in Israel!

And there were more to come! Most came from the Tigre province where Feredeh's family lived. This was a time for celebration and humility. I immediately sent a telegram to Prime Minister Begin congratulating and thanking him for this first major rescue since we had met in the Knesset building nearly a year ago. Trying to be extra cautious while writing to him in case my telegram were to be intercepted, I did not mention the Ethiopian Jews or any African country. To my surprise, a few days later I received a telegram from the prime minister addressed to my home in Costa Mesa, California. In touching words, he expressed his commitment to "our brothers...[for] we are our brothers' keepers."

My first chance to get to Israel was in July 1980. My goal was to visit the new immigrants living in absorption centers in Beersheba and at nearby Ofakim. Rahamim met me at the airport, and we headed unannounced to Beersheba. He found someone at the Beersheba bus stop who knew the route to the absorption center. It was the last bus stop on that route, bordering the desert. Jewish Agency bureaucrats had a pattern of settling new Ethiopian immigrants in the far edges of towns. Such isolation did not help the integration of the Ethiopians with the rest of Israel's multiethnic population. We joked that whenever we wanted to go to a Beta Yisrael absorption center, we would tell the bus driver, "*l'gvul, b'vakasha*" (to the border, please).

We could hardly believe our eyes. Hundreds of Ethiopian Jews were strolling the yards, kids were playing games, the old folks were chatting. Just think: in 1974 there were but 168 in all of Israel. With Feredeh's rescues in 1980, in one fell swoop the population of Ethiopian Jews in Israel more than doubled.

We walked though the facilities. They were not perfect, but it was gratifying to see that the nurse, a male, was an Israeli Ethiopian Jew, and that other longtime Ethiopian residents were assisting the social workers. Some of those social workers were young Israeli soldiers.

They asked me to say a few words to the residents and explain how Jews in the United States were interested in the welfare of the Beta Yisrael and wanted all of their brethren in Ethiopia to come to live as free Jews in Israel. A large crowd was gathered in the courtyard between the apartment buildings. While giving my short pep talk, I noticed a young mustached man, crouching on his haunches, scowling at me. When I finished, he stood up and, in good English, started to shout and criticize me for jeopardizing his rescue efforts in the Sudan and not caring for the Ethiopians who came from the Tigre area.

Surprised by his diatribe, I suddenly realized – this must be Aklum Feredeh! Excitedly I hurried over to him, grasped his hands and said: "Feredeh. I am so happy to finally meet you. Please, let's not argue in front of our brothers. They have been through hell in the Sudan. They should not see Jews arguing. Let's go inside and talk together, and I will try to answer all of your questions." He hesitated for a moment, but then agreed.

We had a heated discussion about the goals and plans of the AAEJ and how we worked in Israel. It soon became apparent that Feredeh mistakenly thought the AAEJ did not care about the Ethiopian Jews of Tigre – that we favored instead the Beta Yisrael from the Amhara regions. When we began to talk more about the rescue, I asked him if more were coming, and he said, "Yes, maybe three hundred more." Then he told me that his activities had caught the attention of the Sudanese authorities. Twice he was arrested, and each time he was able to get out by bribing his captors. Finally it was getting too dangerous, and he had returned to Israel to be with his family. I must have answered his questions favorably, because after a half hour, we shook hands, embraced, and he insisted that Rahamim and I stay for supper and sleep overnight in his apartment in the absorption center.

In the meantime the crowd had dispersed, and after supper the residents returned to the courtyard dressed in their finest Ethiopian garb, most of which they had made themselves since arriving in Israel. Soon a group of musicians came out with their homemade *krar* (Ethiopian guitar) and drums. By nine o'clock they started to dance, sometimes in circular patterns with the dancers gently swaying back and forth, and in other styles that were more vibrant as the dancers' backs shimmied though the rest of their torsos seemed not to move. Sometimes the dancers held onto towels and moved their bodies up and down as their backs shimmied. Those vibrant dances, I learned, were more popular among the Amharas and the Ethiopian young people, whereas the gentle swaying was more a tradition of the Tigrenians.

While the adults danced, the younger children sat on the ground with their legs crossed, clapping their hands rhythmically. The older women clapped as well, but also enhanced the festivities by emitting their unique ululations as their tongues wagged back and forth from side to side in their mouths. Feredeh, dressed elegantly in his *shamma*, a traditional white Ethiopian toga-like garment, came over and said: "Lenhoff, this is the first time they have celebrated like this since they came to Israel a few months ago. They think constantly of their relatives who are still in the Sudan and Ethiopia. But today is a time for celebration. This is for you." I appreciated his remarks, but suspected he was trying to charm me. Rahamim told me that they were celebrating because the next day they would be going on a tour of Jerusalem for the first time. They danced until after midnight. Exhausted, my heart full of joy, I slept on a cot in Feredeh's room, knowing that from then on Feredeh would be a friend, which he is to this day.

Before leaving the rescue achievements of the remarkable Aklum Feredeh, there is a special story to be told about his family. In 1982 Feredeh's mother had heard that "Professor Howard" was in Israel, and she wanted to see me. She knew that Feredeh was now working for the AAEJ; she had not heard from him for a while and hoped to find out if Feredeh was safe. Assuring her that nothing had happened to him, I could not tell her that her son was planning to go to Djibouti to find an alternate escape route for the isolated Jews of Quara.

Her eyes lit up when I mentioned that I was planning to meet with Feredeh in Paris in a few weeks on my return trip to the United States. She asked me to sit down, went into her bedroom, and returned with a colorful handmade, double-tiered basket (*mossab*) that she had woven herself. Again she believed in photographs. "This basket is for you. But take it with you to Paris. When you meet with Feredeh there, have someone take a picture of both of you holding this basket and send the photograph to me. Only then will I be sure that he is safe." At that moment, I realized where Feredeh had gotten his cunning. He, however, never showed up in Paris as planned. A few months later he returned to Israel only to leave the country again, this time for Kenya to participate in another AAEJ rescue effort.

Memories of that incident came back to me in October 1997, six and a half years after Operation Solomon, and four years after the AAEJ had dissolved. One evening that month I received a call from Helen Arfin, a family friend who had done the bookkeeping for the AAEJ in California. She and her husband are Orthodox Jews who that week were hosting an observant Ethiopian Jew who was a guest of the Jewish Anti-Defamation League (ADL) on a tour visiting American schools.

They invited me to their home to meet Shmuel Yilma. After chatting for a while, he said that he was a nephew of Aklum Feredeh and one of the members of Feredeh's family who, at the urging of Feredeh's mother – his grandmother – had gone to the Sudan. As I was describing to him some of my experiences involving Feredeh, Shmuel stopped me to say that he was one of those clapping children I had seen during my visit to the Beersheba absorption center in July 1980. Recalling my meeting with Feredeh's mother and her basket, I suggested to Yilma, "Let's have the Arfins take a photograph of you and me holding the *mossab* that your grandmother gave me, and when you return to Israel, you can give her the photo as a memory of the meeting that she and I had in the winter in 1982." He seemed a little uneasy at first, but then agreed. When he returned to Israel, he sent me a copy of his book, which I read immediately. Only then did I learn that Feredeh's mother, Shmuel Yilma's grandmother, had died in 1992. That is so typical of Ethiopian Jews. He did not tell me that she had died, as he had not wanted to disappoint me.

To the best of my knowledge, 1980 was the last year that Israel used Feredeh to rescue Ethiopian Jews. The AAEJ, on the other hand, realized that he could be of great help; he assisted us in two other efforts, first in a Kenya route (chapter 16) and then in a futile attempt to rescue the Beta Yisrael isolated in the hills of the Quara region of Ethiopia.

Feredeh was a trailblazer. Numerous times he risked his life while demonstrating that it was possible to encourage large numbers of the Beta Yisrael to leave their homes in Ethiopia and walk to the Sudan and to get them from there to Israel. For that alone he should be celebrated.

Looking Ahead

The year 1980 marked a turning point for the AAEJ. The Association had survived a potentially damaging encounter with the Jewish Agency in the fall of 1979 and had regained the publicity and rescue initiatives we might well have lost. Israel started to rescue larger numbers of Ethiopian Jews using the Sudan route. Yet we still had recurring nagging questions: Would the Israeli rescues continue? Increase in number? If not, what should we do next?

Emma and Graenum Berger, founders and longtime leaders of the AAEJ, at the opening of its office in the Los Angeles Jewish Federation building, 1977.

Murray Greenfield, AAEJ volunteer representative in Israel (left), two Ethiopian Jews (center), and Nathan Shapiro (right), third president of the AAEJ. Ofakim, Israel, 1982.

Howard Lenhoff with three children of Telahun
(Rahamim Elazar's brother). The younger child, Yisrael,
was Telahun's first Israeli-born child. Lod, Israel, 1979.

Professor Aryeh Tartakower, leading sociologist and President,
Israel Committee for Ethiopian Jews. Jerusalem, Israel, 1981.

*Yona Bogale (left), leader of Ethiopian Jews in Ethiopia.
Rahamim Elazar (center), important activist among Ethiopian
Jews in Israel. Rabbi Yosef Adani (right), first Ethiopian
Jew ordained in Israel as a rabbi. Tel Aviv, Israel, 1982.*

*Chief Ashkenazic Rabbi of Israel Shlomo Goren, with new immigrants
a few days before the "circumcision caper." Afula, Israel, January 1978.*

Bernard Alpert (left), pioneer AAEJ officer who immigrated to Israel in 1976. Haim Halachmi (right), employee of HIAS "on loan" to the Jewish Agency specifically to arrange for the immigration of the Ethiopian Jews. Tel Aviv, Israel, 1978.

Barry Weise, student activist, subsequently an employee of the Los Angeles Jewish Federation, and then of the NJCRAC. Photograph is from Israeli passport, 1977.

William "Bill" P. Halpern convinced the AAEJ that Ethiopian Jews could be rescued via the Sudan. He, along with Baruch Tegegne, led the AAEJ rescues from the Sudan in 1979. Photograph, taken in the USA in about 1981, was supplied by his brother, activist Elie Halpern.

Aklum Feredeh (left) and Baruch Tegegne (right). Two pioneer Ethiopian Jews who were the first to rescue their brethren from Africa, sometimes working with the government of Israel, and sometimes with the AAEJ. Jerusalem, 1986.

Senator Alan Cranston (D-CA) (center) met with California rabbis during the ARNEJ "Rabbinic Call to Conscience" for the rescue of the Ethiopian Jews. Left to right, Rabbis Daniel Zucker, B'nai Tikvah, Los Angeles; Philip Posner, Beth El, Riverside; Jonathan Miller, Stephen S. Wise Temple, Los Angeles; Bernard King, Shir Ha-Ma'alot, Newport Beach; Steven Kaplan, El Torah, Freemont; Ira Book, Beth Shalom, San Leandro; Ben Beliak, Claremont College Hillel, Washington, D.C., 1986. Photograph from files of AAEJ and ARNEJ.

Henry and Mildred Rosenberg. Veteran AAEJ members who visited Ethiopian Jews in 1973 and were instrumental in AAEJ rescues from Ethiopia and the Sudan. New York, 1983. Photograph courtesy of Sandy Leeder.

President George H. Bush (left) congratulating Jerry Weaver (right) for his work in Operation Moses. Khartoum, Sudan, March 9, 1985. Photograph supplied by J. Weaver.

LaDena Schnapper, major AAEJ figure in rescues from Ethiopia, 1985–1991. In village with Ethiopian Jews. Ethiopia, 1992. Photograph supplied by L. Schnapper.

*Dr. Will Recant, Executive Director of A A E J,
1986–1993. Key in developing and cementing A A E J programs
as the organization grew and took an active role in
Washington. Photograph supplied by W. Recant.*

*Berhanu Yiradu, Ethiopian Christian who aided the A A E J in
its rescues and who developed "The Committee," a group of
Ethiopian Christians and Jews that was instrumental in laying
the groundwork for Operation Solomon to occur. Addis Ababa,
Ethiopia, 1992. Photograph supplied by L. Schnapper.*

CHAPTER 13

Winning Hearts and Minds: American Rabbis Join In

Zionism is color-blind. The vicious canard that Zionism is racism would be effectively undercut by the rescue of this black Jewish community. The Falashas are a precious strand in the incomparable tapestry of Jewish history. Jewry would be terribly diminished by the loss of this group. Without reducing the urgency of the action for Israel or Soviet Jewry, here again is the question: "Am I my brother's keeper?" We dare not fail to respond to its call.

          – Rabbi Irving "Yitz" Greenberg, May 1980

Early in the development of the AAEJ, we realized that we needed the strong endorsement of North American rabbis. As leaders in their communities, they set the moral tone and often the action agenda for millions of observant and affiliated Jews. If we could convince these leaders of the danger to the survival of the Ethiopian Jews and the correctness of our concern that they be brought to Israel under the Law of Return, we felt that the American Jewish community would rally to the cause. But how to win the support of the rabbis?

In the early 1970s, as the plight of the Ethiopian Jews became known, the response of American rabbis varied from firm commitment to open rejection. When I assumed the Association's leadership, it seemed a daunting task to win their widespread backing. Nonetheless, we developed a strategy to do so.

Some rabbis who were children of the 1960s quickly came to

143

equate the rescue of the black Jews of Ethiopia with the American civil rights struggle which they firmly supported. My good friend and backer, Rabbi Bernie King, saw the similarities and took up our banner. Many in the American rabbinate perceived the rescue of the Beta Yisrael as a call to conscience. As teachers of the high standards of morality expected of Jews, they were pledged to the *mitzvot* of *pidyon shevuyim*, the ransoming of captives, and of *pikuach nefesh*, the saving of lives. These were themes of the AAEJ Chai Campaign. The AAEJ showed that not only governments could redeem the imprisoned and save lives; the ordinary man-in-the-street Jew could also participate in these lifesaving *mitzvot*.

But while the late 1970s brought increased support from the rabbinate, some continued to ignore or oppose our activities. An oft-repeated response to AAEJ demands for action was the assertion that the Ethiopians were not Jews. Yet there was ample argument to the contrary from American rabbis. Solomon Schechter, founder of the Conservative movement in the United States and famed discoverer of the Cairo Genizah documents, had written at the turn of the century that self-governing Jewish communities existed in Ethiopia as far back as the sixth century, and that the Ethiopian Jews were the last of a continuous chain beginning with the ancient Zadokites.

Among Reform rabbis, Alfred Wolfe of the prestigious Los Angeles Wilshire Boulevard Temple was one of the earliest advocates for the Ethiopian Jews after he visited Ethiopia in the early 1950s. Wolfe was one of the few rabbis fortunate to have been rescued from Germany; perhaps his salvation sensitized him to the danger facing the Beta Yisrael in Ethiopia. His commitment to rescuing them was instrumental in stimulating and motivating two women who later became active board members of the AAEJ: Eleanor Kahn and Jane Fellman. Officially, Reform Judaism resolved the argument regarding Falasha Jewishness in 1973 when Rabbi Solomon Freehof, considered the master of Reform Jewish responsa, concluded that the Beta Yisrael are Jews.

At about the same time, Freehof was joined by Orthodox Rabbi J. David Bleich who wrote in the journal *Tradition*:

> Of the (black) groups and individuals claiming to be Jews…the only ones who have a fairly well substantiated claim to Jewish ancestry (and who have been accepted without conversion by some rabbinic authorities) are the…Black Jews of Ethiopia…. They have been recognized by many renowned rabbis and scholars throughout the ages as being Jewish.

Almost immediately after Chief Rabbi Ovadia Yosef of Israel declared in 1973 that the Beta Yisrael of Ethiopia were Jews according to *halachah*, the Synagogue Council of America, which represents an affiliation of the Orthodox, Conservative, and Reform congregations, adopted a resolution asking that American Jews "allocate necessary funds" to protect the Jews of Ethiopia from impending danger. The resolution warned that recent events indicated that their existence "has been further imperiled and they could well become the targets of anti-Israel elements from within and without Ethiopia." The council recommended that "mechanisms be set up immediately to aid the immigration of those Falashas who wish to leave Ethiopia as well as to safeguard those who wish to remain [there]."

A simple and direct statement, free of ambiguity, along with a call for action, came from the revered and recognized *halachic* authority Rabbi Moses Feinstein. In a letter written for him by his grandson and corresponding secretary, Rabbi Mordecai Tendler, Rabbi Feinstein declared:

> I am constantly praying for the safety of all Jews, especially those in Ethiopia, and we hope that our prayers will be answered. I commend you and your organization for the excellent work you are doing, and for having undertaken this big *mitzvah* of *pikuach nefashot*. Of course all Jews should join in whatever way they can to aid the Falashas, be this aid material or spiritual.

That message, in 1979, was given by the great rabbi to Yehuda Shapiro, a young, observant member of the AAEJ board. I still treasure the memory of opening a letter from Rabbi Feinstein containing his personal donation to the AAEJ.

Even in the face of endorsements by leading rabbis, others remained noncommittal and said that the question of whether or not the Beta Yisrael were Jews was a matter for Israel to decide, not American rabbis. For instance, a rabbi who was a leader of a major rabbinical organization wrote to AAEJ board members Edith and Henry Everett, saying: "My hands are tied at the present time because the *halachic* issues involved concerning the Falashas have not as yet been resolved or clarified for me." Henry sent me a copy of the letter and wrote: "We will battle this!"

Rabbi Robert A. Alper put the question of the Jewishness of the Ethiopian Jews a little more plainly in his Yom Kippur sermon of 1981 (5742) when he said:

> We Jews are really strange people! Look what happens when someone wants to join our synagogue. They don't even have to come to our office. Phone calls and mailings do quite nicely. All one must do is fill out a blue membership form, enclose a check, and chick chock they are "members of Beth Or."
>
> But with the Falashas, how do we react? Of course, the first question: "Are they really Jewish? What are their credentials? What are their backgrounds? How can they prove they are Jewish?"
>
> We don't say that of Russian Jews who have not practiced their religion for fifty years. We don't say that of those American Jews who have never set foot inside a synagogue. But the Falashas are another story.

Meir Kahane the Peacemaker

History has a way of sometimes placing well-known actors in unusual roles. So it was when firebrand militant Meir Kahane entered the drama of the rescue of the Beta Yisrael as peacemaker. It began in August 1981 when Rabbi Sholom Klass, editor of the Brooklyn *Jewish Press*, wrote an outrageous letter to one of his readers, in which he claimed:

> As to the Falashas, there is doubt if they are Jews. To be considered a Jew you must behave like a Jew, observe Torah, be circumcised, etc. Otherwise a person is not a Jew just because he says so.
>
> It is only those Russian Jews, who are fighting to get out of the Soviet Union and they began practicing our religion and by so doing this they endanger their lives. They are the ones to be helped. Very few Falashas observe any part of our religion nor do they circumsize [sic] their children or themselves. Therefore there is grave doubt to their identity.... They have no proof of their claims.
>
> May I suggest you join a Torah education class or enter a Yeshiva, then you'll begin to understand what our religion is.

Responding to these errors in fact and judgment, Rabbi Abraham Cooper of the Wiesenthal Center wrote to Klass that Rabbi Moshe Feinstein had brushed aside *halachic* questions regarding the status of the Ethiopian Jews as "secondary to the need to save them from physical destruction." As to the Jewishness of the Beta Yisrael, Rabbi Cooper related his experiences with several Ethiopian Jews he met "who spoke of *Shabbas* and *kashrus* and love of Israel with a level of dedication and love I only wish will be matched by other young Jews around the world today.... [These] *mitzvot* have been part of their tradition for a very long time in Ethiopia."

Rabbi Cooper was firm, but kind. I, on the other hand, wrote to Klass that our activist students in New York were going to picket his newspaper office and tell readers to stop subscribing. Our board member Yehuda Shapiro, the young man who had obtained a copy of the Feinstein letter, would lead the demonstration.

Within a week, Rabbi Meir Kahane, the national leader of the Jewish Defense League (JDL), sent a letter to Yehuda Shapiro and me. The JDL was notorious for espousing violence to solve problems. To our surprise, Kahane's message was low-key and diplomatic. He asked that we initiate a dialogue with Klass, rather than take to the sidewalks, in order to convince Klass – as he himself was convinced – that: "The *Halachic* authorities, in the main, DO consider the Falashim Jewish." Such a reasonable appeal from such a normally uncompromising figure convinced me; I asked Shapiro and his friends not to picket the publication.

Educational Campaign Begins to Pay Off

In late 1979, another major rabbinical organization, the New York Board of Rabbis, appealed to its membership to alert their congregations to the "pathetic plight of the Ethiopian Jewish community," and to observe November 2–3 as "Solidarity Shabbat with Ethiopian Jewry." We were happy to see this commitment; and even happier when the rabbinical organization of the Reform movement (CCAR), spearheaded by Rabbi Robert Bergman and Rabbi Joseph Glazer and known for its strong activities in community and social action, endorsed the AAEJ's efforts and sent us $3,000 to support our rescue program.

Other rabbis were more equivocal in their advocacy; they appeared caught in a troubling dilemma. For instance, as Rabbi Sol Roth, a leader of the Rabbinical Council of America, an organization of Orthodox rabbis, wrote: "We are not prepared to direct any criticism to the Government of Israel for failing to meet its obligation with respect to Falashi (sic) Jews…. We will…inquire about these Jews and their well-being with Israeli officials whenever the opportunity presents itself, not in order to criticize but to exhibit interest in the well-being of those who are…at present persecuted and the targets of inhuman and intolerable treatment."

Yet Rabbi Roth was concerned about the welfare of the Beta Yisrael. He and some of his colleagues at Yeshiva University in New York sent an important letter to Prime Minister Begin about the Beta Yisrael. The signatories included Dr. Arthur Hyman, professor of philosophy; Rabbi Dr. Israel Miller, senior vice president;

Rabbi Shlomo Riskin, Lincoln Square Synagogue; and Rabbi Pinchas Stolper, executive vice president, Union of Orthodox Jewish Congregations. In that letter they wrote: "We urge you to exert every effort to assist in bringing the Falasha Jews of Ethiopia to Israel. We hope that this crucial issue be made a top priority for the Israeli government."

Setting a Goal and Devising a Strategy

How to harness and unite the large and diverse community of Jewish religious leaders in the United States to devote time and energies to the rescue effort? We needed their help in educating their congregants. We needed them to pressure American Jewish organizations and members of Congress. We needed their influence on the policymakers of Israel and the United States to place the *aliyah* of the Ethiopian Jews high on their agenda. Achieving the challenging task of aligning the American rabbinic community with us proved to be easier than I had expected.

From the many requests the AAEJ received for speakers and for information, and from letters rabbis wrote us reflecting their interest in our press releases, we were confident that we were reaching many; yet we wanted to reach even more – and quickly. A path to our goal lay through the organizational hierarchies which incorporated almost all rabbis in the United States.

The AAEJ wrote to the executive directors of the three umbrella rabbinical organizations: Rabbinical Council of America (Orthodox), Rabbinical Assembly (RA, Conservative), and Central Conference of American Rabbis (CCAR, Reform), requesting they provide us mailing labels of their membership lists. With these lists, we could provide their member rabbis accurate, up-to-date information about the Ethiopian Jews. How delighted we were when all three sent us their lists and labels. Before long, we compiled our own list of those rabbis who replied to our mailings.

In our first mailing to the rabbis, we sent material on the dire situation of the Ethiopian Jews and asked them to give a sermon on the subject and to place some of our stories in their synagogue newsletters. In later mailings we provided details about the availability of members of our speakers bureau along with a booklet suggesting ways in which they could help, such as writing to Israeli and American politicians and influential national Jewish organizations. Some mailings contained posters showing conditions in Ethiopia; these were suitable to display in day schools and recreation centers. We gave details of our "Chai" program during such holiday seasons as Rosh Hashanah, Chanukah, and Passover. From businessmen on our board came the idea of asking for donations during the end of the tax year; a little charitable giving could reduce Uncle Sam's take while helping fellow Jews in need.

As rabbis took up our cause, we expanded the board of directors to include them so that they could serve as liaison with other rabbis. These included, for example, Rabbi Allen Krause, who went to Israel and prepared his own slide show on the Ethiopian Jews living there. Others, who were not board members, contributed in their own creative ways. For example, Rabbi John Rosove became an influential member of his Federation's Community Relations Council. A group of rabbis at the Hebrew Union College prepared and distributed "A Creative Service Focusing on the Plight of the Falasha Jews of Ethiopia." Others, like Rabbi Daniel Isaak, submitted pro-Beta Yisrael resolutions to their national rabbinical umbrella organizations. Rabbi Ira Youdovin submitted such a resolution at a meeting of the Association of Reform Zionists of America. Many Hillel rabbis, such as Rabbi Albert Axelrod of Brandeis University, guided pro-Beta Yisrael college activists. In St. Louis, Rabbis Benson Skoff, Jeffrey Stiffman, Alvan Rubin, and Zalman Stein co-sponsored an Ethiopian Jewry program for their Rabbinical Association. In Rochester, New York, Rabbi Judea Miller became a strong voice in the eastern U.S.

Rabbi Irving J. Block of the Brotherhood Synagogue of New York allowed the AAEJ board to hold its annual meeting in his synagogue. Rabbi Shalom Singer of Highland Park, IL, not only was a strong activist but also invited the AAEJ to use his synagogue to house the national office of the AAEJ when Nate Shapiro became president. Columnist Rabbi David Polish of Chicago wrote often about our responsibility to save the Ethiopian Jews. The list goes on and on, and I apologize for not recognizing the many other rabbis who responded to our call and to their consciences.

American Rabbinic Network for Ethiopian Jewry (ARNEJ)

One of the most important outcomes of the AAEJ's endeavor to enlist the support of American rabbis was the formation of ARNEJ, primarily through the efforts of Jane Fellman. Her dedication to rescuing the Beta Yisrael dates from 1955, when, as a teenager, she attended a slide show presented by Rabbi Alfred Wolfe at a summer camp in Los Angeles. Memories of "the gaunt, handsome faces and the Ethiopian Jews isolated in Africa" haunted her. As the AAEJ publicity campaign mounted, in the late 1970s, she thought again of the Ethiopian Jews. Her memories began to turn to action. While visiting Israel she met Ran Cohen, a member of the Knesset, who told her in 1979 of the terrible conditions of the Ethiopian Jews, their desire to return to Israel, and the unwillingness of the Jewish Agency to help them.

Shortly after her return from Israel, Jane and her attorney husband, Gary, attended my lecture sponsored by the Pasadena Jewish community. After the lecture, a group of activists gathered to discuss strategy in the Fellman kitchen, seated around a large antique wooden table, warmed by an old potbelly stove. Unlike many of the younger activists, Jane had clear and direct ideas on what needed to be done. Having been influenced as a youth by Rabbi Wolfe, she was convinced that we must get more rabbis involved so they too could influence their congregants. Jane was a dynamo, and I asked her to join the board of the AAEJ. Getting rabbis actively engaged was her obsession.

Jane Fellman initiated meetings with a number of activists, including Nell and Bob Mendleson and Rabbi Daniel Zucker. These get-togethers resulted in the formation of the Organization for Ethiopian Jewry-Los Angeles (OEJ) with Rabbi Zucker as its first president.

In 1983, Jane attended a meeting of the Central Council of American Rabbis. Together with Zucker, she met Rabbis Allen Krause, Phil Posner, Haim Asa, Haim Beliak, and Myron Kinberg. Rabbi Krause was in regular correspondence with the AAEJ; Rabbi Kinberg had helped mobilize the small Jewish community of Eugene, Oregon and had spoken at other synagogues. Jane and the rabbis communicated with each other until Phil Posner and Jane agreed that an organization was needed through which rabbis could raise the moral voice of Jewish leadership on behalf of the Ethiopian Jews. Posner ran the plan by a few colleagues; they concurred, and ARNEJ was created.

On the founding board were Rabbis Phil Posner, Haim Beliak, Jonathan Miller, Daniel Zucker, and Steve Kaplan. Each was already involved in various projects dealing with social justice and civil rights. Posner had served time in an Alabama jail for his efforts in the civil rights movement; Haim had been in a Displaced Person's camp as a child; Daniel Zucker's father had been among a group rescued from Nazi Germany; Jonathan was heir to his parents' commitment to social change; Rabbi Kaplan had been on one of the first missions to Ethiopia and had met a Beta Yisrael *kes* there (chapter 6). Fellman wrote that the ARNEJ rabbis, having grown up through the post-Holocaust experience and coming of age during the decades of the Vietnam War, and under the influence of Martin Luther King and of Rabbi Abraham Joshua Heschel, who was active in the civil rights movement, spoke of feeling a profound connection to God through the prophetic cries for justice, peace, and care of the poor. "The Holocaust," she said, "underscored their passion for the rescue of the Ethiopian Jews."

The AAEJ board invited the rabbis to join and become part of our rabbinic network. But they declined, because they viewed themselves as leaders and facilitators, desirous of creating and sustaining harmonious relationships with all activist groups assisting the Ethiopian Jews. Further, they believed that their independence from any one organization's agenda would enable a larger number of people to embrace ARNEJ's programs.

In 1987, ARNEJ hired Jane Fellman as executive director. The AAEJ, on the recommendation of Nate Shapiro, provided ARNEJ with $20,000 start-up money. It was a good investment. After another advocacy group (NACOEJ) refused to work with ARNEJ, the rabbinical group gave $350,000 of its funds to the Association. About $250,000 of that sum went to the AAEJ rescue program in Ethiopia that began after Operation Moses. But ARNEJ made contributions far more important than the monetary ones.

Through thirteen major mailings dealing with the Ethiopian Jews, ARNEJ regularly furnished seven thousand rabbis, congregant activists and educators with sermons, ceremonial materials, posters, political updates, action programs, media presentations, and historical and cultural materials.

The ARNEJ executive director, rabbis, and lay volunteers made hundreds of presentations on behalf of Ethiopian Jewry. Jane Fellman and the officers of ARNEJ were advocates for the Ethiopian Jews at national and regional rabbinic and lay conferences. Over one thousand rabbis, student rabbis, and religious school educators contributed to ARNEJ in support of its goals.

At the "ARNEJ Call to Conscience" in 1986, representatives from the Israeli embassy and U.S. State Department met with forty-five rabbis in the Foreign Relations Committee Hearing Room of the Senate building. Later that day, the ARNEJ delegation met with key members of Congress who had expressed interest in helping the Ethiopian Jews.

At its second advocacy campaign in 1989, called *HINENU* ("we are here"), ARNEJ brought fifty rabbis and congregants to Capitol Hill to meet with State Department and Israeli representatives and to deliver to them twenty-five thousand signatures on behalf of family reunification of the Beta Yisrael. Copies also were sent to President George H.W. Bush and individual members of Congress.

ARNEJ rabbinic delegates went to Ethiopia and met representatives of the Ethiopian, United States, and Israeli governments. ARNEJ rabbis impressed upon them American Jewry's serious concern for the family reunification of the Ethiopian Jews.

In August 1990, ARNEJ published eyewitness accounts and photographs of the critical health and safety conditions afflicting the Beta Yisrael in Addis Ababa. ARNEJ mobilized a grassroots letter campaign directed to Israeli and U.S. officials urging alleviation of the conditions.

ARNEJ also initiated the national B'nai Mitzvah Twinning Program linking youngsters and their families to a Beta Yisrael child and his or her family.

Were the ARNEJ rabbis effective? Did the AAEJ have the right idea when it took a proactive step and sought the help of American rabbis? The answers to those questions lie in the reaction of the Jewish Agency and the Israeli government, which subsequently formed their own committee to involve U.S. rabbis. They too realized the importance of American rabbis in influencing their congregants.

An Exceptional Rabbi

Among the wonderful rabbis who participated in the effort to bring the Ethiopian Jews to Israel, one deserves special mention: Rabbi Irving "Yitz" Greenberg. The influence of Rabbi Greenberg, a scholar with a Ph.D. degree from Harvard, is described in a book by Professor Steven Katz: "No Jewish thinker has had a greater impact on the American Jewish community in the last two decades than Irving (Yitz) Greenberg."

I first met Yitz Greenberg in 1979, and we started a dialogue which continues to this day; it dealt with ways to get the Israeli authorities to address the complex issues regarding the Jews of Ethiopia. He was a steadfast supporter and friend, although we differed in our strategies: Rabbi Greenberg encouraged the AAEJ to work *with* rather than *against* the government of Israel, the Jewish Agency, and establishment functionaries, and vice versa. He was tireless in arguing his concern for the Ethiopian Jews and advocating their rescue. His moral authority was a major asset for the AAEJ in the struggle to rally public support.

Greenberg had impeccable credentials. From 1974 he served as president of the National Jewish Center for Learning and Leadership (CLAL), a pioneering institution in the development of adult and leadership education in the Jewish community; as leader of CLAL he also headed the National Jewish Resource Center. Before CLAL, he was rabbi of the Riverdale Jewish Center and associate professor of history at Yeshiva University. He also had founded the Department of Jewish Studies at City College of the City University of New York where he had been chair and professor.

The rabbi was early into the skirmish when, in April 1980, his National Jewish Resource Center published a comprehensive, detailed twenty-three-page booklet by Diane Winston entitled: *The Falashas: History and Analysis of Policy Towards a Beleaguered Community.* The paper reached a wide audience. It also provoked a strong response from Yehuda Dominitz of the Jewish Agency (chapter 11).

Rabbi Greenberg responded to Mr. Dominitz with respect, but informed him in no uncertain terms how a growing number of Americans felt about the situation. Winston was right: more had to be done. Undeterred by official bluff and bluster, the rabbi continued to challenge the Jewish conscience in America with a constant flow of commentaries. His remarks were published widely in the Jewish press.

Shortly after the Winston booklet appeared, Rabbi Greenberg wrote "Open Letter: Plight of the Falashas." Some newspapers titled the same article "The Eleventh Hour." Another widely published commentary came out in January 1982, headlined in the *Los Angeles Community Bulletin*: "Falasha Rescue: Silent Diplomacy or Shrill Cries?" Rabbi Greenberg had originally called it: "Israel, American Jews and the Falasha Problem."

Rabbi Greenberg did not forget the Ethiopian Jews after Operations Moses and Sheba. In 1985 and 1986, he published two more commentaries. In the first, he took on the rabbinate of Israel for imposing such restrictions as the hated symbolic circumcision. He concluded the article with: "How many more Jews must be lost...? When will we ever learn?" In his January 1986 article, titled:

"Ethiopian Jewry: Urgent Unfinished Business," his final words on the Ethiopian Jews were prophetic:

> Business-as-usual is the enemy of this matter. The sense of destiny and history moved American Jews to a high-powered response to Operation Moses; pledge levels and the speed of cash payments were outstanding. Let integration of the Ethiopian Jews get the same priority and attention as their rescue; let a total plan be formulated – and world Jewry will respond. The alternative could well be an immigration failure, deculturation, and social pathology. I fear the creation of an underclass in Israel with different skin pigmentation that will besmirch the miracle of redemption of the Beta Israel.

Unfortunately, Rabbi Greenberg was on target. A positive response to his message of 1986 is still needed today, twenty years later.

CHAPTER 14

American Jewish
Establishment Drops Out

The American Association for Ethiopian Jews...is proposing
to engage in their own independent rescue operation to save
Ethiopian Jews.... They allege that "for the price of $3,000,
the life of an Ethiopian Jew can be saved." ... Any donation to
the American Association for Ethiopian Jews will increase the
chances that the currently successful operations [by Israel] will
be endangered.... We ask that you join us in our efforts to do
our part to aid Ethiopian Jewry.

From letter of June 22, 1982, to
"Dear Rabbi" by president of the Jewish
Federation Council of Greater Los Angeles

By 1982 the board of directors originally selected by Graenum
Berger had changed significantly. Berger was a star of the New York
Jewish establishment, but in one respect a renegade one. Employed
by the Jewish Philanthropies of New York, he was the maven of
Jewish Community Center directors, and he had trained a legion of
disciples. But they rejected Berger's pro-Beta Yisrael campaign and
did not lend their full support to assisting the Ethiopian Jews. That
was hard for Graenum to take. Nonetheless, he had put a number
of his colleagues on the AAEJ board, many of whom were executive
directors of major establishment organizations. As the Association's
base of operations moved to the West Coast, quite a different set
of individuals moved onto the board. Most were younger, more in

touch with ordinary men and women, and decidedly more proactive. The AAEJ needed action, not names.

My presidency was marked by clashes over style and tactics. Some board members who had risen through the ranks of local, regional, and national Jewish organizations were accustomed to defending the government of Israel, not questioning it. They were definitely uncomfortable, for example, when some of their board colleagues joined university students picketing Abba Eban or the Los Angeles Israeli consulate. A number of Graenum's early appointees to the AAEJ board started to drop out. They left either voluntarily or because of pressure from a boss.

What Is the "Jewish Establishment" and How Does It Work?

The North American Jewish community is a model of organizational entanglement. There are clubs for every interest in the local synagogue. There is an array of national organizations with local chapters: Hadassah, B'nai B'rith, ADL, American Jewish Committee, American Jewish Congress, Women's ORT, Pioneer Women, Zionist Organization of America, Jewish American War Veterans.

Many of the rich and powerful serve on boards of directors of these national organizations. The boards employ full-time professional administrators who not only run the business of the organization, but also are influential in setting policy. The organizational professionals often are appointed to the boards of other standard Jewish organizations. Along with major donors and elected and appointed officers, these bureaucrats constitute the Jewish establishment. Their linkages are both horizontal and vertical: that is, its members have social, business, and sometimes family ties with one another as well as contacts through their positions in the hierarchy with its regional and local subdivisions. Their control of major Jewish institutions allows them to set the agenda for national meetings, to influence Jewish media, and to reward – or punish – ambitious individuals seeking community recognition to move up the organizational ladder. These organizational pacesetters have learned well from the entrenched WASP models.

The government of Israel usually listens most to three groups within the American Jewish community. One is the umbrella out-fit called the Conference of Presidents of Major American Jewish Organizations (CPMAJO), which now claims to represent fifty-two national Jewish organizations and to be the voice of organized American Jewry. Of similar influence is the National Jewish Community Relations Advisory Council (NJCRAC), since 1997 called the Jewish Council for Public Affairs (JCPA). Also consequential, especially in dealings with Congress, is the American Israel Public Affairs Committee (AIPAC) lobby in Washington.

By 1980, it was clear that almost all major Jewish organizations opposed the AAEJ's confrontational tactics. Although many estab-lishment individuals supported the goal of rescuing the Ethiopian Jews, they shied away from endorsing the Association's demand for quick, positive action by Israel. There seemed to be three intercon-nected factors at work blocking their endorsement of the AAEJ: a deep-seated belief in the correctness of Israeli policy; concerns over reinforcing the virulent idea that Zionism equaled racism; and fear of undermining their positions as representatives of the American Jewish community should they come out forcefully demanding the large-scale immigration of the Jews of Ethiopia. In addition, there was the typical organizational fear that that the AAEJ might be a serious competitor for charitable donations.

Belief in Israel

Although at that time many American Jews were too young to re-member the Holocaust, most were heavily influenced by its horrors. They remain deeply grateful that in the State of Israel there is a safe harbor for endangered Jews, and proud that Israel is willing and able to defend Jews from attack by men determined to eradicate the Jewish state. Millions of American Jews send their dollars, and some their sons and daughters, to Israel as a sign of their commit-ment to its survival.

Out of this love for Israel has grown a widespread belief among American Jews that Israel can hardly do wrong. If an American

Jew should criticize the government of Israel, he or she often is castigated by the American Jewish establishment for providing ammunition to anti-Semites or Arab terrorists, or for being a self-hating Jew. And I pretty much agreed – until we had lived and worked in Israel.

In Israel for extended periods as "temporary residents," we learned that there are righteous Jews and true heroes, and there are also Jewish gangsters and drug dealers; there are Jewish "women of valor" and Jewish prostitutes; there are religious Jews and Jewish atheists; there are Jewish scholars and Jewish retarded. "Israel is a sovereign nation with representatives of all strata of society," Israelis told me.

My colleague and dear friend, the late Professor Menachem Rahat of Hebrew University, said: "Here we do not pretend to be all professors, media stars, and wealthy businessmen. We do not need to hide our warts to please our neighbors as you American Jews seem to need to do." He called that attitude the "*Galut* (Diaspora) mentality," the albatross that hung around the necks of American Jews. By that he meant that the American establishment makes great efforts not to antagonize our non-Jewish neighbors in hopes of being accepted by them as worthy compatriots.

Because many American Jewish functionaries erroneously interpreted the activities of the AAEJ as implying that Israel was racist, they led major organizations into joining those Israeli bureaucrats who were attempting to discredit our motives.

Not so the Israeli citizens who freely mock their political leaders and are even more critical of the Jewish Agency which employs so many political cronies. Once, after I told a Tel Aviv cab driver to go to the Jewish Agency headquarters on Kaplan Street, he said: "To the *sachnut* (Jewish Agency)? Don't you mean the *Beit ha-Teh* (The Tea House)?" It took only one visit on Kaplan Street to know what he meant. The Jewish Agency is charged with assisting new immigrants, and there were lines of people in most of the offices waiting for service. Yet invariably, the clerks took their tea and pastry breaks leaving their clients standing in line.

Especially from 1974 forward, after becoming an advocate for the Ethiopian Jews, it became clear to me that American Jews and organizations do a disservice to the citizens of Israel by placing virtually all Israeli diplomats or representatives on a pedestal and treating them as heroes. Though some certainly are, others are not. In Israel it is different. The Israeli citizen is more realistic and recognizes that politicians in Israel are the same as politicians everywhere. They have self-interest, constituents to please, cronies to hire, and political debts to pay. For reality to set in, one has only to witness a debate in the Knesset where some members have been known to resort to fisticuffs.

Just as Israeli citizenry encompasses both good and bad individuals, so are its government's policies open to critical examination. But when the AAEJ demanded changes in the scope and pace of rescuing the Beta Yisrael, we were attacked as irresponsible enemies of Israel. Jewish American organizational functionaries seemed not to understand that it is possible to love the State of Israel and its principles and at the same time be critical of a particular Israeli government. Had they been correct in viewing such criticism by the AAEJ leadership as self-hating or anti-Israel, they would have had to tar with the same brush such distinguished Israeli backers of the *aliyah* of the Beta Yisrael as Knesset Member Haim Ben Asher, paratrooper Moshe Bar Yuda, Professors Erlich and Tartakower, and Ambassador Hanan Aynor (chapter 5).

A corollary of uncritical acceptance of Israeli policy is the "trust us, we are doing all we can" mantra. We met this attitude regularly when we asked leaders of American Jewish organizations to inform their membership and to participate in the movement to assist the Jews of Ethiopia. Their typical response went this way: "We are told by high-level Israeli officials that any public discussion of the Ethiopian Jews will endanger their lives, that Israel is committed to their rescue, and that they are doing all they can under very difficult circumstances in Africa."

A 1981 letter between establishment figures is relevant and revealing in the matter of granting trust to Israeli officialdom. Irving

Kessler, executive director of the United Israel Appeal (UIA), which funds the Jewish Agency, at that time wrote to Carmi Schwartz, associate vice president of the Council of Jewish Federations, which collects the funds for the UIA. Kessler described a report by Yehuda Dominitz, director of immigration and absorption for the Jewish Agency, which stated that Israel was caring for the Ethiopian Jews in the refugee camps of the Sudan. He told Schwartz of the need for unquestioning support: "I am positive that no written description of this program will ever be given to us. We must act without evidence."

That was it from the man charged with transferring to the Jewish Agency the money the UJA collects from loyal American donors! As Kessler advised, American Jews were expected to support the Jewish Agency's programs to care for and rescue the Ethiopian Jews simply on faith, without any evidence of success or explanation of why so few were getting out.

Does Zionism Equal Racism?

In 1975, the United Nations General Assembly passed Resolution 3379 which equated Zionism with racism. That this indictment is both untrue and deeply offensive is obvious to all who have seen the multiracial Israeli community. That is the way we saw it. In 1968 we became good friends with two families of an Israeli community of dark-skinned Jews from Yemen. We attended their colorful wedding and henna ceremonies and visited them on the Sabbath several times a month. When on sabbatical in Haifa in 1973–1974, we were friends with a family of dark-skinned Jews from India and their Jewish friends who had immigrated to Israel from Burma. One had simply to walk the streets of Tel Aviv or Jerusalem to see Jews not only from Europe, but from Morocco, Iran, Iraq, Uzbekistan and many other countries; also Arabs, Druse, and Ethiopian Christians milled the streets. What a refreshing experience after having lived in John Birch country in Southern California.

But the resolution was an effective piece of anti-Israel propaganda. In consequence, American Jews rallied to Israel's defense. In

1975, the AAEJ was a tiny organization of a few hundred adherents. But five years later it had thousands of members. And we were critical of Israel's lack of progress in rescuing the Beta Yisrael. Some of our opponents, both in North America and Israel, demanded we be silent: our charges could be seen as accusing the Israelis of racism for their failure to rescue the Jews of Ethiopia.

American Jews had reason to be concerned about being labeled racists. At home a second worrisome predicament had arisen. In 1978 the Anti-Defamation League (ADL) and the American Jewish Committee (AJC) presented briefs supporting Alan Bakke's case at the U.S. Supreme Court. Bakke, a white male student, sued to overturn the University of California's "affirmative action" policy. Support of Bakke by the ADL and AJC did much to shatter the previous special relations between African Americans and Jews nurtured during the civil rights movement. The harm was done; American Jews were considered racist by many African Americans.

Sylvia and I published full-length articles in the Jewish press challenging the right of the ADL and the AJC to act as if they were representing American Jewry, because they certainly did not represent our views. Our challenge got a mixed response. A number of prominent grassroots Jews supported us including the editor of the *Jewish Spectator*, scholar Trude Weiss-Rosmarin, and Richard Giesberg, who later became a leader in the North American Conference on Ethiopian Jews (NACOEJ). At the same time, certain members of the AAEJ executive committee itself chastised us for our stance.

The "Zionism is Racism" charge and the growing alienation among African Americans were sensitive issues for American Jews, and the Jewish establishment was not pleased with the AAEJ's publicity campaign. A number of establishment editors were caught in the trap of refusing to publish AAEJ articles. Graenum Berger describes one who had requested him to write a "hard-hitting" article regarding the rescue of the Ethiopian Jews, but then did not publish it. To quote Berger, after Operation Moses, when it became "permissible" to talk openly about the Ethiopian Jews, that same editor wrote that he had been "confident that Israel would come through, and was glad that he hadn't published [Berger's] critical material."

Striking a Financial Nerve

People rarely give money to organizations they consider irresponsible, dangerous, or crooked. With millions of dollars annually going to the UJA and other Jewish organizations, the few thousand reaching the AAEJ during its early years were easily ignored. But by 1982, twelve thousand members and several major donors on our board changed the arithmetic.

Long-time AAEJ board members and philanthropists Henry and Edith Everett were already viewed as generously supporting a number of "marginal" charities. When Barbi Weinberg and Nate Shapiro joined the AAEJ board, however, establishment bureaucrats began to show concern. A number of Federation leaders in Los Angeles, San Francisco, and Chicago became alarmed when we asked donors to demand evidence from the UJA that a designated portion of their contributions was going to projects supporting the Ethiopian Jews. If the Federation and the UJA did not provide that evidence, we asked that donors give instead to the AAEJ. Irving Kessler of the UIA was concerned after he "heard through [the] UJA and the Oakland Jewish Federation that the AAEJ is beginning a campaign to solicit allocations from federations [July 10, 1981, letter to Carmi Schwartz]." After suggesting that the federations consider challenging the AAEJ for evidence that our funds were being spent to assist Beta Yisrael refugees in Africa, he reconsidered and wrote: "I would hate to get into an argument with their leadership as to whether or not they are able to fulfill their promises."

Graenum Berger wanted to place advertisements in major newspapers stating that Israel was not getting the Ethiopian Jews out of Africa fast enough, and that Jews should contribute their donations directly to the AAEJ. We did not publish that ad, but we did ruffle a few feathers when some bureaucrats saw the page layout for the ad Berger was ready to place in the *New York Times*.

How effective our campaign was in challenging the establishment organizations was evident when a high-ranking elected officer of the Los Angeles Federation confronted me during a meeting
in Los Angeles, lost his cool, and grabbed me by my tie and shirt
collar, warning me about going too far. I shrugged him off, not
making a big fuss because of my respect for the man's past record,
and also because he took the AAEJ seriously. (See the quote at the
head of this chapter.)

As more and more rank and file Jews came to support the Association, we began to receive invitations to speak or serve as pan-
elists at their major conferences, such as those sponsored by the
National Jewish Community Relations Advisory Council and the
Council of Jewish Federations. An unusual opportunity occurred
in the fall of 1980 when the AAEJ brought Nachum ben Yosef to
lecture throughout the country. Nachum, a college graduate and
former employee of ORT in Ethiopia, was a credible and effective
spokesman. In his talks, Nachum asked members of the audience
to pledge $3,000 to the AAEJ "Chai" campaign to be used for the
rescue of one Ethiopian Jew. After he gave a major presentation
in San Diego where Ruth Bennet and Morris Shovel had gathered
about a thousand guests to hear his talk, Peter Jackson, a wealthy
new resident of San Diego, formerly of England, wrote out a check
to the AAEJ for $3,000, and then cornered me for half an hour
wanting to learn how he could help. We took to each other in-
stantly, partly because we both had a mentally handicapped child;
we seemed to connect.

At that time, the AAEJ was in the process of closing its Los
Angeles office. An employee in the office of our host, the Community Relations Council (CRC), opened our incoming mail before
sending it to our Costa Mesa office. We asked CRC director Murray
Wood to tell the staffer to send our mail unopened. Still, in spite
of the request, the envelopes came opened. Murray was a prince
of a man and trustworthy, but he had an eager employee who apparently wanted to find out if the AAEJ were getting significant
contributions from California donors.

That "eavesdropping" elicited a brainstorm, a bit of chicanery, that also might help get Peter Jackson more involved with the AAEJ if he would agree to participate. That evening I phoned Peter and explained the plan. After hearing it, he laughed heartily and agreed: "Sure. I'm game. Let's try it." According to the plan, Peter wrote a $100,000 check as a contribution to the AAEJ and mailed it to our Los Angeles address, supposedly by mistake. With the check, he included a letter emphasizing that he wanted to keep the gift anonymous, and that absolutely no one else should know that he was the donor. One evening, about 3 days later, Murray Wood called.

"Howard," he said. "I have some bad news."

"What's wrong, Murray?"

"A letter came for you with a check for $100,000 and –"

"Murray, that is great! Best news we've had in a while. But I don't get it, why is that bad news? Is it a hoax?"

"No, it's real. But the donor asked that only you were to know of the donation. I'm sorry, but the letter was opened and others have seen it."

"Yeah, I wish they would stop prying so much. Please put a stop to it. But what the hell. It's our largest gift ever. Can you send it right away by certified mail?"

Two days letter I received the check, made a photocopy for my archives, destroyed the original, and called Peter Jackson to tell him what had happened.

Soon afterwards there were rumors that news of Peter's "megagift" was spreading. And as expected, invitations increased for the AAEJ to speak about the Beta Yisrael at major establishment events.

Did the ploy work? Possibly it made the establishment think twice about the AAEJ because they knew that big donations meant greater credibility for our cause. Did it get them to side with the AAEJ in assisting the Beta Yisrael? Not really. They did not join in until November 1984, when the UJA prematurely began to raise money during the time that Operation Moses was in process. Then it became not only fashionable but profitable to advocate helping Ethiopian Jews. Mention of the Beta Yisrael has since become routine for fundraisers supporting projects in Israel. How much of those donated funds go directly to helping the Ethiopian Jews someone else will have to answer. One thing is for sure: according to current (2005) official statistics, 72 percent of the Ethiopian Jewish children in Israel live in households where the income is below the poverty line.

CHAPTER 15

An American Vatik *in* *Israel Enters the* Fray

In the crazy fabric known as *aliyah* (immigration to Israel) –
and I have had some experience because of my involvement
in the illegal Aliyah Bet in 1947 for Holocaust survivors – the
program to rescue the Beta Yisrael of Ethiopia and get them
to Israel was one of the more unusual and creative ones that a
group of volunteers ever undertook.

Looking back, there is no doubt in my mind that the AAEJ's
approach of open confrontation worked. It is also clear that
Operation Moses and Operation Solomon could not have succeeded were it not for the Government of Israel. But the heroic
rescue by Israel of virtually the entire community of Ethiopian
Jews might not have happened for many years to come and
with the loss of many Jewish lives, had it not been for the AAEJ.
I feel privileged to have been a part of this effort.

– *Murray Greenfield, 2002*

As the AAEJ continued to expand its base during 1981 and 1982,
more and more of our attention and energy came to focus on improving the absorption process for the approximately two thousand
Ethiopian Jews in Israel and on preparing for Beta Yisrael immigrants who would come in the future.

Successful absorption of the Beta Yisrael into Israel society
had been a major interest of mine since first meeting Rahamim.
His achievements in Israel and those of his veteran Beta Yisrael
friends were impressive and could be a model for other Beta Yisrael

immigrants. The rescue of the Beta Yisrael community from Africa and its successful absorption in Israel would be such a fitting story of what this tiny democracy in the Middle East truly stands for.

The absorption would not be easy. Even in the United States, it usually took three generations before immigrant Jews and others were fully assimilated. Wouldn't it be grand for the Ethiopian Jews who reached Israel to do it in two?

During my trips to Israel in 1975 through mid-1977, much of my time there was spent visiting as many Ethiopian Jews as possible; there were fewer than two hundred then. In December 1977, we got to know the group of fifty-eight new immigrants who had just come from Ethiopia. In addition to the Beta Yisrael, we also met a number of Israelis who had befriended members of that small Ethiopian community and had helped with their problems. Among them were Sarah Levin of Ashdod, a social worker who assisted local Tigrenian families; members of Kibbutz Netzer Sereni, who accepted two families of Ethiopian Jews; Chanan Lehman and Mordechai Paran of the Israel Colonization Association (ICA), who helped the Association of Ethiopian Jews (AEJ) of Israel; Shoshana Ben Dor, recent American immigrant activist, who was concerned about the Beta Yisrael maintaining their unique culture; and my science host, Professor Menachem Rahat, who helped me with most phases of my earlier work with the Ethiopian Jews while we cooperated on our scientific research.

The information gained from these interactions was crucial in designing an absorption plan to prepare for the anticipated arrival of more Jews from remote African villages so that they would integrate successfully in modern Israel. The plan listed problems especially pertinent to Ethiopian Jewish immigrants in contrast to other immigrant communities and ways to deal with those problems. Also included was a directory of names and contact information for individuals having a wide variety of expertise, who were knowledgeable and concerned about the Ethiopian Jews and ready to help the government with absorption matters if asked.

But what to do with that plan? Would it interest famed archeologist Professor Yigal Yadin, the deputy prime minister under Prime Minister Menachem Begin? AAEJ board member Henry Everett arranged for me to see Professor Yadin. We met twice in mid-February of 1978, the second time with Education Minister of the Cabinet Zevulun Hammer and a few other officials also participating. What, if anything, came out of these meetings? Did they ever use that information? Who knows? But one thing we do know is that the prime minister's office received in a two-month period both an absorption plan and a rescue plan (with Tegegne) from this new vice president of the AAEJ. The government of Israel in the spring of 1978 knew that the AAEJ was becoming deeply involved with rescue and absorption issues, more than any other American organization, and had to be reckoned with.

Help from Bar-Ilan University

It was not possible for visiting AAEJ board members to micro-manage the absorption process during the short periods we were in Israel, or long distance from the United States. After a few visits with the veteran staff of the Jewish Agency at a number of absorption centers, it became clear to us that the staff of the Jewish Agency was not prepared to handle the special needs of the Beta Yisrael. One glaring shortcoming was the lack of Israeli Ethiopian Jews who spoke both Hebrew and Amharic, preferably trained in social work or nursing, who could communicate with the new arrivals and act as intermediaries for the agency staff.

To ameliorate the situation by bringing in the expertise of Israel's universities, we sought out Dr. Emmanuel Rackman, president of Bar-Ilan University near Tel Aviv. Rabbi Rackman had written an article calling for the rescue of the Beta Yisrael, and he was a colleague of Graenum Berger. In response to my request, Dr. Rackman invited me to meet with him and Professor Florence Mittwoch, an expert in social work.

Rahamim, then a student at Tel Aviv University and an example of a well-adapted Ethiopian immigrant, also was to participate in the meeting. While we were on the bus to Bar Ilan and discussing our strategy, a Bar Ilan co-ed offered me her seat. Startled, as this had never happened to me before, I politely thanked her while flirting in my limited Hebrew, and remained standing, clinging to the strap hanging from the ceiling of the bus. That co-ed, however, was perceptive and sensed an exhausted middle aged man. During this trip and during most of my stays in Israel since becoming an advocate for the Ethiopian Jews, there were many eighteen-hour days crisscrossing the country to meet with most anyone who might be able to help the Beta Yisrael or who needed our assistance. Finally it became obvious that the AAEJ itself needed such help from an Israeli well versed in the day-to-day customs and politics of the country.

Arriving weary at Bar-Ilan, we were ushered into the president's book-lined office. Rabbi Rackman and Professor Mitwoch were warm, hospitable, and interested in learning what they could do to improve the absorption of the Ethiopian Jews. They offered to give one full scholarship towards a bachelor's degree to a qualified Ethiopian Jew who was a resident of Israel. In addition they liked and agreed to implement my proposal to have Bar-Ilan sponsor an evening program to train veteran Amharic-speaking Israeli Ethiopian Jews in procedures for helping new immigrants, although they said that the AAEJ would need to recruit the students for them.

Such a program would be a positive step, but who would recruit the students? Who would advocate for the new immigrants in solving their problems in housing, health care, employment, and other social and personal services? They deserved an effective advocate who was an experienced and accessible Israeli resident, someone who could take their individual and collective problems before relevant agencies. No doubt about it, the AAEJ needed a permanent liaison in Israel who would handle day-to-day activities and work on behalf of the interests of Beta Yisrael residents, new and old. Knowing Rackman's concern for the welfare of the Ethiopian Jews, I asked him if he could recommend someone who could be trusted with this important assignment. Without hesitating, he replied, "Murray Greenfield."

Murray Greenfield's Immigrant Programs

Greenfield's name was not new to me. His reputation and track record were promising. His commitment to Zionism and to Israel was clear. As early as 1947 he was a volunteer in the "illegal immigration," serving as an officer on a ship manned by volunteer North Americans who sailed from the U.S. to Europe and picked up Holocaust survivors there. He remained with them till they were captured by the British and incarcerated in Cyprus. Greenfield later was one of the founders of the Association of Americans and Canadians in Israel (AACI). While working with the AACI, he gained experience in dealing with the bureaucracy of the Jewish Agency on behalf of its members, and he became schooled in the workings of the corridors of power. Greenfield shared our concern. He already was aware of the plight of the Beta Yisrael from his friend, author Meyer Levin, who was living in Israel and had produced the classic film documentary on the Ethiopian Jews.

Rabbi Rackman was exactly on target in recommending Murray Greenfield. But would he take on the huge responsibility? Fortunately for us, Murray held Rackman in such high regard that he felt it an honor to be recommended by him. But he also realized it would be a major undertaking that would cut into his already busy life. While mulling the offer, he attended a meeting of Israeli officials where the problems of rescuing the Jews of Ethiopia were discussed. "As soon as Yehuda Dominitz of the Jewish Agency demanded absolute secrecy from those attending," Murray told me later, "I blew up, recalling how the demand for secrecy by other bureaucrats at the time of the Yom Kippur war led to the death of many brave unsuspecting Israelis." Greenfield agreed to help the AAEJ in Israel, to serve as the eyes, ears, and hands of the AAEJ in Israel, but only as a volunteer. He recognized that the AAEJ had limited funds for social service projects in Israel and thought it irresponsible to rent an office for the AAEJ or to hire employees. The assistance in Israel of someone of Murray Greenfield's caliber, experience, and connections was sorely needed. We had found just the right person.

Murray had challenges to face, some seldom encountered in Israel before. Most Beta Yisrael immigrants came from impoverished isolated rural villages; most had little or no formal education. Clearly there existed a huge cultural gap which had to be closed if they were to adjust successfully to Israeli society. Greenfield made the AAEJ's first priority in absorption matters that of assisting students and supporting educational programs, like the short courses proposed for Bar-Ilan University. We also provided sophisticated hand-held calculators to graduates of technical schools. When pictures were published showing the students using the calculators, Israelis commented that they were impressed by the young Ethiopians making such a rapid transition to modern Israeli life.

So that new arrivals would receive the best education possible, the AAEJ believed that we had to supplement established programs. Some students, many with parents still in Africa, were placed by the Jewish Agency in schools on religious kibbutzim. The Jewish Agency also placed about thirty at a technical high school near Beersheba. I went to a number of the schools, met with the principals and staff, visited with students to find out how they were acclimating, tried to inspire them and give them hope, and even slept overnight in a student dormitory. By chance, the student who gave me his cot that night, Addisu Messala, went on to become the first Ethiopian Jew to serve as a member of the Israeli Knesset. The principals and staff were committed and concerned for these students whom they saw as capable, but having a difficult time adjusting. Most of the students, they said, were concerned about their families still in the Sudanese refugee camps. We called those students "orphans of circumstance" and got special help for them.

Greenfield, who saw the students year-round, knew that they had unmet needs. He recommended that the AAEJ provide these students grants while they attended school. The amounts would vary depending on the need, marital status, and school level of each student.

The amount of our assistance and the number receiving it grew each year as universities set up preparatory programs for the

Ethiopian students similar to those offered immigrant students from other countries. Because many a young Beta Yisrael arrived with limited formal education, the universities extended their preparatory program to two years; the AAEJ helped fund this extra year. We also helped Beta Yisrael students who wanted to participate in vocational projects sponsored by ORT, AMAL (an educational network operated by the Histadrut, Israel's labor federation), Lady Davis, and similar training programs. These were ways to help young women and men to get employment. Murray had a knack for creating opportunities as he perceived the need. Nurses, for example, were desperately needed in Israel; by offering AAEJ study grants, we encouraged hospital officials to train Ethiopian nurses. As news spread of the generosity and concern of the AAEJ, sometimes Greenfield was approached by Israelis who wanted to start projects in their own communities to help Ethiopian Jews. Thus the AAEJ provided seed money for a synagogue wishing to start a nursery school for children of Ethiopian working mothers.

Murray was also to secure the help of a number of national organizations in Israel, such as the Mizrachi Women, WIZO (Women's International Zionist Organization), and the AACI (Americans and Canadians in Israel).

In order to get political support for these educational programs, the Israeli AAEJ committee – Murray, Bernie and Fran Alpert, Attorney Mordechai Horowitz, and Chanan Lehman of the Israeli Committee – were able to get committed Knesset members to be advocates for the education of the Beta Yisrael immigrants; those members were Yael Rom of the Likud and Tamar Eshel of the Labor Party.

Many of the newcomers were single young adults, mostly men. Lacking the extended family structure they had grown up with in Ethiopia, they often were lonely. Tuesday was open house at the Greenfields. Hana, Murray's wife, who had lost her mother and father, got the students to talk about their concerns. They called her "our Jewish Mother." She served them snacks, cookies, and juice, and she listened. The students needed to talk, and they knew that this was the day to let off steam. It was easy to open up to Hana. She had a warm smile and twinkly eyes that radiated a mother's caring and understanding.

Hana, a survivor of three concentration camps (the Terezin Ghetto in Czechoslovakia, Auschwitz in Poland, and Bergen-Belsen in Germany) who had lost her mother while they were both in the Terezin Ghetto, served as a compassionate audience. The students poured out their concern for their families, still refugees in the Sudan. They felt guilty for their modest good life as students and wanted to help their families in some concrete way. Would the AAEJ recommend and support another demonstration in front of the Knesset to speed the rescue of their families? There was an urgency in their questions. It was difficult for them to study. The pathos in their pleas was heartrending, Murray said. It moved him to work even harder to pressure the government to increase its rescue efforts.

The open house, as well as reports from the various schools, gave Greenfield a chance to follow the academic progress of many students. He questioned them to see how they were adapting to the Israeli schools.

To help the students in their studies, especially those who knew English, Greenfield requested the Association buy Amharic-English dictionaries. Those were quickly followed by Hebrew-Amharic dictionaries. Murray distributed both of those library-type dictionaries to a number of secondary schools and colleges attended by Ethiopian students. In addition, the AAEJ approved Murray's request to have an Israeli fluent in both Hebrew and Amharic produce a useful smaller dictionary to be provided to each student as well as to language school teachers and social workers.

Many older Ethiopian Jews arrived in Israel with little or no secular education. As the young students gained fluency in Hebrew, many were eager to use their newly acquired skills to help facilitate the acculturation of their parents in Israel. Just think; the first language that many illiterate Beta Yisrael adults could read was their second language, Hebrew!

With Greenfield's assistance, a group of Beta Yisrael students began writing a newsletter, "News of the Ethiopian Immigrants," to be shared across the community. It soon became a useful network of news, tips, and suggestions designed to help newcomers cope with what at times was a very rocky road to integration. Initially, it was written in Amharic, a Semitic language widely spoken by Ethiopian Jews from the Gondar area. But shortly after the first issue appeared, Greenfield learned that the majority of the new immigrants arriving in 1980 and 1981 spoke Tigrean, an Ethiopian tongue having more Hebrew cognates. This linguistic divide cut deeply, as it reflected both geographic and historic differences within the overall Beta Yisrael population. Quick to recognize the language issue, the producers of the newsletter began to print in both languages.

Soon, the newsletter became more sophisticated and included photographs as well as practical information regarding the benefits offered to new immigrants. The first issue was written by hand. It became more professional when the AAEJ provided funds to purchase a typewriter with Ethiopian fonts. This little newsletter found its way throughout the community, and the students took on another important service; they read the newsletter regularly to immigrants who were not able to read.

The older teenage immigrants had another factor to deal with in their absorption: army service. It is a common belief among Israelis that the Defense Force is the great leveler of Israeli society. Almost everyone serves; everyone receives equal treatment, and promotion is based on merit. If an immigrant were having problems learning Hebrew, he or she would learn it quite rapidly in the army. And most important, the Ashkenazis, Sephardis, Sabras, and immigrants from Russia, Ethiopia, and other countries learned to understand each other as they trained and served together.

Greenfield, however, saw that the unmarried Ethiopian soldiers had problems distinct from those of other recruits. Unlike the rank and file, most had no home or families to visit on weekends or on holiday leave. Other than their bare subsistence military

salary, they could not get financial help from families for a trip to
see friends or to buy a few modest luxuries. Murray presented their
case to the AAEJ and obtained funds for small but useful grants
to needy soldiers.

The AAEJ's grants to the single Ethiopian soldiers were so successful that after a few years, embarrassed army officials met with
Greenfield to learn more about our grant program. Murray told
them of plans to broaden our program to award grants to high
school age orphans of circumstance enrolled in the pre-army program. Perhaps shamed by our offer, the responsible military officials refused to accept the AAEJ's financial help and started to fund
the program from their own budget. They said that it was wrong
for outsiders to subsidize a project of the Israeli army.

One AAEJ project which gave us particular pleasure involved
securing large amounts of good quality used and some new clothing from the United States. Murray, Rahamim, volunteer Israelis,
and Ethiopian students distributed them to needy Beta Yisrael families, especially those who came half-starved and in rags from the
Sudanese refugee camps before and through Operation Moses.

The AAEJ started this project after my wife noticed a need for
good clothing during one of our long visits to Israel in 1979. In
particular, we met one Ethiopian family in Lod who needed warm
winter clothing for their eight children. The father was one of the
Hebrew teachers tortured in Ethiopia, who had been trained in
Kfar Batya in 1955. We took the family by bus to Jerusalem where
we had an appointment with an elderly Orthodox Jew from Brooklyn. He had an apartment near Jaffa Street that was stuffed with
used clothing he collected in Israel. Although the family was able
to get some items there, the overall selection was of rather poor
quality and we could see that the parents, though gracious, were
disappointed.

The experience troubled us, and when a group of Jewish students in California heard about it, one of them arranged for me
to see her uncle who owned a clothing store in Anaheim. He took
us into a storeroom in back of his warehouse and pointed to shelf

after shelf of surplus new working clothes that were either out of style, or were miscellaneous items from batches of clothing that he needed to discontinue. He would be thrilled, he said, if we took the clothing off his hands. And, of course, a tax deduction for gifts in kind also would be helpful!

But it took six months and another trip to Israel before we could work out most of the details. It was not a simple matter; the clothing had to be collected, shipped to Israel, stored there, and later distributed to needy families. Murray set up a meeting to discuss the project with representatives of Israel's largest women's service group, Women's International Zionist Organization (WIZO).

It was a positive meeting, and we developed an efficient low-cost procedure that worked with hardly a glitch: (1) *Source of Clothing:* The clothing came mostly from U.S. Jews who were aware of our program primarily through articles by the AAEJ they read in the American Jewish press.(2) *Method of packing and shipping:* We advised our donors to wash all the clothes and to label them as used. We later learned that some of the donors even washed the new clothes that they were giving and did not iron them, thereby rendering them an appearance that was not new and nontaxable. Still other donors hid in the middle of their bundles other gifts that might be taxed, such as shoes or toys. Most of the clothing was shipped directly to WIZO in Israel. Donors who were air travelers to Israel often packed the used clothing in a large duffle bag and checked it with the other luggage they were taking on the airplane. (3) *Pick-up and storage of clothing in Israel:* Before the air travelers left for Israel, they would inform the AAEJ in the U.S. of their flight plans, time of arrival, and the name and address of their hotel. We relayed this information to Murray. He, or one of his friends with a car, and an Ethiopian student would pick up the clothing, either at the airport or at the traveler's hotel, and then transport it to one of the WIZO chapters for storage. (4) *Distribution:* From this point, the distribution was handled almost completely by members of WIZO. They had a well-organized network throughout Israel, had contact with social workers and the absorption centers that housed the new immigrants, and used good taste in distributing quality clothing to the newcomers, efficiently and with sensitivity.

The response was immediate and positive. By having such a supply of clothing collected and available in 1984, WIZO and the AAEJ were prepared to provide for thousands of Ethiopian Jews brought to Israel during Operation Moses that year. They literally came from the Sudanese refugee camps with only the tattered clothing that was on their backs. The Jewish Agency simply was not prepared for such a sudden need.

It was heartwarming to get letters of appreciation from the fine women of WIZO. Some ran outstanding programs in their home districts. Edith Geiger, for example, served a large population of refugees and she even raised money from her friends in Florida. On the other hand, "Don't distribute clothing to the Ethiopian Jews; Israel could handle it all" was the essence of a letter we received from a high-ranking officer of the American section of the World Zionist Organization.

In addition to clothing, Murray learned from an Israeli rabbi that most Beta Yisrael new immigrants could not afford the relatively expensive *tefillin*, the ceremonial phylacteries used by devout Jewish males; these serve as a reminder of the constant presence of God and are used in morning prayers after the age of bar mitzvah when the youth are required to take on the responsibilities of manhood. Greenfield advertised this need in Israeli newspapers and received numbers of donations. Even more came from the U.S. after the AAEJ publicized the need. We soon had an ample supply to give to many needy Beta Yisrael youths at their bar mitzvahs.

As the population of the Falasha increased during the early 1980s, their religious leaders, *kessim*, wanted to celebrate "Sig'd," a religious holiday unique to Ethiopian Jews. The custom is to travel to a mountaintop to commemorate the renewal of the covenant between God and the Jewish people; the ceremony also expresses a longing for Jerusalem. Now that there was a growing population of Ethiopian Jews scattered throughout Israel, the *kessim* wanted their people to observe the holiday by gathering on a hilltop in

Jerusalem. For this first Sig'd in Israel, Ethiopian leaders asked the Jewish Agency to pay the cost of renting the necessary buses. When the agency refused, they approached Greenfield, and without hesitating, he allocated A A E J funds to pay for the buses and other expenses of their sacred and highly anticipated celebration of Sig'd.

Murray understood the system. After he approved the A A E J funding, he turned to top officials he knew in the Israeli government, told them about the holiday, which none had heard of previously, and convinced several to attend and take part in the celebration. Once the Jewish Agency learned that A A E J money and top Israeli officials were involved, it announced that it would pick up the tab. The holiday is now celebrated yearly in Israel.

The celebration of Sig'd recalled Greenfield's experience of embarrassing the army to take over the A A E J's program of helping single Beta Yisrael soldiers. An impish glee lit Murray's face as he told me: "If I ever wanted to get the Jewish Agency to sponsor a project for the Ethiopian Jews, all I needed to say was: 'the A A E J will pay for it.' It wouldn't be long until the agency came up with the funding."

The Greenfields, who live close to the Diaspora Museum, served on the board of the Friends of the Museum. With the help of the museum's able Dr. Natalie Berger, the A A E J supported the development of a full exhibit for the general public on the Jews of Ethiopia. From that exhibit, the museum designed a smaller exhibit and displayed it in many countries including the United States. Murray helped recruit one of the A A E J students to serve on the staff and provided the impetus for the museum's program to educate Ethiopian immigrants. This project brought busloads of Ethiopian families, young and old together, to see their own unique history, and also to learn about the rest of the Jewish world. Greenfield got the "Miriam's Dream" organization to help with this concept of intergenerational teaching.

The A A E J was concerned that the Beta Yisrael immigrants receive adequate and proper services from the Jewish Agency. Knowing how bureaucrats like to give a rosy picture, we were determined to get an objective view. Board member Edith Everett recommended a meeting with Professor Alex Weingrod, formerly of Brandeis University and now at Ben-Gurion University, and a contract with him to conduct an objective report on the progress of the many Ethiopian Jews settling in the Beersheba area. A year later I returned there to participate as a guest fellow of the Hubert Humphrey Institute at Ben-Gurion. But the workload was too much, and again we turned to Murray who became our liaison for the project. Professor Weingrod and his colleague, Dr. Michael Ashkenazi, produced a well-documented, reliable evaluation of the absorption of the Beta Yisrael. Their pioneering research stimulated other scholars to broaden the research. Greenfield distributed summaries of their reports to various governmental agencies in Israel.

With Murray Greenfield acting as advocate and liaison, the AAEJ began to develop contacts with important bureaucrats, raise the visibility of its interest in the well-being of local Ethiopian Jews, and bring the plight of the Ethiopian Jews still in Africa more clearly to policy-makers' attention. Murray was in contact with the Israeli press and television news journalists; he sent out news releases regularly in Israel as well as in the U.S. via the AAEJ, and in Australia with the help of Aussie activists Isi Liebler and the Ellinson family.

Murray Greefield gave the AAEJ a year-round presence in Israel. We communicated weekly by mail and telephone. His work in Israel gave me more time to devote to spearheading AAEJ advocacy programs in the U.S. Murray's small cadre of Israeli volunteers and government contacts became even more important in the 1980s when the AAEJ began to augment its advocacy role with direct rescues. But by the summer of 1982 major changes were about to occur within the AAEJ in the U.S., and to some extent those changes involved Murray Greenfield.

Time for a Change
Minor controversies common to boards of directors of growing organizations were ongoing during my years as president of the AAEJ.

This was normal and healthy; trying to resolve them was a valuable learning experience. By 1982, however, certain long-standing differences in approach and style became more problematic.

Several members of the AAEJ executive committee wanted to dump Murray Greenfield and hire a "professional" to run our office in Israel. Internal bickering and haggling about the program in Israel and objections to my confrontational policies, plus the ever growing workload as the AAEJ expanded from a few hundred to twelve thousand members, were wearing me down. We had grown and became a different organization. Perhaps now was the moment for the AAEJ to change its leadership. I decided to resign as president two months before my term was up.

How had I come to that point? Since joining the AAEJ in 1974, I had urged that only by educating the public to the plight of the Ethiopian Jews and to Israel's failure to take remedial actions could our tiny grassroots organization build a base of support that would become the foundation for changing Israeli policy. By 1978, as AAEJ president, I had come to believe that the AAEJ must launch our own rescue missions. Designed primarily by Henry Rosenberg and Nate Shapiro, the AAEJ rescues would prove that the Beta Yisrael could be freed from oppression in Ethiopia and the misery of the refugee camps in the Sudan. We were convinced that our rescues, although small in numbers, would shame the Israelis into a more active role and would evoke more support among American Jews for a full-scale *aliyah*. Our expanding public education campaign and our pressure on establishment organizations were directed to these strategic goals.

My aggressive approach, inherited from Graenum Berger, of attacking the Jewish Agency and the government of Israel for not being more proactive in the rescue of Ethiopian Jews had troubled some board members. They felt that such a confrontational stance alienated not only high-ranking Israeli politicians but also many American Jews and religious leaders.

On another level, the internal conflicts arose from a difference in style: I was a university professor from modest circumstances who felt more at ease with college students and ordinary working people than with multimillionaire social elites. I was "grassroots California" while some of my critics were accustomed to the more formal environment of board rooms and country clubs.

These organizational tensions, however, had little impact on our growing effectiveness. By the summer of 1982, we had a broad base of public support and a number of solid achievements. Our news releases appeared weekly in scores of publications, dozens of well-trained speakers addressed thousands each year, and thanks to all these efforts and the support of key senators and representatives, we had nurtured the seeds of what was to become an active caucus in Congress. A workable and firm infrastructure was in place.

The time was right to consolidate our gains, I believed, and the right person to do it was Nate Shapiro. He seemed to span the divide within the board: he was a successful businessman and deeply committed to our rescue program. He was a vice president on the executive committee, thus well known to those with differing opinions on tactics. He was our major contributor, respected by wealthy potential donors. He was equally at ease sharing his views with a U.S. senator or an Israeli official.

I asked Nate to fill in for me from July 10, 1982, when I would resign, through September when the AAEJ would hold its yearly election. He agreed to the interim appointment and in September was elected to become the last person to serve as president of the AAEJ.

Early in his presidency, Shapiro, trying to placate a few of my critics, employed a "professional" to run our office in Israel; that hire proved to be a major disappointment, accomplishing little in two years. Nate eventually replaced that person with two others, another arrangement which proved unworkable. When Dr. Will Recant became the first and only executive director of the AAEJ in 1986, he recommended that we no longer retain hired personnel in Israel, and he closed our Israeli office. Once again, the AAEJ turned primarily to volunteer Murray Greenfield and to Rahamim Elazar to continue the successful programs we had initiated in 1981 and to give much-needed support to LaDena Schnapper's efforts to rescue Beta Yisrael after Operation Moses.

MAJOR LOCATIONS OF THE BETA YISRAEL IN ETHIOPIA AND IN REFUGEE VILLAGES IN SUDAN

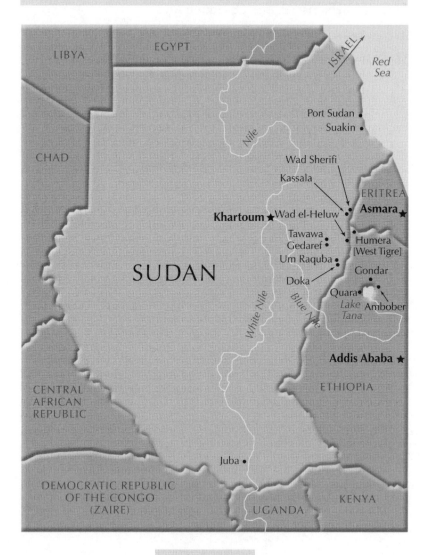

PART V

JERRY WEAVER AND OPERATION

MOSES, 1982–1985

CHAPTER 16

A Flare Illuminating the Landscape

It had taken members of the AAEJ more than six years of intense activism to witness the rescue of significant numbers of the remnant ancient Beta Yisrael community of Ethiopia. The government of Israel brought out of Africa about seven to eight hundred Beta Yisrael yearly during 1980, 1981, and 1982. We were beginning to see a flicker of light regarding their rescue from refugee camps in the Sudan. Near the end of 1982, the AAEJ learned that the number of Beta Yisrael crossing the border from Ethiopia had increased, and that those who made it were trying to survive in the Sudan under the harshest of conditions. We needed to decide what kind of role, if any, we should take in their rescue.

Two major players were to dominate the scene during the 1983 rescues from the Sudan: Henry Rosenberg of the AAEJ, and Jerry Weaver, refugee affairs counselor stationed in the Sudan for the American State Department's Bureau of Refugee Affairs. Those two gutsy trailblazers met but once in the Sudan in the fall of 1982. Never did they imagine then that their brief unplanned encounter would become the catalyst leading to the historic large-scale airlift of Operation Moses two years later.

I am pleased to present in this chapter, and in the following two written by Jerry Weaver himself, an exclusive report revealing his critical role in the rescue of over ten thousand Ethiopian Jews. As Weaver puts it, Henry Rosenberg was the "flare that illuminated the landscape," allowing Weaver with his mostly non-Jewish professional collaborators to participate in the *mitzvah*

189

of rescuing Ethiopian Jews who were suffering in the squalor of Sudan's refugee camps.

Israeli Rescues from the Sudan

The cunning and courage of Aklum Feredeh in his Israeli-supported rescue of 677 of his Ethiopian brethren in 1980 gave the AAEJ hope. Would Israel continue to rescue large numbers of Beta Yisrael from the Sudan, and if they did, could they be pressed to do still more? Past experience led us to believe that we needed to keep pressuring Israel by carrying out our own rescues, no matter how small the number of people we brought out in comparison to those rescued by the Israelis. Among the board members of the AAEJ consensus grew stronger after we saw the yearly *aliyah* from the Sudan stuck in a steady state figure of around seven hundred per year (681 in 1981 and 800 in 1982). Some of us questioned whether the Jewish Agency, regardless of opportunities for rescue, had set a yearly quota of about seven hundred Ethiopian Jews, a number that could be handled by existing absorption centers in Israel. Nonetheless, we were cautious. While investigating possible options for rescuing some of the Beta Yisrael from the Sudan, we kept a watchful eye on Israel's rescue activities so that we would not interfere.

We usually knew when Israel was in the Sudan preparing to bring a group of Beta Yisrael to Israel because they needed the help of Israeli Ethiopian Jews who knew both Hebrew and the major Ethiopian tongue of Amharic, and who also could help in distinguishing Ethiopian Jews from Ethiopian non-Jews who would like to get out of the Sudan and into Israel. My friends in Israel knew the identity of those veteran Israeli Beta Yisrael, and would phone me in the United States to let us know when one of their cars was sitting idle for days, even weeks. We had guessed that during the "times of idle cars," those individuals were in Africa, a guess that was usually confirmed within a few weeks when we got reports of the arrival of more Ethiopian Jews from the Sudan.

Do not think that we were reckless talking about such delicate matters over transatlantic telephone lines that could be tapped. We used code words which we changed periodically. For example, at one time our code word for "Israel" was "library." The code word for "Beta Yisrael immigrant" was "book." An Israeli agent involved in the rescue was called "mailman." So a message stating that "the mailman brought sixty new books to the library this week" was quite clear.

As we watched and weighed the Israeli rescues versus the need, the news that Israel brought to its shores nearly four hundred Ethiopian Jews in January 1981 gave hope that larger numbers of Beta Yisrael would be rescued that year. "See, Lenhoff," bureaucrats of Jewish organizations in the U.S. would tell me, "You are wrong. At this rate Israel will bring in thousands this year." At the end of that year, however, fewer than seven hundred had arrived.

Activists advanced a number of reasons for there being a "quota," as they called it. One explanation involved Israel's receipt of significant funding from U.S. government sources to assist in the absorption of Russian immigrants. But because of the bad relations between Israel and the Soviet Union at the time, immigration from Russia came only in trickles. Some think it was not a coincidence that the U.S. funds continued during the period when the shortfall from Russia was compensated for by the seven hundred Ethiopian Jewish immigrants yearly, especially because the Jewish Agency appeared not to have increased or to have planned any increase in the number of absorption centers for new immigrants that full-fledged larger rescues from Africa would have required.

In describing the January 1981 rescues, the expression "Israel brought to its shores" was not a figure of speech. On three different occasions during 1981 and 1982 Israel rescued from the Sudan numbers of Beta Yisrael ranging in the hundreds. For those three rescues Israel gathered the refugees secretly and placed them on boats at Suakin near Port Sudan. From there they sailed to Sharm el Sheikh at the southern tip of the Sinai Peninsula and then were taken to absorption centers in Israel.

These boat rescues were complex to carry out and fraught with danger. With a few modifications, they closely resembled Baruch

Tegegne's 1978 plan, which I had delivered to General Poran, Prime Minister Begin's military advisor. Poran claimed it was a coincidence that the procedures were similar, that Israel had thought of the model first. But it was no coincidence that after I gave the plan to the general in 1978, he contacted Tegegne to report to the Mossad. What really counts, however, is that Israel used this route successfully, and more power to the brave Israelis who carried it out, and to Baruch Tegegne who paved the way for developing the route. Tegegne was utterly dedicated to Israel and to saving his people.

As for this naval route which brought to Israel perhaps a thousand souls, a quirk of history intervened in 1982. Pursuant to the historic Israeli-Egyptian peace treaty of 1979, Israel by 1982 was required to evacuate Sharm el Sheikh, a resort city on the coast of the Red Sea, and the rest of the Sinai Peninsula. The saga of large-scale naval rescues of the Beta Yisrael from the Sudan to Sharm el Sheikh was over.

My records and sources tell us that during the years 1980 through 1982, in addition to using the boat method three times, Israel employed two other methods for getting Beta Yisrael from the Sudan to Israel. One was the refugee route using the detailed procedures as first executed by Feredeh and Israeli operatives. They flew the Ethiopian Jews as refugees from Khartoum by commercial airlines to a European city, such as Athens, and from there to Israel. To get on those flights at the Khartoum airport, we believe that those helping the Beta Yisrael would of necessity have followed official tight Sudanese regulations and operated via international refugee organizations.

Once, possibly twice, according to the Sudanese State Security, Israel landed a C-130 military cargo plane in the desert of eastern Sudan. Approximately 130 individuals could be carried in one flight. Because the Israeli ground crew left sufficient telltale litter there, such as empty plastic Evian water bottles and "Product of Israel" food wrappers, local peasants became suspicious and reported their findings to the police. Word from the Sudan got to Israel and Washington via the American embassy in Khartoum, conveying warnings from its Sudanese contacts that if the Israelis were to try such a method again, orders would be given to shoot the planes down. This message ended the cargo plane scheme. It probably would have continued for a while, if not for the careless-ness of the Israeli ground crew. Sensitive to that carelessness, the Mossad told distinguished journalists Dan Raviv and Yossi Mel-man in 1990 that "the Mossad made sure not to leave anything on the ground that might indicate Israel's involvement, not even an empty cigarette pack or a matchbook."

To Rescue or Not?

While the AAEJ was exploring various rescue options, we decided to find routes that would complement the Israeli operations and not interfere with them. Because Israel had been focusing its main rescues in the eastern part of the Sudan, we would keep out of their way by devising an alternate route for taking Beta Yisrael safely out of the refugee camps of the Sudan.

It was Aklum Feredeh himself who came up with the idea for an alternate route which would take the refugees from the Sudan to Kenya. During one of my trips to Israel in the winter of 1982, he recommended that the AAEJ speak to his friend in Beersheba, Yitzchak Yieyas. According to Feredeh, Yitzchak, who had arrived from the Sudan in 1980, was quite familiar with the area and knew individuals who, on their own, had escaped from the Sudan by get-ting to Kenya via Juba in southern Sudan. Intrigued by Feredeh's suggestion, later that spring Murray Greenfield and I arranged to meet with Yitzchak in Beersheba. He was home for the weekend and was dressed in his army fatigues. Thin, mustached, he hardly smiled the whole time we were with him. This was serious business, and he proceeded to reveal a detailed escape route which would take the refugees in the Sudan southwest to the southern regional capital city of Juba, and from there to Kenya. His proposal was comprehensive; he had thought of almost everything. Nothing could be done, however, until the AAEJ executive committee, and especially Henry Rosenberg, approved.

Later that year, Nate Shapiro joined me in Israel. Together we met Yitzchak Yieyas, and Nate heard the Kenya proposal directly from him. I assume that Nate, who succeeded me as president of the AAEJ that summer, transmitted the essence of Yitzchak's proposal to the secretive Henry Rosenberg, our board member who was aching to direct the AAEJ rescue of Ethiopian Jews from the Sudan. The executive committee gave Henry the green light.

Henry Rosenberg

Henry is my senior by a few weeks. Tall and trim, he sported a thin mustache and was a committed jogger, and was known by his friends for standing on his head and hands as part of his regular exercise. Beyond appearances, Henry was the perfect person to lead the AAEJ rescue team in the Sudan. Although professionally he is an extremely successful lawyer in New York dealing in commercial real estate, he prefers identifying himself as a humanitarian. And that he is. Fresh out of high school at age seventeen he enlisted in the U.S. Army. After graduating from City College and Brooklyn College Law School, for many years he was involved in aiding minorities and ex-convicts to obtain good jobs through admission to craft unions. He was active with Big Brothers and served pro-bono as a lawyer for Native Americans belonging to a New York intertribal council.

But it was the plight of the Ethiopian Jews that consumed most of his humanitarian energies. After the 1974 revolution in Ethiopia, he had spent about two months there in a number of visits before he went to the Sudan in 1982. On his first visit, he was accompanied by his wife, Mildred, also an idealist who had served as a nurse for the Israeli Haganah during the 1948 War of Liberation. Henry's last visit to Ethiopia before initiating the Sudanese rescue was in 1981. During that trip he surreptitiously smuggled a young Jewish couple out of the country with him. He also played key roles in extracting other key Beta Yisrael from Ethiopia, including Bill Halpern's friend Semu Desta, and Gedaliah Uria, a teacher who had been imprisoned and tortured by the Ethiopians.

Henry was well connected with liberal politicians. On August 5, 1982, he testified in the U.S. House of Representatives for the AAEJ on behalf of the Ethiopian Jews. His audience there was the Subcommittee on Human Rights and International Organizations of the Committee on Foreign Affairs. Henry had just returned from Israel where he had attended the funeral of his Israeli son-in-law, who had been stabbed to death by an Arab terrorist.

Henry Rosenberg's dedication inspired confidence, and it did not take him long to recruit a number of capable volunteers to help develop further and implement a Kenya route. Because of the potential dangers from possible leaks about Henry's rescue work, most board members, including me, were never given details of those undertakings.

Some journalists have attempted to describe the Rosenberg rescues in depth. To my mind, although these writers knew many of the facts, they did not use the best judgment in checking the veracity of the partisan remarks of many of those whom they interviewed. These particular authors appear to have focused on the controversial, presenting charges made mostly by Israeli spokesmen that the AAEJ team jeopardized the larger-scale Israeli efforts. The critics were also quoted as accusing Rosenberg and other active members of the AAEJ of being egomaniacs having mid-life crises and seeking self-aggrandizement.

In my experience, the Jewish establishment handles the egomaniacs, usually because they are *nouveau riche* large donors, by taking their money, patting them on the head, and giving them plaques at dinner parties.

By contrast, it is hard for me even to begin to describe the courage and selflessness of members of the AAEJ team, including men in their fifties, scurrying in the Sudanese desert and countryside to find Ethiopian Jews in order to help them start a new life in Israel. That was what Henry Rosenberg was doing with a number of dedicated colleagues. Among them were my friends, Jerry Strauss and the late Murray Narell of California; Jerry Strauss's friends Sandy Leeder, Joel Neuberg, and Jerry Koloms (former

Peace Corps buddies in Africa); Aklum Feredeh and his Christian Ethiopian friend, Allem Seged; American Thomas O'Rourke and Scotsman Jack Charity; Israeli Gabe Galambos; and the Ethiopian Jews, David Seyum, "Tadessa," Tesfaye Aderju (a translator), and Robel Adane, who helped identify Ethiopian Jews in the refugee camps. The Rosenberg team kept a record of hundreds of Ethiopian Jews they had found. Because they could not rescue all of the Beta Yisrael they had identified, they transmitted their lists containing those names and their locations to the Israelis.

Many of the Kenya rescues were daring, and some did not always work the way that we wanted them to. Nonetheless, from spring 1983 to just before Operation Moses in November and December 1984, the AAEJ rescues were responsible for bringing to Israel 128 Beta Yisrael. The first rescue via Kenya arranged by Henry was managed by former Peace Corps worker Sandy Leeder, in the spring of 1983. Henry knew I would be thrilled when, in a letter with accompanying photograph, he told me that Leeder had brought to Kenya a group of eighteen Beta Yisrael, among them the elder Mengistu Elias. He was the Faitlovitch-trained, learned father of my friend, the handsome veteran Ethiopian Jew in Israel, Elias Mati.

Leeder told me with glee how he and his two helpers sat in the front seat of their Toyota van, carrying the eighteen refugees, including the patriarch, Mengistu Elias, sitting in the first row of seats behind them. The rescue of the eighteen and the journey to Nairobi was in Leeder's words, "an adventure similar to those depicted in [the movie] *Raiders of the Lost Ark*."

No wonder Leeder was excited to have been involved in the rescue of Mengistu Elias. The elder Elias was a giant of a man, a fervent Zionist. Not only was he leading his villagers in the Sudan so they would reach Israel; he was also preparing them for their new life "in Jerusalem."

How did I learn about that second activity, not having met the man? Through another one of those beautiful chance encounters so frequent in Israel. It was the spring of 1984, about a half year before Operation Moses. Rahamim brought me to visit some new immigrants from the Sudan staying at the absorption center in Atlit, a city built at the site of an old Roman fortress just south of Haifa. A good-looking teenager, about sixteen years old, recognized Rahamim and asked to join us. We had an animated discussion of his adventures as he told us how happy he was to be finally in Israel.

"Your Hebrew is excellent."

The young man seemed embarrassed by my compliment.

"You must have had some fine instructors at your *ulpan* (Hebrew language course)."

He looked at me quizzically. "What *ulpan*?" he said. "There is no *ulpan* at this absorption center."

"But where did you learn your Hebrew? You have been in Israel less than a month. In your school in Ethiopia?"

When he said no, I was really confused. Then with a big smile, he said, "Mengistu Elias taught us while we were in a refugee camp in the Sudan."

His response flabbergasted me. It took me full circle from my early meeting with Elias Mati at Kibbutz Netzer Sereni, to my photograph of Elias Mati's father, Mengistu Elias, taken when Sandy Leeder had brought the elder out of the Sudan to Nairobi, and now to this Hebrew-speaking new immigrant. How fortunate I was to be a witness to this marvelous story of the strength and unity of the Jewish people. That was one of the great gifts the Ethiopian Jews gave to all of us who had the luck to be part of their remarkable odyssey. We look back at those days as among the richest parts of our lives.

Were those rescues organized by the AAEJ important? You bet they were, for a number of reasons beyond the gift of bringing Mengistu Elias in the group of eighteen to Israel. When Rosenberg started his work in the Sudan, Ethiopian Jews were leaving their ancestral villages in Ethiopia because of the intolerable political situation there. As Rosenberg testified in Congress in August of 1982:

I have been there [Ethiopia] twice in the last few years since the revolution…[and] I visited many of the Falasha villages.

Hundreds of Falashas have been imprisoned and tortured and killed. They are called Zionists and CIA agents.

[Their] crimes ranged from distributing matzohs to teaching Hebrew and the ultimate crime, trying to emigrate…. I have seen the physical evidence of this torture. [The Communist political party the Dergue] took…[the Falasha] leaders, the teachers…and used them as an example.

[Rosenberg describes the conditions of two of the tortured teachers he met.]

Torture is a way of life and the fear it inspires in the rest of population has a way of dehumanizing them…[as were] the Jews in Europe at the time of the Holocaust.

All you need is a small spark in this area. It is an area where famine and disease are no strangers.

Whether or not the Kenya rescues by the AAEJ were necessary at the time to spur the rescue efforts by the Israelis, we may never know. But the activities of the Rosenberg team were heroic. They made it possible for 128 Beta Yisrael to reach their long dreamed-of "Jerusalem" where they could lead a life free of intolerance and persecution. What a good feeling it must have been for Rosenberg and his "boys" in Kenya to have played a major role in fulfilling that dream for those 128 refugees. That's much better for the soul than receiving a plaque.

Inconsistency in the Numbers

Between Greanum Berger and me, we usually had accurate records – sometimes a month-to-month count of the numbers of Ethiopian Jews brought to Israel from Ethiopia and the Sudan (Appendix B). Our figures for 1983 were slightly less than seven hundred, a number which accorded with the steady annual rate that the AAEJ thought to be a yearly quota. In addition there were the 128 Ethiopian Jews whom Henry Rosenberg and his cohorts brought in via Kenya. Hence the total was closer to 830. Yet the appendix of Stephen Spector's book on Operation Solomon lists the number of Beta Yisrael immigrants for that year as 2,227. Spector received his information from the Jewish Agency, Department of Immigration and Absorption, Office of the Director-General, and confirmed for 1977 to 1991 by HIAS.

In response to my question, LaDena Schnapper, who kept the records in Nate Shapiro's AAEJ office in Illinois, responded that the number for 1983 was in the neighborhood of 830 if we included the 128 rescued by Henry Rosenberg. A few days later, however, LaDena called me because she found a memo that she had received from Israeli authorities in January of 1984. It stated that the number of Beta Yisrael immigrants arriving in Israel in 1983 was 2,227. She too could not account for the discrepancy.

It was not till January 2005 that the inconsistency was resolved. The answer was provided by Jerry Weaver, a former Foreign Service officer serving in the U.S. Embassy in the Sudan. He was the Refugee Affairs Counselor (RAC) in charge of the U.S. program for resettling refugees from Africa from 1982 to 1985. But before describing Weaver's official role in the rescue of the Ethiopian Jews from the Sudan, you need to know something of Jerry Weaver the man – a remarkable and unique down-to-earth individual, part scholar, part Lawrence of Arabia, and part Indiana Jones.

That Weaver had played a key role in Operation Moses was not news to me. Mitchell Bard and I wrote about him in our 1987 article about how President Reagan had helped facilitate Operation Sheba. But I did not realize the extent of Weaver's involvement until reading part of his story in *The Arabists* (1993) by Robert D. Kaplan. Impressed with Weaver's background, accomplishments, and independent free spirit, I felt impelled to talk with the man. But, even with Google, he was hard to find. First of all, Weaver is a common last name, and Jerry could be a nickname for Gerald or Jerome.

Kaplan gave a hint when he wrote in 1993 that Weaver had been living somewhere near his hometown of Newark, Ohio.

After learning through some Google searches that a Gerald "Jerry" Weaver from his high school had died, I was able to contact the chairwoman of a class reunion, the one for the class of the deceased Jerry Weaver. In a passing remark, she suggested phoning another Jerry Weaver who had a farm nearby. When he answered my call and confirmed that he was the Jerry Weaver who used to work in the Sudan, my instant response was, "My God, you're alive!" Since then we have been exchanging notes and filling in gaps of our respective recollections of the rescue of the Ethiopian Jews. Finally we met in early June 2005 at the "Blue Nile," his farm in Newark, Ohio.

In *The Arabists*, Kaplan describes how Jerry Weaver, a star high school football player with a love for guns, joined the Ohio National Guard at sixteen. After high school he went on active duty with the U.S. Army and married his girlfriend. When he was nineteen, he got out of the army and accepted a football scholarship to Ohio University. He got his bachelor's and master's degrees there. With his new thirst for knowledge he went to the University of Pittsburgh and earned his Ph.D. in political science. After some teaching stints at California State Long Beach and the University of Texas, Austin, he joined the faculty of UCLA (University of California, Los Angeles) as a full professor. While in California, he gave some lectures and participated in a research project at the University of California at Irvine, which was my campus at the time. We were unaware of each other then.

Weaver went to Washington in 1977, working for the State Department's Agency for International Development (AID). He resigned from UCLA in 1978 when he was sworn in as a Foreign Service officer. Later that year he went to the Sudan, starting out as a social science analyst, which gave him a unique opportunity, as he said, "to roam the hinterlands." Weaver had already served various agencies of the U.S. government in Guatemala, Thailand, Nicaragua, Bolivia, and Pakistan. Being an avid big game hunter, he surmised that he would "enjoy the wildlife" of those hinterlands. It was through those excursions that he learned the landscape and made important contacts with the Sudanese which were later to help him in getting Ethiopian Jews from the Sudan to Israel.

In the fall of 1982, one of Weaver's major responsibilities was to facilitate the resettlement of African refugees to the United States through the International Committee for Migration (ICM). This Geneva-based organization was first established in 1951 to deal with the migration and resettlement of displaced persons and refugees. Currently 105 nations, including Israel, are members of the ICM (now renamed International Organization for Migration, IOM).

Although there were over a half million refugees in the Sudan in those times, most from Ethiopia, it was the policy of the United States then to accept only 2,500 refugees per year from all of Africa. Weaver said in hindsight that through the ICM, he probably handled the migration of relatively few Ethiopian Jews per month. That was changed shortly by two events: one, the meeting with Henry Rosenberg of the AAEJ in the U.S. Embassy in Khartoum in late 1982; second, a large influx in the number of Ethiopian Jews entering the Sudan during early 1984.

Visit of Henry Rosenberg, the "Flare"

A series of critical events took place after Henry Rosenberg arrived in the Sudan and before he and his crew rescued the 128 Ethiopian Jews as described earlier in this chapter. The following narrative replays some of Rosenberg's story as seen through the eyes of Jerry Weaver. One fall day in 1982 while Weaver was at his desk working on a report regarding a visit he had made to some UNHCR camps in southern Sudan, the ambassador's secretary called and said that the boss wanted to see Jerry "right away."

Ambassador C. William Kontos, once head of the United States' "Sinai Mission" designed to keep Israeli and Egyptian forces apart after the Yom Kippur War, had arrived in Khartoum in 1980. He and Jerry got along quite well, often traveling together when the ambassador wanted to familiarize himself with parts of the Sudan distant from Khartoum. From the tone of the secretary's voice, Jerry sensed that Kontos was angry. Jerry described the meeting that followed, a meeting which he later described to me as "the flare that illuminated the landscape" regarding the involvement of the United States in the movement of Ethiopian Jewish refugees out of the Sudan. These are Jerry's words:

> When I entered the ambassador's office, I could tell that something was up. He introduced me to Henry Rosenberg, an American from New York. Rosenberg launched a heated criticism of the embassy for not protecting the "Falashas." He said that "hundreds" were being mistreated in the Tawawa refugee camp and that he was there to straighten things out. He had already seen the UNHCR representative, Robert Muller. Rosenberg handed Ambassador Kontos a sheet of paper which Bill studied and then passed to me. It was a letter signed by Congressman Stephen Solarz, a man well known to us as chair of the House Appropriations Committee's subcommittee for Africa. The letter read like an injunction stating that "we" give Mr. Rosenberg, who Solarz identified as an important personage, all help possible.
>
> Ambassador Kontos assured Rosenberg that his staff would do everything necessary to facilitate his trip to Gedaref. Rosenberg was barely out the door when Kontos, red-faced and upset, barked at me, "Who are the Falashas and why is the United States interested in them?" He was furious. Neither he nor his staff had ever been briefed about an American concern for the Ethiopian Jews, and in walks this VIP and demands that the embassy do something for a group of people of whom he was totally unaware.

To find out what was going on, Jerry, using a secure telephone, called the Refugee Bureau in Washington. After much delay, he finally reached Deputy Assistant Secretary Arthur E. Dewey. A former White House Fellow and retired army lieutenant colonel who had flown helicopters in Vietnam, "Gene," as he was called by his friends, had visited the Sudan in 1981 to size things up. Jerry was definitely a friend of Secretary Dewey; it was Dewey who had recommended that Jerry Weaver be appointed RAC for the United States in the Sudan. Carefully and clearly, Dewey explained who the "Falashas" were. Then he revealed that the United States government, working through the ICM, had a special interest in moving as many Ethiopian Jews as practical out of the Sudan. Jerry was instructed to contact the ICM. Jerry told me of the ICM meeting in his distinctive colorful language:

> At Gene's direction, I called on "Ruth," who was head of the ICM office. Before the meeting, I knew that the ICM handled the paperwork for getting the necessary travel documents and airline seats for refugees who were to go to the United States. Bob Muller of the UNHCR told me, with just the hint of a Gallic smile, that "Ruth" was a lady of some parts. I had by this time served more than four years in Sudan and had faced angry lions, belligerent buffalo, and overly protective cow elephants. My first encounter with Ruth ranks right up there. I learned later that Ruth was an Israeli and was not surprised.
>
> Probably in her early fifties then, with gray-streaked hair and nicotine-stained fingers, she made no pretenses of welcoming me. She blew smoke from purple-papered Indian cigarettes in my face. With this kind of foreplay, she informed me that she had heard of me from ICM in Geneva and gave me ten strong minutes. The meat of her tale was that "somebody" moved "some one" from "somewhere" to "some place" where they stayed while travel documents were arranged. Clearly, the "who, what, where, and how" was none of my business. Ruth mentioned that the Netherlands had provided many visas for her refugees. Because I knew Dutch Ambassador DeYoung, I went to see him.

DeYoung, a career diplomat, had met Jerry many times at social gatherings hosted by the Mullers and knew Jerry well. He was helpful and open, revealing that several hundred Ethiopian Jews had been taken out of the Sudan each year for several years, mostly on Dutch travel papers. He thought that the number could be increased if the United States wanted to get involved, and did not think there would be any problems.

Muller also spilled the beans to Jerry for the first time. He told Jerry that he and one other UNHCR staffer were aware of the movement to take the Ethiopian Jewish refugees out of the Sudan and bring them to Israel. Muller also confided that although Sudan's Commissioner of Refugees knew little about the movement of the Ethiopian Jews, key Sudanese security personnel were aware that Ethiopian Jews were being taken from Gedaref to Khartoum and out to Israel through the ICM channel, and that they had no plans to stop that movement. The cooperation of the Sudanese startled Jerry at first, because Sudan was officially in a state of war with Israel. I write "at first" because Jerry had much respect for the Sudanese people and had worked with them before on other humanitarian projects.

As per normal embassy procedures, Weaver cabled this information to Washington and sent a copy to the U.S. Mission in Geneva. Within days he received a response instructing him to fly to Geneva and meet with Carl Beck, the refugee affairs coordinator in the mission. He was well known to be supportive of efforts to assist African refugees. Beck knew little or nothing about specific efforts of the United States in assisting the Jewish refugees from Ethiopia, but he could tell that there was a new and significant interest coming from the State Department.

Beck had Weaver meet with Robert Paiva, a former U.S. Foreign Service officer who then was working for the ICM in Geneva. Paiva was close-mouthed about details, but knew much. He told Jerry that Israel, as a member of the ICM, received help in moving "people of interest," the code lingo for Ethiopian Jews. He made it clear that the Dutch played an important role in the movement of those people. It was Paiva who also knew of Israeli connections. It was he who first told Weaver that Ruth was an Israeli. He also told Jerry that the ICM funded other individuals who might not be Israelis but who helped move the Ethiopian Jews.

"A month or two after Rosenberg's visit," reminisced Jerry Weaver, "it became clear that the United States government, or at least its Refugee Bureau, had been energized to move the Ethiopian Jews out of the Sudan." Jerry explained that the ICM in Khartoum was to be responsible for the movement of Ethiopian Jews. It would do the work and would bear the risk if something went wrong. Israel would underwrite the costs, including those of the airline tickets.

What did this new policy mean to Weaver? He was responsible for monitoring the ICM's progress, making periodic reports to the State Department, and intervening as troubleshooter and liaison should problems arise between the ICM and the Sudanese authorities. Though not anticipated at first, Weaver also intervened whenever nongovernmental volunteer rescue groups caused problems. Jerry Weaver summarized this major change in U.S. policy and in his "job description" as follows:

> To me, the main points were two. First, the U.S. resettlement program was now open to Ethiopian Jews who either wanted to come to the U.S. or who would use the U.S. as a transit point to Israel. Second, it was my job to serve as liaison between the Sudanese authorities, the ICM and UNHCR, and to troubleshoot should problems arise.

Mystery Solved

This collaborative program between the United States, Israel, Holland, and the ICM was extremely successful. During 1983 and early 1984, some 100–120 Ethiopian Jews per month came through the ICM channel, mostly young men and a few women. The approximately 1,440 Ethiopian Jews, about 120 per month, who were moved through the ICM/U.S. collaboration probably account for the discrepancy in the total number of Ethiopian Jews rescued in 1983 as noted earlier in this chapter. I had projected that Israel would have rescued about seven hundred during that year, the steady state yearly number it had rescued in each of the previous three years. Assuming that Israel had rescued seven hundred through its usual methods, and adding to that number the 128 rescued by Henry Rosenberg and his AAEJ friends, and then adding the approximately 1,440 brought out though the ICM/U.S. collaboration, we get 2,268 – a fairly close match!

While all of this was going on, both the UNHCR and the Sudanese government officials essentially turned a blind eye to what became an obvious migration of Ethiopian Jews to Israel.

The ICM movement continued smoothly through 1982 and 1983. Nonetheless there were always some problems. For example, members of the Ethiopian Peoples' Revolution Party (EPRP) living in the Tawawa refugee camp got wind that the Ethiopian Jews there were getting help from the outside. In an attempt to extort money and food from them, a small cadre of the EPRP would torch the *tukuls* (traditional straw huts) inhabited by the Ethiopian Jews in the camp. After Jerry was told of the torchings by his contact in Sudan's State Security, Lieutenant Colonel Musa Saeed, the local Sudanese security in Tawawa identified the perpetrators and the torchings stopped.

Weaver was called upon to help resolve other problems that could interfere with the relatively effective movement of Ethiopians generated by the ICM/U.S. collaboration. Mistakes were made by inexperienced, though well-intentioned, private individuals who were attempting to rescue Ethiopian Jews in the Sudan. The Sudanese security knew what those volunteers were doing and would stop and sometimes arrest them. When Weaver was told, for example, that some American volunteers were being held in the prison in Juba, he rushed there to get them out. "The Juba prison," Jerry told me, "is one of the most primitive and cruel in Africa. That is a prison no one should experience." Weaver got the volunteers out of the Juba prison as well as the fourteen Ethiopian Jews they had brought with them from the refugee camps. "Happily," said Jerry, "the fourteen refugees were sent to Khartoum where they were processed by the ICM and sent on their way in a few weeks."

Fortunately, no one was harmed, and the ICM program continued uninterrupted.

Another example of Weaver's troubleshooting and liaison roles was alluded to earlier in this chapter. When Israel started to fly C-130 cargo planes to the Sudan to take out Ethiopian Jews illegally, it was Jerry Weaver, under instructions from Lieutenant Colonel Musa Saeed, who warned Israel that if they tried to do that again, the airplanes would be shot down.

The AAEJ Rescue Program in Retrospect

How are we to evaluate the impact of the visit of Henry Rosenberg carrying the letter from Congressman Solarz to Ambassador Kontos in the fall of 1982? Was the AAEJ action the catalyst for getting the United States Embassy in Khartoum involved in the movement of Ethiopian Jews out of the Sudan and then to Israel? The AAEJ never made this claim; had we done so it would have been interpreted as self-aggrandizement. Jerry Weaver, the man responsible for the United States refugee affairs in the Sudan, however, speaks to this issue. Because the AAEJ got lots of criticism for Rosenberg's efforts, I asked Weaver a number of related questions. Here are his responses:

> First let me say in no uncertain terms, Henry Rosenberg's arrival in Bill Kontos's office was quickly followed by a major change in policy of the United States government, which in turn led to changes in the role of the ICM in moving large numbers of Ethiopian Jews.
>
> I do not think that Rosenberg's activities in the Sudan endangered the Israeli rescue efforts or the lives of the Israeli operatives in the Sudan. Sudan's State Security was aware that "refugees" were being smuggled to Khartoum. Sudanese security became "concerned," however, when an Israeli military airplane landed in the desert. Had Sudan's security known of the movement of Ethiopian Jews via Port Sudan, they probably

would have cut it off. The government of Sudan could not have turned a blind eye to clandestine Israeli operations.

Rosenberg did not endanger the Israeli operations, but Israel's own indiscretions, as with the military cargo airplane(s) incident(s), did. Nor am I aware of any Israeli operatives in the Sudan losing their lives or being arrested because of Rosenberg. Probably half a dozen or more "tour guides" were detained after I got involved, but none were harmed. This I am certain of because I had lots of contact points and would have been informed by the Sudanese security, Peter Parr (the UNHCR representative in Gedaref), or by PVO (Private Volunteer Organizations) personnel that the U.S. was funding in the refugee camps.

You ask, "Did Rosenberg's efforts interfere with or hurt the ICM program?" No, not at all. His efforts were such low scale as to be nonfactors. I made a trip or two to Juba, a couple of visits to Gedaref, and one or two meetings with Colonel Musa when someone from a PVO – usually the International Rescue Committee – was caught with undocumented refugees. But given what the ICM and the U.S. and Sudanese governments were doing, and given the Sudanese attitude of extreme forbearance, Rosenberg's operation was as prominent as a bottle floating on Lake Erie.

The Mossad probably considered you guys as a pain in the ass. It saw itself as the supreme pros. They of course distrusted and disliked "amateurs," especially ones that embarrassed the government of Israel. I think their intentions to rescue the Ethiopian Jews were genuine. Personally, I feel that the Mossad did a terrible job in Sudan, especially in regard to its efforts up to 1984. But more on that when we go into Operation Moses. In all fairness, however, once a rescue plan was agreed upon, the Israelis did great work.

As pointed out earlier in this chapter, most previous commentators on Operation Moses, when describing Rosenberg's efforts, focused on partisan remarks implying that his rescue campaign brought to Israel only miniscule numbers of Beta Yisrael, and that it also jeopardized the larger-scale efforts of the Israelis. The details described on these pages show that Rosenberg's efforts were significant and filled an important gap in the rescue of Ethiopian Jews from the Sudan.

But even more important, were it not for Rosenberg's unexpected colorful entrance to Ambassador Kontos's office in Khartoum in the late fall of 1982, the role of Jerry Weaver and the U.S. government in the rescues of 1,440 Beta Yisrael via the ICM in 1983 and of another ten thousand through Operations Moses and Sheba in 1984 and 1985 might have been delayed or might never have happened. I attempted to ask Rosenberg about his role in catalyzing the American effort, but he interrupted and would not hear me out. He claims no credit in being in that link, nor even visiting the ambassador. Despite his modest denials, Dawn Calabia, a senior aide of Congressman Stephen Solarz who handled most of the congressman's affairs dealing with the Ethiopian Jews, referred me to a memorandum in the Solarz archives in the library of Brandeis University in Waltham, MA. The memo described a request of Nate Shapiro, who had just become president of the AAEJ, that Congressman Solarz write letters of introduction for Henry and some of his crew as they prepared to go to the Sudan that fall.

Turning Point

Late in 1983, Ambassador Kontos was replaced by the highly respected Arabist-scholar diplomat, Hume Horan. Weaver reported to him early in 1984 that from the rate of arrivals of Ethiopian Jews in Tawawa and the rate of their departures via the ICM, there would be no more Ethiopian Jews in the Sudan in another month or so. Soon afterwards circumstances changed dramatically as droves of Beta Yisrael started to enter the Sudan in 1984, and Jerry admitted that he could not have been more wrong. Because conditions were so bad in the Sudan, especially in its rainy season, we need to ask "why did so many Beta Yisrael leave Ethiopia for the Sudanese refugee camps at such an inopportune time?"

They could have left because of the volatile political situations in Ethiopia. There fighting between the Tigrean People's Liberation Front (TPLF) and Dergue forces moved in early 1984 into the areas where there were many villages of the Beta Yisrael, and some were set afire. In other areas, the Dergue was trying to recruit Beta Yisrael men into their army. In still other locations, the Beta Yisrael were caught in the cross-fire of the fighting between the Dergue and the Eritrean People's Liberation Front (EPLF).

Or they could have been encouraged to go to the Sudan as a means of getting to Israel. The encouragement could have come from a number of sources: letters from relatives who had already arrived in Israel; from pro-Beta Yisrael activists in Ethiopia, including those from the AAEJ; from Israeli operatives, some posing as tourists, in East Africa; or from Beta Yisrael who had been in Israel and returned to Ethiopia. In 1984, a group of American Jews from the Reform movement traveled to Ethiopia to deliver religious items to the Beta Yisrael. "Acting in coordination with Israeli officials, they provided money to Jews who were willing to risk the long and dangerous trek to the Sudan."

About the strangest "encouragement" came from Christian fundamentalists who believe that the second coming of Christ will not occur until all Jews return to Israel. In June or July 1984, Peter Parr and Jerry Weaver visited Wad El-Heluw and met a small group of young Americans running a health clinic there. When Weaver asked why so many Ethiopian Jews were coming to the Sudan at this most inopportune time, one replied that "American Christians" were flying to Addis, taking buses to Falasha villages, and trying to persuade the village elders to leave Ethiopia – "next year in Jerusalem." To help stimulate this movement, these fundamentalist Christians provided maps to reach Sudanese refugee camps and cash to buy supplies for the journey. Weaver believes that there is some truth to that story, because he was contacted by the Sudanese State Security when they had arrested a couple of American fundamentalist expatriates trying to cross into Ethiopia from the Sudan carrying maps and undeclared currency.

Those were horrible times for the large numbers of Ethiopian Jews in the Sudan during the summer rainy season of 1984. Hundreds of Ethiopian Jews died while walking to the Sudan, and still others, possibly a thousand or more, died of malnutrition, dehydration, and disease in the Sudanese refugee camps while waiting for help to get them to Jerusalem.

When in Israel, both before and after Operation Moses, I made it a point to go from one absorption center to another to visit with many of the survivors who eventually got to Israel. After they would serve me *bunnah* (Ethiopian coffee) and some cookies, they would tell me about their ordeals. It always was a similar tragic story. I cannot recall a single instance in which a survivor of the Sudan had not lost at least one family member there. Some families reported the loss of all their children. Others told me that to prevent the other refugees from knowing that they were Jews, they needed to bury their dead according to Jewish law secretly in the nighttime. Often they would dig a grave with their bare hands in the confines of their own straw hut (*tukul*). One needed only view the TV footage of the Jews rescued during Operation Moses to see that they were mostly skin and bones, calling to mind images of the Holocaust victims we had seen in archival photographs of starving Jews in Nazi concentration camps. To learn the details of how Operation Moses and later Operation Sheba were conceived and implemented, read Jerry Weaver's words in the following two chapters.

CHAPTER 17

The Untold Story behind Operations Moses and Sheba

By Jerry L. Weaver with introductory comments by H.M. Lenhoff

Secrecy has shrouded much of Jerry Weaver's role in the rescues of the Ethiopian Jews during Operations Moses and Sheba. Weaver's sense of loyalty and honorable professional behavior constrained him until now from revealing the complete story. To have done so earlier, he believed, would have risked the lives of a number of key players, without whose help Operations Moses and Sheba could never have happened. A part of his story has been told, especially by the late Charles Powers of the *Los Angeles Times* in 1985, and a bit more by Robert. D. Kaplan in his 1993 book *The Arabists*, and an abbreviated version of the same in the November 2005 *Reform Judaism Magazine*.

To the best of my knowledge, no scholars or journalists are currently investigating the first major large-scale rescues of the Ethiopian Jews from Africa. Operation Moses is generally accepted as one of the great achievements of the State of Israel. Most informed Jews are aware of the terrible conditions of the Ethiopian Jews languishing in the Sudanese refugee camps that sparked the rescue and know that over eight thousand of them were taken out of the Sudan in the last two months of 1984. Knowledge of the full particulars of how those rescues actually came about, however, lay with one elusive man, Jerry Weaver. After months of emails and phone calls, I finally had the opportunity on June 4–5, 2005, to meet with Jerry Weaver and to learn the intriguing details of those secrets of twenty years standing.

Who were the unnamed players whose identities he was protecting for two decades? Many were Sudanese Muslims, some of them members of the Sudanese government, others of the secret police of Sudan, and still others just friends of Jerry Weaver. Did they do it for money? After all, Sudan was officially at war with Israel then and still is as of this writing. No. They did it because Weaver sought their help in taking from the Sudan some ten thousand suffering Jewish refugees and allowing them to leave the Sudanese refugee camps to pursue a better life in Israel. The situation was very different from Operation Solomon in 1991 when Israel had to raise $26 million to pay off Mengistu, the dictator of Ethiopia (See *Operation Solomon* by Stephen Spector, 2005). In fact, the Israeli with whom Jerry worked, Ephraim HaLevy, later to become head of the Mossad, told Weaver that of all the rescues Israel has ever made of distressed Jews in foreign lands, Operation Moses was the least expensive.

I am privileged to have the trust of Jerry Weaver in sharing his amazing story with me. As we got to know each other, we learned that we had started out with similar academic careers just forty-five miles apart on Interstate 405 in southern California. We both served as professors of the University of California. He arrived in 1975 as associate director of public administration in the Department of Political Science at the flagship larger campus of the University of California, Los Angeles (UCLA). I had joined the smaller and younger campus at Irvine (UCI) in conservative Orange County as associate dean of biological sciences six years earlier. He went on to become director of his program, and I became dean of UCI's graduate division. My first academic position was the one at UCI where I started as a full professor. Jerry, ten years my junior, was also a full professor.

Yet, we were very different from each other. Weaver was a college football player, a hunter, and an adventurer. I was more introverted, a lousy athlete, squeamish with animals, and sought my adventures in the laboratory. Certain attributes we share, however: both of us are sticklers for detail, more interested in deeds than in talk, intolerant of bureaucracy, and more comfortable when working alone. We were particularly restless individuals, and we both became adept in political dealings: he in "sun-baked" Khartoum; I as an activist at the university and in the Jewish community.

In April 1978, after a two-year leave of absence from UCLA working as a social science analyst in the State Department in Washington, D.C., Weaver resigned from the university to take a similar job in the Sudan with the U.S. Embassy in Khartoum.

In September 1978, I became president of the AAEJ. In April 1979, the AAEJ had Bill Halpern and Baruch Tegegne in the Sudan finding Ethiopian Jewish refugees there.

Weaver, in 1982, accepted the challenging job of Refugee Affairs Coordinator in the Sudan for the United States Refugee Bureau. In July 1982, I stepped down as president of the AAEJ after having had four years building an infrastructure for the organization and making it a powerful political voice in Washington and in Jewish circles, a voice that got the support of many members of Congress.

Soon after I stepped down, Henry Rosenberg of the AAEJ went to the Sudan carrying a letter signed by Congressman Stephen Solarz and created a scene in the Khartoum office of U.S. Ambassador C. William Kontos, a scene that soon sucked Jerry Weaver into the business of rescuing Ethiopian Jews.

To paraphrase Shakespeare, if these episodes were played on a stage, the critics "could condemn [them] as an improbable fiction." In this and the next chapter, both by Jerry Weaver, and in my chapter that follows, you will read for the first time most of the nitty-gritty details and politics surrounding Operations Moses and Sheba.

After Jerry Weaver describes the intolerable conditions in the Sudanese refugee camps where Ethiopian Jews were dying at an alarming rate, he reveals the political drama, playing out mostly between September and late November 1984, that led to Operations Moses and Sheba. You can understand Weaver's unique contribution as he describes the confusion and infighting of President Reagan's political appointees on "the Seventh Floor" in Washington with the professional staff in the State Department; the Sudanese offer of help; how he and Sudanese security officers brainstormed a workable plan; the meetings in Geneva of the Americans, Sudanese, and Israelis to negotiate the roles that each would play; and how he helped set up the final arrangements for those remarkable humanitarian rescues.

– HML

Death in a Small Place

By late March 1984, thousands of Ethiopian Jews were arriving at the refugee villages of Um Raquba, Wad el-Heluw and Tawawa. They found scant food, miserable shelter, and almost no medical services. It soon became apparent that a human tragedy of epic proportions was taking place, particularly at Um Raquba. Established in the early 1970s, Um Raquba – ironically "Mother of Shelter" in Arabic – had become a successful refugee settlement with medical care, housing, potable water, and food for three thousand residents. But the sudden influx of thousands of Ethiopian Jews, coming at the onset of the rainy season which made access by vehicles all but impossible, overwhelmed the meager facilities.

Much has been written about Um Raquba and the tragedy that occurred there. Even from the perspective of a quarter century, what happened there and why so many Ethiopian Jews died remains an enigma. But this we know: most Ethiopian Jews arrived in Sudan malnourished and exhausted after a twenty- to thirty-day trek across desert and mountains; many were sick. They entered a lowland environment much different from their highland homes. Diseases of all types, familiar and new, attacked hundreds. The rainy season brought contaminated water and more health problems. Food was in extremely short supply, in part because the tracks used by relief trucks across the local heavy clay soil became impassable. For cultural and religious reasons, the Ethiopian Jews rejected some of the available food, such as beef and goats. Resident Christian Ethiopians demanded exorbitant prices for locally grown commodities. Insufficient housing or none at all was available; it was common to find ten or more people in a single tent or rude hut. Sanitation facilities were nonexistent.

When I first saw Um Raquba after the rains began, I thought immediately of the infamous Civil War prisoner stockade at Andersonville, Georgia, as described by McKinley Cantor – death by squalor; death by inattention; death by ignorance.

Two or three health workers from the Swedish Council of Churches as well as a nurse from the Sudanese Council of Churches were present, but they lacked the resources to treat the overwhelming influx of sick, malnourished, and exhausted Ethiopian Jews. The vulnerable – the very young, the elderly, and the ill – died first. Within weeks, all became vulnerable.

The camp staff of the Sudanese Commissioner of Refugees had no resources to meet the swelling demands of the Ethiopian Jews, so they turned to the UNHCR (United Nations High Commissioner for Refugees) for help. At the Gedaref field office, a thirty-year-old American who grew up in Ethiopia and was educated in Alexandria, Egypt – Peter Parr, the UNHCR's eastern regional representative – recognized the emergency and sent a stream of messages to Khartoum requesting food, medicine, tents, and health care workers. In April, Parr and I went to Um Raquba and saw the crisis gathering momentum. Drawing on an emergency account set up by the United States Refugee Bureau, I purchased food and medicine and contracted some lorries to break through the muddy trails to Um Raquba.

In late June, as the crisis deepened, Anders Maltson of the Swedish Council of Churches came to Khartoum seeking more aid from UNHCR. Feeling rebuffed by the high commissioner's office, he came to me and emotionally vented his frustrations. Parr continued to press for more aid, but by July the situation was out of hand. After Parr and I visited Um Raquba again, he produced a file folder containing dozens of requests for supplies that he had forwarded to Nicholas Morris, head of the UNHCR office in Khartoum, with little meaningful results. When I spoke with Morris in his office about the tragedy of Um Raquba, he replied, "We aren't going to give them any special treatment."

Why, in the face of clear and accurate reporting and the body count mounting daily, was so little done to relieve the appalling conditions of the Ethiopian Jews at Um Raquba? Others have speculated about means, motives, and malice. But in the final analysis, it is the responsibility of UNHCR to care for refugees. Its failure to react with alacrity at the onset of the influx resulted in hundreds, perhaps thousands, of deaths. At no other time and at no other location in Sudan was UNHCR's blundering so lethal. Nicholas Morris never visited the site. Instead, he left Sudan in June for vacation. By the time he returned, worldwide publicity was focused on the calamity that had befallen the Ethiopian Jews. Demands for action were coming from humanitarian interests across North America and Europe and could not be ignored.

Because of Washington's mounting concern and growing frustration over the UNHCR's mishandling of the Um Raquba tragedy, I was ordered to Geneva to discuss the crisis with Richard Schmisser, the UNHCR's deputy high commissioner. Schmisser, a distinguished former U.S. Foreign Service officer who had been part of Dr. Kissinger's team that negotiated the armistice ending the Vietnam War, gave close attention to my briefing. He agreed that the UNHCR in Khartoum had dropped the ball and promised to get things moving. Unfortunately, the next twelve months revealed that the UNHCR, like the North Vietnamese, was hard to get moving in the direction Washington desired.

Scrambling for a Solution

As the magnitude of the crisis at Um Raquba became apparent, several individuals emerged who would play key roles in attempting to develop a viable solution. In Washington, the main players were Eugene Douglas, a wealthy political appointee with the title "Coordinator for Refugee Affairs" and an office on the elite "Seventh Floor," and his deputy, Richard Krieger, another Reagan appointee. Also present at a series of meetings held during the spring and early summer of 1984 were career Foreign Service officer and deputy assistant secretary in the Africa Bureau Princeton Lyman; James Purcell, director of the Refugee Bureau; and Gene Dewey, deputy assistant secretary of the Refugee Bureau.

By July, it looked like the only solution they could come up with was an expanded role for the ICM (the Geneva-based Intergovernmental Committee for Migration) rather than a more heroic, and thus more dangerous, "cowboy caper." Gene Dewey, my boss, contacted James Carlin, head of the ICM, to ascertain if his people in the Sudan could expand their operation. Carlin told Dewey that he was working closely with Yehuda Dominitz of Israel's Jewish Agency to find a way satisfactory to Israel and within ICM's capabilities. Carlin reported that Dominitz was concerned that Krieger was pushing for a more accelerated program of action. Dominitz wanted a low-profile operation. A sealift was his preferred method. Carlin said that ICM was prepared to handle an augmented exodus and agreed that a sealift was the most feasible course, but wondered who would pay for such an effort – the Refugee Bureau or the Israelis? Dewey briefed Purcell about the anticipated financial issues in the rescue of Ethiopian Jews and relayed Carlin's concern that Krieger was pushing ICM to act faster than the Israelis wanted to move.

Within a week of Dewey's conversation with Carlin, Krieger stopped Dewey on the street in Washington and said that he regretted that Dewey and Purcell knew of the Ethiopian Jews' situation. Krieger claimed that only he, Douglas, Carlin, and Dominitz were players. Krieger asserted that he could raise all the necessary funds from private sources to cover any ICM shortfall. Moreover, Dewey was not to worry about gaining the longer-term financial support necessary to move the Ethiopian Jews because he, Krieger, could deliver the Hill and get whatever public funds might be necessary.

During mid-July 1984, Krieger attended an international conference on African refugees in Geneva. While there, he contacted Sudanese Refugee Commissioner Mohamed Al Ahmadi. Returning to Khartoum, Al Ahmadi told me that an American (Krieger) had approached him in Geneva claiming to be the representative of "Ambassador Douglas." Commissioner Al Ahmadi had met Douglas during his one trip to Sudan, and asked that he meet with him and other "interested parties," including unspecified international organizations, to discuss issues regarding the Ethiopian Jews. Al Ahmadi said that he did not know Krieger, nor did he want to discuss the issue of the Ethiopian Jews with anyone. He was disturbed that such a close-held and potentially explosive subject could be vented so openly, and questioned aloud why the U.S. government could not control someone who represented himself as an official of the State Department.

Three days later, Commissioner Al Ahmadi called me to his office in a state of fury. The source of his anger was a commercial telegram sent to him by Krieger via the Sudanese embassy in Washington through the office of the Sudanese minister of the interior in Khartoum. The cable asked the commissioner to meet Krieger outside the Sudan to discuss the Ethiopian Jews. The minister, who had not been informed about the ICM's movement of Ethiopian Jews out of the Sudan, asked what the message was all about. Al Ahmadi came to see me, and I remember his exact words: "It will cost me my head if it is known that I'm helping Jews get to Israel." Commissioner Al Ahmadi went on: "If Krieger meddles in this business one more time, I wash my hands of the entire matter."

I reported this meeting to Purcell in an "eyes-only" cable. Because only two Sudanese senior officials knew of the ICM movement of Ethiopian Jews, the other being vice president and head of State Security Omar El-Tayeb, it seemed likely that any further meddling by Krieger would result in their denying their involvement. As a consequence, without El-Tayeb's protection, ten thousand Ethiopian Jews could be rounded up and shipped without delay back to the Ethiopian border.

Attempting to rein in a political appointee, especially one with a patron on the State Department's "Seventh Floor," can be a daunting task, even for a senior professional. Yet Krieger's good intentions were about to produce the very tragedy he had fought for years to forestall. After conferring with Purcell, Dewey sought out Princeton Lyman. Lyman, point man in the Africa Bureau for East Africa issues, said that his boss, Assistant Secretary of State for Africa Chester Crocker, also had become concerned about Krieger's behavior when he saw "Not for Distribution" (i.e., classified) cables being forwarded to ICM by Krieger. Crocker, therefore, had ordered that a small group be assembled within the State Department's Bureau of African Affairs to deal with matters of the Ethiopian Jews. This excluded, among others, Douglas and Krieger.

That was a gutsy and shrewd move by Crocker because Douglas had powerful connections within the Reagan White House. Henceforth, only a handful of individuals would receive cable traffic concerning Ethiopian Jews. Of course, these arrangements dealt only with the American side. Lyman spoke of his concern that Israelis continued to use multiple channels simultaneously to promote their interests: the State Department, the White House, and Congress. By August 8, however, Princeton Lyman was made coordinator of a new task group that would take control and attempt to limit damage and stop other channels and individuals from interfering. Crocker had won the turf war, and African Affairs, not the Refugee Bureau or Douglas's shop, would lead on all issues involving aid to the Ethiopian Jews.

Jumping ahead for a moment, from that time on, and throughout the preparation for and implementation of "Operation Moses," Princeton Lyman played the key role in Washington. He coordinated the flow of information, was the point man in contacts with

American Jewish organizations, and was the operation's link to the Israelis. I considered him my "handler." For instance, during early December of 1984, when news of the movement of the Ethiopian Jews out of the Sudan and to Israel appeared in North American newspapers, Lyman met me in Geneva and suggested ways I could try to keep the Sudanese from jumping ship. As Kaplan wrote, "He [Lyman] held the fort in Washington, assaulted by American Jewish groups, even as he knew that a secret rescue operation was in progress that he couldn't tell them about" (p. 214). After the successful rescue, while Douglas and Krieger boasted of roles they did not play, Lyman remained silent. Always the consummate professional, Princeton Lyman is an unsung hero of the Ethiopian Jews.

Despite Lyman's new task force, I still had to provide information to government officials who asked. This was especially true in early September when there was a growing sense of urgency because no viable operational plan emerged to save the Ethiopian Jews as conditions worsened in the Sudan. One of my first of a series of round-robin meetings was with Douglas and Krieger. Krieger was clearly annoyed by the increased involvement of the Refugee Bureau in the exodus of Ethiopian Jews and urged me to "stay out of the Ethiopian Jewry business." Looking at me from across his desk, Krieger growled that he had friends in the CIA (sic) and any more interference by me with his attempts to reach Al Ahmadi "will not be career-enhancing."

A more congenial tone was set by Assistant Secretary of State for Human Rights Elliott Abrams. Abrams, whose father-in-law, Norman Podhoretz, was editor of the widely read journal *Commentary*, was seen as well connected with important Jewish Republicans. He said that he had received several conflicting sets of mortality and morbidity figures concerning Um Raquba Ethiopian Jews and wondered aloud if sending in a military medical unit might not be the best solution. He said little else and seemed only mildly concerned about finding a quick solution.

After a week of consultations, no consensus emerged for a plan of action. After a careful review of the sealift scheme, however, we agreed that moving ten thousand Ethiopian Jews from the settlements to Port Sudan posed overwhelming logistic and security problems.

A Breakthrough at Last

Returning to Khartoum in mid-September, I was swept up in a new crisis. All summer long, informants among the Eritrean and Tigrean insurgent fronts had warned that the combination of drought, spreading combat, and the Ethiopian government's new military conscription program was pushing tens of thousands toward the Sudanese frontier. By September, five to six thousand Ethiopians were arriving each week along the border. Spontaneous settlements of twenty-five to thirty-five thousand drought victims – technically not refugees – arose within days; some of the established camps doubled, then tripled. These were the vanguard of 250,000–300,000 Ethiopians who fled into Sudan in two or three months. Meeting with UNHCR's Nicholas Morris to review his contingency plans, I was surprised to hear that Morris had underestimated the crisis and was reporting to Geneva that he expected "around twenty-five thousand" new refugees.

A talk with Commissioner Al Ahmadi found the Sudanese far more pessimistic. His eastern region staff was reporting major shortfalls in food, shelter, medical supplies, and health care workers and, above all, potable water. Al Ahmadi urged the U.S. to pressure UNHCR for more supplies and medical help. To get things moving, he suggested a joint meeting of Morris, the Sudanese minister of the interior, and the U.S. ambassador to the Sudan, Hume Horan. When it became clear that neither the UNHCR nor the World Food Programme could or would meet the needs of the new arrivals, Washington ordered U.S. commodities already in the pipeline to be diverted to the Ethiopians. This led to a major conflict within the U.S. Mission in Khartoum when the director of the United States Agency for International Development (AID) refused to redirect food supplies donated by the United States destined for western Sudan to the Ethiopian settlements in the east. It was months before a significant volume of U.S. supplies reached the new Ethiopian arrivals.

I briefed Commissioner Al Ahmadi on what I learned in my meetings in Washington and assured him, with more confidence than I felt, that salvation for the Ethiopian Jews would soon be forthcoming from the U.S. Al Ahmadi replied that he wanted the problem of the Ethiopian Jews solved soon because the negative publicity about conditions at Um Raquba hurt Sudan's image internationally. This publicity was particularly worrisome because of his country's desperate need for external assistance in overcoming Sudan's developmental problems.

As we walked out of his office building, our conversation focused on Um Raquba. I had visited it the previous week. Although some supplies and personnel were starting to reach the camp, I told Al Ahmadi that the high mortality and the overall squalor remained unacceptable.

When I asked Al Ahmadi what it would take to move many more Ethiopian Jews to Khartoum and hence out of Sudan through the ICM channel, he replied that the Sudanese State Security would have to issue more internal travel permits. The head of security, Omar El-Tayeb, already knew of the ICM movement and would have to approve an expanded operation. Because I knew that Al Ahmadi was a college classmate of Omar El-Tayeb, I asked him if he could arrange a *fetur*, a breakfast of beans, eggs, and bread, for Omar and me. The commissioner's face would have served a professional poker player holding no cards: "I'll ask him," he replied.

The next day Al Ahmadi reported that Omar would meet me for breakfast. Ambassador Horan cabled Washington requesting guidance before approving the meeting. After Horan received the go-ahead, he conferred with the CIA station chief, Milt Bearden, and me. Milt recommended that he and Ambassador Horan dine with Omar El-Tayeb because agreement between State and CIA required that contacts with Sudan's security service be handled through the station chief. Since I did not know Omar El-Tayeb personally, Milt thought it best that I not attend the meeting.

Omar agreed to consider the Americans' proposal to extract the Ethiopian Jews from Sudan. But before a deal could be struck, Omar wanted to meet me because Horan had designated me as the embassy's point man. The next day, Milt Bearden and I went to Omar's office at security headquarters in Khartoum. At this meeting, no specifics were discussed, only that a plan would have to be worked out between the Americans and the Sudanese. We talked about hunting, the importance of solving the financial drain on Sudan of half a million refugees, my traveling throughout the vast territory of Africa's largest country. After sizing me up the way a cattleman looks over a potential herd bull, Omar said that he would order his officers to cooperate.

The following afternoon Bearden called me and said that the Sudanese counterparts would be introduced at his house that evening. Still lacking even the outline of a plan, the next chapter in the Ethiopian Jews' saga was about to be written.

On September 21, 1984, Ambassador Horan cabled Washington that the Nimeiri government had agreed in principle to the removal of the Ethiopian Jews and that discussions had been initiated. A breakthrough had been achieved.

A Merry Band of Plotters

After more than five years in Sudan, I knew many Sudanese military and security officers. Some were card-playing tablemates; others shared duck or gazelle hunting trips. Several were frequent guests at my dinner table, and I at theirs. Moslem or Christian, northerner or southerner, I found none I would not value as a teammate. I looked ahead happily to meeting the men Omar had called off his deep and talented bench.

Both of the men he had selected were lieutenant colonels, seasoned senior officers. I knew one, Musa Saeed. Thanks to his help, we had been able to resolve the incident in Tawawa where Eritreans were setting fire to Ethiopian Jews' straw *tukuls* after Rosenberg visited the village. One of Musa's main jobs was to monitor the Ethiopian liberation movements operating out of Sudan. The other officer, El-Fatih Erwa, was Omar El-Tayeb's operations man. They were members of the Sudan's elite State Security, which was an equivalent of a combination of the FBI and CIA set up by the East German secret service at the request of President Jaafar Nimeiri after he seized power in 1969. State Security paid better than any other Sudanese agency and took care of its employees. It subsidized housing, provided educational allowances for children, and allowed officers to import luxury goods duty-free. Add that to the pride that comes with protecting your nation, and it is not hard to see why State Security was able to attract many top university graduates to the service. Musa and El-Fatih were prime examples of the men Omar commanded.

In many ways, these two officers represented the "yin and yang" of Sudanese society. Musa was light-skinned, quiet, and thoughtful. He said little, preferring to sit and listen. But he had a brilliant tactical mind and proved masterful in analyzing operational issues, such as deciding which officers to bring in and which should be kept at arms' length. All told, there were a dozen officers and forty or fifty security men to manage. Quietly yet effectively, Musa quarterbacked our squad.

El-Fatih, dark and sporting what in the U.S. was called an "Afro," was outgoing, quick with a joke or laugh. He drove an expensive car equipped with all the extras. He was self-confident and free with advice. He focused easily on major issues such as maintaining the security and secrecy of the movement. His love of new gadgets proved invaluable when it came to selecting appropriate state-of-the-art communications gear. Nor did it surprise us later on when, at the beginning of the movement, he suddenly "needed" a small airplane to improve contact between Khartoum and Gedaref. During our initial meeting, El-Fatih saw a .45 caliber revolver on Milt's desk and played with it as we talked.

We held several meetings at State Security headquarters the following week. From the outset, the two colonels rejected the plan to move the Ethiopian Jews overland to the Red Sea for a massive "sealift." There were just too many police and military checkpoints to slip past and too many logistical obstacles. El-Fatih told me that "your friends" had tried some airborne and sea escape operations before, but they were small-scale; they just will not work with such large numbers of refugees. Above all else, he repeated, secrecy had to be maintained, because Sudan was technically in a state of war with Israel. If his Moslem neighbors learned that Nimeiri was aiding the Zionists, his regime might well be toppled.

After discarding the sealift option, we considered expanding the ICM movement of refugees. Here again, the size of the potential passenger population seemed to rule it out. With ten thousand Ethiopian Jews to take out of the Sudan, and more coming into the country every day, it was beyond belief that secrecy could be maintained over the months the ICM channel would need to complete its mission. Already too much attention and too many prying eyes were being focused on Um Raquba. To protect Sudan's requirement of strict security during the movement, something had to be done quickly and soon.

Slowly the germ of an idea began to take shape. If a sealift is impractical, an Israeli air rescue out in the desert was unacceptable to the Sudanese, the ICM route too slow – what's left? How can speed and secrecy be achieved? Why not have the whole thing done by Sudanese State Security? We reasoned that the safest, quickest escape was by air through Khartoum International Airport. Would the operation be visible to others at the airport? Not if we used remote areas of the airport that could be cordoned off; it might be tough to control access by airport workers, but it can be done. How do we get the Ethiopian Jews to the airport? Collect them from Um Raquba and Wad El-Heluw and bring them to Tawawa, a large refugee settlement near the highway linking Port Sudan and Khartoum, and close to Gedaref. Then we can bus them to Khartoum. The local security detachment there was commanded by a reliable young officer, Fuad El-Amin Bander, whom the colonels assured me could be counted on to cooperate.

For a trial run of the plan, the two colonels and I ran the route. We noted police and military checkpoints along the Port

Sudan highway to Gedaref. We estimated that, once the buses were loaded in Tawawa, the driving time to the airport would be about five hours. Tawawa was a long-established settlement containing several health clinics staffed by experienced, well-trained personnel. Here the sick and weak could be treated, while all transit passengers enjoyed adequate shelter, food, and potable water. Fuad identified an area on the edge of the camp where several hundred Ethiopian Jews were thought to live. Another favorable point was that adjacent to "Falashaville" there was an open area that could be used to assemble and board the passengers on the buses.

The road from Gedaref to Um Raquba was rough, but it was passable because the rainy season was over. Many lorries carrying supplies to the camp returned to Gedaref loaded with Ethiopians bound for work on the nearby large commercial agricultural schemes. We figured that once our buses began extracting Ethiopian Jews from the camps, no doubt other "travelers" (our code word for Ethiopian Jews) would hop a lorry to Gedaref and make their way to Tawawa. The much smaller community of Ethiopian Jews at Wad El-Heluw would require a few bus trips, but when the movement got underway, we assumed that some would find ways to get to Tawawa on their own.

After we arrived at Um Raquba, the two colonels went first to the settlement security officer, who reported the presence of five or six thousand Ethiopian Jews, a number later to be found low. As at Tawawa, the Ethiopian Jews lived apart from the long-term Christian Ethiopian residents. The local security officer thought that even if the Ethiopian Jews' exodus could not be concealed from the other residents, security would not be a problem. Their unwilling hosts would be glad to see them go.

The impact of Um Raquba on the Sudanese colonels was powerful. Neither said much as they perused the Ethiopian Jews' quarter and passed by a makeshift cemetery. They saw that they were segregated in an area prone to flooding, that they were using contaminated ditch water, and that there were neither food stores nor medical supplies being distributed to them. The sites, the wailing sounds, but mostly the smell seemed to blanket us, making conversation inadequate and unnecessary. These were hard men who had done hard things. Back in the car, several minutes down the lorry track, El-Fatih remarked in a barely audible whisper: "I've never in my life seen anything like that." We proceeded in silence.

In Gedaref we met with Lieutenant Colonel Daniel Deng Laul, a Dinka Christian who commanded the local security forces. Deng was one of only a handful of former southern rebels who had integrated into the national security service after the 1972 peace accord that ended the civil war which began in 1957. Well over 6'6" and physically formidable, clearly he was a no-nonsense guy. He agreed that Ethiopian Jews could be gathered at Tawawa and that a staging area for movement down to Khartoum could be created. Colonel Deng indicated that he knew of the Ethiopian Jews and of previous efforts to move them. He offered no objections to the plan and volunteered to find safe-houses for drivers, guards, and mechanics, and storehouses for supplies.

The next day back in Khartoum, we met to further refine our plans. "How do we move the Ethiopian Jews to Tawawa?" By overland buses, and as quickly as possible. "Who will provide shelter and food for the Ethiopian Jews?" Give the Ethiopian Jews' leaders cash before moving them to Tawawa and tell them to distribute it to their followers so they can buy food and other necessities after arriving. "Who will protect the Ethiopian Jews from prying eyes or hateful neighbors?" Fuad's men. "Who will pay the 'overhead' for the security men?" I will see to this and other purchases.

We calculated that three or four buses would be required plus two all-terrain cars, one to carry a security officer to escort the buses through police and military checkpoints and another following the convoy. Later we bought a minivan to haul air crews from the airport to their overnight hotel rooms. We also purchased a small airplane for El-Fatih to speed up his visits to Gedaref. To our list we added powerful radios so Gedaref and Khartoum could contact each other outside the official radio network. And then there were more radios for the escort cars plus hand-held radios, food for the drivers, repair facilities in Khartoum and Gedaref, fuel, and spare parts. The list kept growing.

Finally, El-Fatih and Musa were satisfied that we had an operational plan that made sense. Since their concurrence reflected Omar's benediction, I drafted a cable for Ambassador Horan's review. He sent it immediately, and shortly Washington replied that it was a go. The fine tuning, and acceptance or rejection, would come in Geneva at a conference with the Israelis during the October meeting of UNHCR's executive committee.

Walking Hand in Hand

The final review session for the rescue plan was set for the executive committee because it provided excellent cover: all three principals sent delegations. Commissioner Al Ahmadi headed the Sudanese delegation. With him was a senior State Security officer who would report directly to Omar. Dewey, Lyman, and I were among the U.S. representatives. During the long flight to Geneva, I sat next to Al Ahmadi. He discussed current trends in Islam, his daughter's decision to join the ultraconservative "Moslem Brothers," nineteenth-century British poetry, and how he had been twice elected president of the student union at the University of Khartoum – first as a communist, then as a Moslem Brother. He seemed perfectly at ease going into an adventure he could not control with people he did not know, the outcome of which might well put his head on the chopping block.

After reviewing the plan over breakfast in the Intercontinental Hotel dining room, Lyman, Dewey, and I drove to the ICM building for our first head-to-head meeting with the Israelis. Jim Carlin of the ICM hosted the meeting. The Israelis had reviewed our draft exit strategy and argued for a sealift. After considerable debate, they came around and agreed to the air option. Breaking for the day, I drove to the executive committee meeting in the old League of Nations building and briefed Al Ahmadi and his companion from State Security. Overnight came Khartoum's agreement to cooperate. They had, however, one major proviso: no Israeli could touch ground in Sudan.

Back at ICM, we threshed out the details. The Israelis would provide the aircraft, someone to handle the planes in and out of Khartoum International Airport, a "Falasha-finder" to identify bona fide Ethiopian Jews from other Ethiopian refugees, and the money to purchase local supplies and services. Again that afternoon, Al Ahmadi and I walked the marble halls of the league building, hand in hand, the way Arab men do, I in a light cotton safari suit, he in traditional headdress (*keffiyeh*) and flowing white *jelebiah*. No handshakes, no formal agreements; just two friends making a deal.

Next morning brought official approval from Khartoum. At the Geneva airport that evening, the first installment, $250,000 in hundred-dollar bills packed in a Samsonite attaché case, was handed to me by a short, balding man with a limp. Was it Ian Fleming or Dorothy Sayers writing the scene?

On the flight home, I shared a row of seats with ICM's newly appointed resident representative in Khartoum, Robin Goodman, a French Jew whose family had escaped the Nazis to England. The attaché case occupied the center seat. As part of the agreement, it had been decided that, in addition to those to be rescued by a massive airlift, the ICM would continue to process Ethiopian Jews at the same rate it did since 1983 – about 120 per month. Robin was clearly relieved that the main burden would be placed elsewhere. When the airplane stopped over at Athens, I asked Robin to keep an eye on the attaché case while I deplaned to visit a friend. A former coworker in the refugee office, Anna Kriticopoulou, who now worked at the U.S. embassy in Athens, was waiting in the transit lounge to see me. Returning to the airplane, I noticed that Robin's seat was empty and that the case was gone. About the time an adrenaline rush reached my brain stem, Robin returned. He retrieved the case from the overhead luggage bin, where he had placed it for safekeeping. Weeks later on another trip from Geneva, with the case replenished, Robin learned its contents.

A Tight Schedule

The Israelis said the air transport would be a Boeing 707 that could carry about 240 passengers. They wanted the lift to begin quickly – November 1 if possible. The buses available in the Sudan carried around sixty passengers each; thus, four would be needed to make the Tawawa-Khartoum run to fill one airplane. In addition, a shelter of some kind would be needed near the airport to safeguard the Ethiopian Jews if a pickup was aborted after the buses had rolled. We also needed to have food and water for at least forty-eight hours, as well as blankets for 240 guests. Fortunately, this backup was never needed. Now that we knew the size of the passenger load to be carried, quantities were set quickly for fuel, spare parts, and drivers, plus on-board guards. Orders went out to State Security detachments at Um Raquba and Wad El-Heluw to alert the Ethiopian Jews that they were soon to be brought down to Tawawa.

El-Fatih sent his men looking for vehicles. The SUVs were found, but no new buses. His man in the Sudanese embassy at Jeddah, Saudi Arabia, reported that new Toyota truck chassis were available and could be shipped within days to Port Sudan. My assistant, Nicholas Mandrides, and I flew to Jeddah and bought four chassis plus a ton of spare parts. Mandrides, a twenty-eight-year-old Sudan-born Greek, who spoke perfect Arabic and English, was my indispensable right hand throughout the extraction. His skills in dealing with a wide variety of problems were surpassed only by his talent at poker. John Kriticopoulos, a skilled mechanic and a friend of mine, agreed to fabricate the bus bodies and install them on the chassis. Another member of his family, Theodore, a frequent card-playing companion, bought blankets, water barrels, and boxes of dry rations. He handled the negotiations with a Pakistani black-market petroleum dealer that secured fifty tons of diesel fuel and five tons of gasoline. Pending the arrival of the new buses, El-Fatih suggested a relative of his might be willing to hire out some buses he owned to begin transporting some Ethiopian Jews to Tawawa.

Predictably, schedules slipped. Finally November 21–22 was set for the first flight. A few days prior to liftoff, two key people were in place: the Falasha-finder and the air traffic controller. The latter, "René," was a seasoned professional. An Arabic-speaking North African French Jew, René was introduced to the tower crew by the airport's head of security. With an admixture of Arabic, charm, technical expertise, and "gifts," he performed brilliantly. René met Ambassador Horan, who was impressed: "I felt comfortable with him. I felt that he knew what he was doing." (See Kaplan, *The Arabist*, p. 227.) Kaplan, however, incorrectly identified René as Georges Gutelman, the Jewish owner of TEA, the Belgian-based Trans European Airlines.

The second key man, dubbed "James-the-Falasha-finder," inspired less confidence. About 5′6″, slightly built, quiet, and seemingly ill at ease with the rustic conditions of his Gedaref safe-house, this man, later identified as Zecharias Yona, proved brave and resourceful. I assigned Nicholas Mandrides to be his minder: should anything happen to "James," the entire operation would flounder.

Several writers claimed after "Moses" and "Sheba" that dozens or scores of Mossad agents roamed the Sudanese countryside, directing movements and controlling the extraction. They may very well have done so. But if they did, they left no footprints in Sudanese sand. Only René and James definitely walked there. They left lasting impressions.

CHAPTER 18

Operations Moses and Sheba Continued

By Jerry L. Weaver with commentary by H.M. Lenhoff

The previous chapter revealed that to conduct a rescue of Jews from a country officially at war with Israel required a cunning and a wide network of local connections that could not be expected of the typical diplomat nor even of the most capable member of the Mossad. There could not have been a more perfect man for the challenge than Jerry Weaver. In this chapter we see still another side of Weaver: that he is one tough character when he is dealing with unscrupulous individuals, especially those who try to interfere for selfish reasons with lifesaving events. Should his behavior be admired? Some may think not. I like to go back to the number one *mitzvah, pikuach nefesh*; it is permissible to do most anything in order to save a life. Weaver was trying to save and did save more than ten thousand people.

– HML

Operation Moses

The first flight of what eventually became known as "Operation Moses" began on the afternoon of November 21, 1984. About dusk, "James" entered "Falashaville" at Tawawa intent on gathering the 240 or so sick, elderly, and vulnerable Ethiopian Jews he had previously identified and alerted to be ready to move. The four newly fabricated buses pulled into the loading zone at camp's edge. Fuad's

235

detachment of a dozen heavily armed security troops circled the loading area, intent on discouraging sightseers. Musa and El-Fatih remained in the escort vehicles, waiting. Mandrides and I stood next to the door of the first bus. Ten, then twenty, then thirty minutes passed. The desert air was cold, but sweat began – pre-game jitters. After what seemed like hours, a handful of Ethiopians emerged into the circle of light emanating from the buses' head lamps. Behind them a trickle, then a torrent burst out pushing, struggling, fighting to board the bus. Chaos bordered on riot. Too late, we learned that our loading area was an outdoor toilet used frequently by thousands.

Finally the four buses were filled; the plan to seat sixty had been erased by the onrush. The Sudanese security men dispersed the desperately disappointed. The convoy drove off with El-Fatih and me in the lead car, Musa and Nicholas at the rear. Everyone was nervous; the buses proceeded bumper to bumper. At the first checkpoint, El-Fatih ordered the drivers to slow down. The convoy reached the designated rest stop near the airport and El-Fatih radioed for the Boeing 707's estimated time of arrival. It finally arrived – three hours late.

Although I did not know it at the time, the Mossad hired the rescue aircraft from the Belgian George Gutelman's Trans European Airlines. TEA had flown out of Khartoum many times carrying devout Moslems on pilgrimage to Mecca. Hence, the TEA planes aroused no suspicion among local airport personnel. In order not to reveal to Arab air defense monitors the destination of its passengers, each plane flew directly to Brussels, then on a well-established flight plan to Israel.

As the aircraft came to a halt, the four buses pulled alongside the loading ramp. Slowly the passengers disembarked. A few, too weak to climb the stairs, were carried on board. True to the Geneva agreement, no Sudanese touched the ramp, no Israeli came down it. When everyone was seated, the Belgian pilot came to the head of the ramp and announced that there were too many passengers for the available emergency oxygen masks: "Take back the extras or the plane does not leave," he said. There was momentary confusion when "it was determined" that the co-pilot would fly the plane should the pilot become incapacitated by a 9 mm bullet hole in his head. The pilot temporarily forgot about oxygen masks. Wheels went up at about 0400 hours, November 22, 1984. The *aliyah* was underway.

This first night had not gone well. Perhaps trying to load a riot into a toilet is an apt metaphor. Milt Bearden, the CIA station chief, called me early the next morning and announced that El-Fatih said there would be no more flights unless we guaranteed that everything would go more smoothly. Later, René acknowledged the delay in the arrival of the airplane was caused by a snafu in Europe. He assured me that no more planes would be late. The problem with the pilot had grown out of the overcrowding which in turn came from our inability to control the would-be passengers. Mandrides and I returned to Gedaref that evening and discussed the problems regarding the selection and boarding procedures with James and Fuad. Although James chose only 240 adults, Fuad's men around the perimeter had no way of knowing who had been selected by James or who was a party-crasher. Nicholas suggested we buy a large quantity of different colored cloths, cut them into the required number of ribbons and give a ribbon of only one color to each passenger just before they were to depart for the buses. It worked. The security men could easily identify bona fide passengers. Changing the color each night effectively blocked interlopers.

Forty-eight hours after the initial lift, the second flight went off without a hitch. By the fourth flight, El-Fatih and I had turned supervision over to Nicholas and Fuad. But just as things seemed to be going well, Mandrides radioed me that James had a serious problem.

Slowly at first, perhaps embarrassed, James recounted that from the beginning he had been pressed by a long-time resident Ethiopian Jew to make exceptions to the "most vulnerable" criterion for selecting passengers. This man worked for a health clinic of the International Rescue Committee (IRC) at Tawawa. Together with three or four associates, he collected money from Ethiopian Jews on the promise that they would be selected early in the process. The "travel agent" had threatened James if he refused to cooperate. In hindsight, many of those who fought to board the buses of the first flight did seem anything but vulnerable.

James pointed out the "travel agent" at the IRC health unit. Mandrides approached him and asked for a meeting outside the camp. I drove with Mandrides and the "agent" to a secluded spot not far from the loading area. "Things are going badly with James," I said. "We cannot tell a Falasha from an Eritrean; won't you please help us select and board passengers for tonight's flight?" The "agent" replied affirmatively, saying that he would be glad to help and asked, in return, that when Falashaville was emptied, he be resettled to the U.S.

That evening a very orderly assembly was followed by a quick boarding. As per new rules, the security guard on each bus counted the passengers. I asked the "travel agent," standing beside a bus, to confirm the count. When he reached the rear of the bus, I shouted to the rifle-toting security guard: "Tell that son-of-a-bitch to sit down, and if he moves, shoot him – but use only one bullet!" That was a Sudanese euphemism for "kill him." The remaining thirty flights went off without disturbance and James was never bothered again.

Because of the length of the trip from Tawawa to Khartoum, Nicholas and Fuad urged that a midpoint rest stop be found where the passengers could get down and relieve themselves. This became standard practice. One night a bus had a minor problem and during the rest break, its driver, taking off his uniform shirt, made a repair. When he took up his shirt, he noticed that his wallet containing a few bills and his security identification card was missing. Loss of the card would mean dismissal, perhaps prison. Glancing around, he saw a passenger emerge from the darkness just nearby the place his shirt had hung. He accosted the man, a Falasha, who, in very short order, took the guard to his discarded moneyless wallet.

Hearing about the incident, Mandrides asked the guard what he wanted to do to punish the thief. *"Ma-alesh,"* he replied – it's all right. "These poor people have suffered enough."

Time and again this reaction of pity, charity, and respect came to the Ethiopian Jews from Sudanese. On another occasion earlier that year, sitting with a young paratroop officer in a machinegun nest above a river border with Ethiopia, we watched fifty or sixty Ethiopians cross the river and scramble up a hill to a nearby row of trees. "Who are these people?" I asked, knowing full well that they were Ethiopian Jews. "Oh, they are 'travelers'" (a Sudanese slang term for Falasha), the officer replied. "They are escaping from their homes." The soldier must have known that they were Jews and that Sudan had sent troops to Egypt in 1973 to fight the Israeli army. But instead of opening fire on the "travelers," he went inside the command bunker and radioed a nearby refugee camp. While the Ethiopian Jews waited for the trucks that would take them to the settlement, the soldiers of this combat-ready border guard unit carried jerry-cans of water to their parched guests.

The Best Friends Money Can Buy

Buying fuel and vehicles, renting safe-houses, paying dozens of State Security personnel quickly consumed the initial cash. I had to reach "Ephraim," my counterpart in the Mossad, pronto. Obeying Ephraim's prearranged instructions, I placed two white thumbtacks on the lamppost by the U.S. Embassy in Khartoum, and I received a message to meet him in Athens immediately. On board the flight were Peter Parr and his wife, Kathy, leaving Sudan after two years of struggle and heartbreak as the UNHCR's regional officer in Gedaref. Kathy, an American of Greek origin, wanted to stop over in Athens for a few days before going on to Geneva. Upon arriving, I called Anna Kriticopoulou at the American embassy and arranged for a dinner at our favorite *"taverna."* A call to Ephraim and the party was set.

Anna had known Peter and Kathy when she worked out of the Khartoum refugee office, but Ephraim was a newcomer. Pulling up in front of a shabby no-star hotel, she saw a middle-aged man in a cheap suit holding a bundle wrapped in newspaper. "Who is this man?" she asked in Greek as he squeezed into the back seat. Anna's battle-scarred Russian Fiat had just enough power left to pull the five of us up the hill to the *taverna*. "Do you want to put your bundle in the boot?" "No, thanks; I'll hold it." Two hours later, back at the Athens Hilton, Anna noticed that I now had the bundle. What's in it?" "Oh, probably some dirty clothes. I'll return it in the morning. We're having an early breakfast." Thirty seconds later, Anna's shout of surprise easily reached the bathroom. "You bloody bastard, it's money!"

The next morning, Ephraim asked if Omar El-Tayeb, vice president of Sudan and head of State Security, might be willing to meet him somewhere in Europe. Israel wanted to discuss certain matters with him, especially about obtaining rights for El Al planes to over fly Sudanese air space. I agreed to raise the issue with the Sudanese. That afternoon, I flew back to Khartoum with another $250,000 in hundred-dollar bills.

Handling cash in Khartoum was always a "complicated" matter. The Israelis had given instructions that all their funds should be converted at the official exchange rate – 1.5 pounds to the dollar. The "unofficial" rate was twice this. Obviously, the official rate was a nonstarter. After discussions with several local businessmen, an Italian hunting buddy offered me 3.2 pounds per dollar. He finally accepted 3.4. Now, a quarter of a million dollars makes lots of paper when converted, especially since the largest denomination of Sudanese currency was twenty pounds. Several times during November and December, poor "Luigi" had to lug two huge bags of pounds into the embassy where he and Nicholas spent hours counting and banding the bills in neat piles of one hundred.

Before approaching Omar with Ephraim's initiative, I briefed Ambassador Horan and CIA station chief Bearden. Once they received the go-ahead from their masters, the contact was initiated. At a meeting in Horan's office before going to see Omar, Bearden mentioned a three million-dollar donation to State Security's building fund might be about right to gain Omar's attention. And not surprisingly, before the meeting with Omar the next day, El-Fatih suggested $3 million. Omar had in his office a sand table model of the proposed new office building. It would have a heliport, just like Langley; and it would be a monument to his respect for CIA chief William Casey, the security chief said. After a glass of tea, Omar got right to the point. "Here's my numbered bank account in London. Once the deposit is confirmed, let's talk again."

Another quick trip to Athens and a meeting with Ephraim. Within a week, I learned from El-Fatih that $1.5 million had been deposited. "Omar," said El-Fatih with a smile, "will be glad to meet 'your friends.'"

Apart from Omar's building fund, remarkably little "*baksheesh*" was spread around. "René" saw to it that small gifts went to key individuals at the airport, often in the form of high quality candy from Belgium. Once a Trans European Airline flight brought in a dozen baskets of fruit – the oranges bore stickers "product of Israel." El-Fatih laughed about the gaffe and pronounced them the best he had ever eaten. When René learned that one of Musa's daughters was about to have a birthday, a nice new bicycle arrived. I made Colonel Daniel Deng in Gedaref responsible for disposing of the empty fuel drums, each worth five pounds. He also may have received a "finder's fee" from landlords who rented out storerooms, garages, and safe-houses. Three key security officers at Gedaref received $600 Rolex watches paid for out of the bonus of converting dollars at the unofficial rate.

El-Fatih expressed the need for a "small plane" so we could travel back and forth to Gedaref. Part of the CIA's package of "goodies" for General Omar was an American pilot, "Pete," to fly the general's personal plane. Pete knew that El-Fatih wanted to learn to fly and volunteered that if a suitable plane could be found, he would undertake the necessary training. El-Fatih found a "suitable" plane and negotiations began with its owner. Finally a price of $115,000 was agreed upon. Ephraim concurred.

Both El-Fatih and Musa loved guns. They accompanied me

on several gazelle hunting trips and were especially taken with a Smith & Wesson .44 Magnum pistol I possessed. This scope-mounted weapon regularly took down animals at a hundred yards or more. During a trip to Geneva, I contracted with a first-class gunsmith to create two presentation Magnums, suitably engraved and highlighted in gold, with ivory grips. Unfortunately, events in March 1985 which led to Nimeiri's overthrow and my hurried departure prevented their delivery.

After the exodus was completed, Ephraim told me that "Moses" had cost around U.S. $5 million. He compared this favorably with other major rescues by Israel, such as that of the Yemeni Jews, which cost tens of millions more, largely because of bribes demanded by host government officials. Given the leverage Nimeiri, El-Tayeb, and other key Sudanese had with the success of the operation, their lack of avarice is one of the outstanding and unnoticed features of the rescue.

All Good Things Come to an End

By the third week of the operation, El-Fatih and I agreed that we could and should pick up the pace: reduce the turnaround time from forty-eight to twenty-four hours. Washington had no objections, but it took some time to convince the Israelis. Nevertheless, by early December a TEA 707 carrying 240 Ethiopian Jews was leaving Sudan each night.

Just as we were reaching optimum production, a bombshell exploded that threatened to blow the planes out of the sky. Commissioner Al Ahmadi called me to report that his embassy in Washington had cabled Khartoum typescripts of a newspaper story running in the *Washington Post* and the *Boston Globe* detailing the ongoing movement of Ethiopian Jews out of Sudan. Al Ahmadi feared that the story could not be contained within the Foreign Affairs Ministry's bureaucracy and that once opposition newspapers and conservative politicians in the Sudan picked it up, President Nimeiri would order the flights stopped.

Responding to Ambassador Horan's urgent request for guidance, State passed the ball: prepare for suspension but keep on running. I was ordered to Geneva for a "quickie" with Princeton Lyman. When a week passed with no explosion along Nile Avenue, it seemed that the exodus had dodged a potentially fatal bullet.

Hard on the heels of this episode came another, this one involving journalists working inside Sudan. On December 10, Colonel Deng radioed that his men had detained two expatriates and two staff members of a nongovernmental organization who had been caught attempting to photograph a Khartoum-bound convoy transporting Ethiopian Jews. The paparazzi, minus their film, were hustled out of the country, but their guides posed a different problem. The two men were Gabriel Daniels, an Ethiopian who had settled in the U.S. and who had returned to Sudan, and Nick Miscione, a U.S. citizen who worked for SudanAid's Tawawa health clinic. The two journalists had told Deng that Daniels had approached them with a proposal, in return for cash, to show them the Ethiopian Jews being moved. Since five or six thousand Ethiopian Jews waiting to be rescued remained in Tawawa, we believed that those two entrepreneurs could not be released.

After discussions with El-Fatih, I decided to bring Miscione to the embassy. While he had not been mistreated during his sojourn in Deng's dungeon, his face shouted fear when I eyeballed him across a desk. I suggested that he could either accept a free ticket on the next plane to the U.S., or go back to the refugee camp. In return for the ticket, he would remain silent about "what he thought he had seen" in Tawawa. Four hours later, two of El-Fatih's most convincing stalwarts escorted Mr. Miscione directly to his free seat on an airplane taking him out of the Sudan.

Daniels posed a different challenge. In the first place, he was a member of the Ethiopia Peoples' Revolutionary Party (EPRP), a Marxist organization composed mostly of university students and young intellectuals that had originally supported Colonel Mengistu's overthrow of Emperor Haile Selassie, but had fallen victim to the revolution's "Red Terror." During their struggle with the Dergue, i.e., Mengistu's party, the EPRP had savagely attacked

Falasha villages after a vain attempt to recruit new fighters from them. Daniels was among hundreds of EPRP members who fled to Sudan's refugee camps. He had applied for and received resettlement to the U.S. After he returned to Sudan in 1983 and took a job with SudanAid, Musa Saeed's men placed him under surveillance. When Musa told me of the involvement of EPRP personnel in efforts to extort money from Ethiopian Jews in Tawawa by burning several of their shelters, the Refugee Bureau cancelled in September 1984 its grant to SudanAid. The health clinic and its EPRP cadre, however, continued to draw UNHCR funds. To further complicate an already messy situation, Daniels was well liked by individuals of the embassy community who knew him as a member of the American Club.

After he'd been in confinement for two or three days, I picked up Daniels and a security officer and we drove down to Khartoum. Having made the journey dozens of times, I knew it was customary to stop about halfway near a large *hafir*, an underground cistern. There, herdsmen would lower goatskin bags at the end of long ropes to bring up water for their animals. My driver and I were enjoying a smoke when, inexplicably, Daniels, who apparently had become tangled in the rope, fell headfirst into the water. After a minute or two, he was pulled up – only to fall down again. Try as we might, he went down again. Finally rescued, the poor fellow was nearly drowned. This would have been truly unfortunate, not only for Daniels but for his two brothers who also worked at Tawawa.

Daniels left Khartoum the next day and was later reported to be enjoying the green hills of Vermont. His friends at the "Experiment in International Living" noticed that he shunned swimming altogether. Several others of the EPRP cadre were detained by Deng for the duration of Operation Moses. There were no more nighttime photo-ops.

By December 1984, world attention was turning to the drought and famine engulfing western Ethiopia. Approximately three hundred thousand victims had crossed into Sudan and were threatening to overwhelm the relief system. Slow to react, the U.S. finally began moving hundreds of tons of relief aid to Sudan. Along with expanding U.S. involvement came growing media attention. This hit a peak when Senator Edward Kennedy, his son, and daughter, along with twenty or thirty of his closest journalist friends, fell on Khartoum the day before Christmas. The senator wanted to see and be seen visiting Ethiopian refugees. Members of his party queried Ambassador Horan and me about the verity of newspaper accounts of an ongoing rescue of Ethiopian Jews from Sudan, but did not press us when we denied any such activity.

A day or two prior to the senator's arrival, Colonel Jim Barron, the embassy's military attaché, came by my office with an urgent message from the Pentagon. It seemed that the senator's personal bodyguard had lost his pistol: Could Khartoum supply him with a side arm during his stopover? The cable from Washington had specified a particular handgun that the colonel knew I could supply. Since the senator's party was flying on an Air Force plane, Barron was the control officer. Barron and I were old friends and had hunted together many times, so I was glad to oblige.

Ambassador Horan collected the senator and his family while I picked up "Arnold," the bodyguard, and gave him a handgun. Arnold, a retired Massachusetts highway patrol officer, had been summoned to the Senate office building just before the Kennedy party was scheduled to leave for Andrews Air Force Base. He brought with him a black bag containing two 9 mm pistols and an Uzi machine pistol. He rushed up to the security barrier, handed the bag around the metal detector, and walked through. One of the guards passed him the bag, but retrieved it when the weight caught his attention. Thirty seconds later the bodyguard and his weapons were on their way to the nearest District of Columbia police station. Senator Kennedy managed to get Arnold out, but the weapons remained. So in both Ethiopia and in the Sudan, the senator was defended by borrowed weapons.

Senator Kennedy's visit had taken much of my time and interrupted a previously scheduled holiday in Europe. So, I was most appreciative when the senator offered me a seat on his Air Force jet stopping in Athens on its way back to Washington. Because I had arranged several years earlier to have a custom rifle made by Franf Sodia's gunsmiths, I went to pick it up in Ferloc, Austria. I got it on January 4, 1985. Later that day, while resting in a pension room, Austrian television showed pictures from Israel of Ethiopian Jews being greeted at an Israeli reception center. The news reader reported that they had been rescued from Sudan by the Israelis. "Moses" was blown. [*Details of the news leaks are presented in the next chapter. – HML*]

A Perfect Vessel Smashed

Returning to Athens, I cabled Washington for instructions and initiated contact with my Israeli counterpart. This man, whom I have been calling Ephraim, was Ephraim HaLevy, later head of Israel's Mossad (*Haaretz*, March 18, 1998). He met me in Athens and gave a straightforward account of the security breach that led to the cancellation of "Moses." Two flights had departed after the story broke, allowing both René and James to get out safely. Ephraim had no news about Mandrides or the State Security personnel.

Returning to Khartoum the next night, I walked into the airport's arrival hall; no embassy personnel were in sight. As I waited for my bag to be checked by customs, a firm hand fell on my shoulder. Turning around, I saw El-Fatih, smiling. Overcome by a flood of emotions, we two comrades embraced, unashamed of our tears.

According to El-Fatih, there were no immediate repercussions for the Sudanese personnel; and Mandrides was safe. No problems, except for about five hundred Ethiopian Jews left behind. "Two more flights; just two more flights, and we'd have done it," the colonel groaned. As we drove through the predawn streets, El-Fatih listened with the ears of a professional intelligence officer to the recounting of Ephraim's explanation of the security breakdown. El-Fatih smiled wistfully when I told him that Ephraim said: "We always thought the Sudanese would give it away. In all my years working on extractions, I never saw a better operation."

Life after "Moses"

Immediately upon my return to the embassy, cables flew and arguments erupted over how many Ethiopian Jews had been left behind. With James gone, only second-best sources were available. Fuad and Deng put the number at about 450–500. They reported a few new arrivals were trickling in, some from Ethiopia, others from Wad El-Heluw and outlying sites.

While other people on three continents digested "Moses" and its consequences, the embassy shifted its attention to dealing with the tsunami of drought victims flooding eastern Sudan. Nonetheless, the stay-behind Ethiopian Jews were the subject of much transatlantic paper-passing. Washington peppered Khartoum with requests to verify our estimate – questioned by some in State because other sources were claiming one or two thousand Ethiopian Jews remained in Sudan. In addition to this squabble, Ambassador Horan and I were being drawn into the problems AID was having moving PL 480 (Public Law 480) "Food for Peace" aid to starving Ethiopians.

Princeton Lyman sent me to Geneva in early January 1985 to discuss the critical shortfall of UNHCR food and water assistance for the rapidly growing refugee population. Within hours of my arrival, Lyman flew in. In addition to discussing spurring UNHCR to quicker action for drought victims, we discussed options for rescuing the remaining Ethiopian Jews. Lyman told me to relay the message to Ambassador Horan that State wanted him to become more of "a traffic cop" by signaling the AID director to speed up distribution of famine relief to Ethiopians.

As if the embassy did not have enough to do, we were told in mid-February that Vice President George and Mrs. Bush, along with Assistant Secretary of State for Africa Chester Crocker, the director of AID, Peter McPherson, and about seventy other straphangers were coming to town. One of the purposes of their visit was to check on the status of the "cross-border" operation, a humanitarian project to bring food to the Ethiopian drought victims inundating eastern Sudan. For example, in February 1985, REST (the Relief Society of Tigre) brought nearly seventy thousand Tigreans to one Sudanese village. The politics of those movements and of the distribution of food was complex.

For whatever reasons, a small covert U.S.-backed cross-border operation which for several years had moved supplies into TPLF and EPLF territories from Gedaref and Port Sudan, respectively, was rapidly expanded. Perhaps this CIA-sponsored exercise provided valuable support to U.S. surrogates fighting the Marxist Dergue in Ethiopia.

The expanded cross-border operation became increasingly worrisome to Nimeiri whose policy was to stay out of Ethiopia's problems. Sudan had its own insurgency in the southern region and feared that Addis, if it learned about the cross-border operation, might fight fire with fire. Concern about cross-border moved to the highest levels of the U.S. administration and was a major topic for bilateral talks when George Bush came to Khartoum.

The vice president arrived March 4. That evening Bush, his CIA adviser, and Chet Crocker met with Ambassador Horan and members of the country team. Bush, who had been director of the Central Intelligence Agency, asked for opinions and recommendations about expanding the cross-border operation. He listened attentively and asked good questions about logistical problems and the likely reaction of President Nimeiri. After discussing one or two other issues of U.S.-Sudan bilateral affairs, the meeting broke up. In a brief aside to Ambassador Horan, Bush mentioned that he would raise the matter of the final removal from the Sudan of the Ethiopian Jews in his meeting the next day with President Nimeiri.

After Bush returned to the embassy from his meeting with Nimeiri, a briefing session was held in the conference room for those U.S. government officials who would be joining the vice president on his visit to refugee and drought victim camps. I cautioned them that the inhabitants were infested with lice and fleas, and that unsuspecting visitors often carried away these vermin. As a precaution, I advised them, bottles of GI anti-lice soap would be found in the hotel bathrooms. "Mister Vice President," I said, "you may remember from your World War II anti-VD lectures the proper means of dislodging crab lice." Bush's laughter boomed across the conference table. Later back in Washington, I was told by Mrs. Bush's secretary that the Second Lady had discreetly spread this site-specific hygienic information to the director of the Peace Corps and other females in the party.

During his four-day visit, Bush saw both Ethiopian refugee settlements and displaced Sudanese drought and famine victims. Followed by dozens of journalists, he did much to bring the plight of the Sudanese into focus alongside that of the much more widely exposed Ethiopians. After his departure March 8, the exhausted embassy staff briefly celebrated and went home.

Mandrides and a few close friends had planned a birthday party for me. The usual activities were just getting underway when I was summoned to Ambassador Horan's residence. There, sitting around a coffee table which held no coffee cups, were the ambassador, deputy chief of the mission David Shinn, and Milt Bearden. Horan said that I would be getting a call from Washington on a secure line within a few minutes. Shortly, the ambassador's assistant, a junior CIA officer, appeared and said that the caller was on the line.

For those who remember Maxwell Smart and the "Cone of Silence," no description of the "secure phone line" is necessary. Suffice it to say, the booth was designed for a person leaner, if not meaner, than I was. The caller identified himself as "Robert Mc-Farland" (President Reagan's national security advisor) and told me that a decision had been made to take the remaining Ethiopian Jews out of the Sudan. It would be an entirely American operation. My job would be to design the mission, but the CIA would execute it. The instructions ended with: "...you have the full resources of the United States government at your disposal."

After briefing those present, I returned home. The party was in full swing and continued well past bedtime. At 0700 next morning, my servant, *"Juma"* – Arabic for Friday – wound his way over and around the sleeping party guests to deliver the eye-opener glass of *sha'ay*, hot tea. Sufficiently fortified, I drove to the embassy and began typing. By 1000 hours, "Sheba" was conceived.

Operation Sheba

[*For the political events leading up to President Reagan approving Operation Sheba, see the next chapter. – HML*]

"Sheba" was based on a simple plan. James-the-Falasha-finder would return to Gedaref three days before the scheduled lift. He would spread the word among the Ethiopian Jews so they would know where and when to assemble. On the night of the lift, the passengers would be trucked to a remote airstrip a few miles from Tawawa. A cordon of State Security troops would surround it. A series of U.S. Air Force C-130 cargo planes would come in one at a time until the last Falasha was boarded. No pretense of deception was required: President Nimeiri himself had given the final O.K. to Vice President Bush for the operation to proceed.

The draft plan was read by Milt Bearden and passed to his Arabic translator. Around 1500 hours that day, Milt called me to say that the Sudanese had approved the document without changes. That night the "Sheba" plan was cabled to Langley.

Within a week, two Air Force officers arrived and asked me to show them the intended landing strip. "Strip" perhaps was like placing a rose on a donkey. About nine hundred meters long, undulating sand and gravel; nonetheless, the Air Force thought it would work. One pilot said he had flown into and out of worse places in Vietnam – a comforting thought. The recent failed air operation to rescue the American hostages from Iran simply could not be repeated in Sudan.

After reviewing the plan, Washington decided that Air Force police personnel would control the landing zone. They would come in with the first plane and be deployed between the Sudanese and the runway. Each plane would contain water, blankets, and food for the estimated payload of a hundred civilians. The Air Police personnel would clean the immediate area and depart in the last plane. Ground time was estimated at between fifteen and twenty minutes per load.

El-Fatih was briefed on each revision of the plan. He reported that General Omar El-Tayeb was happy with the plan; he had wanted the CIA to do the original movement. Any hard feelings Omar had towards the Israelis after they exposed Sudan's role in "Moses" had been softened by Israel's contribution of $1.5 million to his "building fund."

All the News That's Fit to Print

In the interval between the termination of "Moses" and the arrival of Vice President Bush, journalists came to Khartoum seeking more information about the *aliyah*. Both the Sudanese and Americans maintained a strict "no comment" policy. While this did not satisfy the news hounds, the embassy was too busy to worry about First Amendment rights. But during Bush's visit in early March, the covers began to slip off the bed. In particular, Judith Miller of the *New York Times* and Charles Powers of the *Los Angeles Times* individually asked me to confirm details of the operation they had received on "deep background" from a member of the Bush party.

Before responding, I asked for a meeting with station chief Bearden and Ambassador Horan. Both journalists had told me that their papers would print the story, with or without confirmation. From what they revealed of the information allegedly from the Bush party, they had a pretty thorough account of Operation Moses. I could tell that they did not know of the coming operation; nevertheless, any publicity about the Ethiopian Jews and Operation Moses might make the Sudanese too gun-shy to cooperate in Operation Sheba. Perhaps the reporters were bluffing, but Miller and Powers seemed to be holding pretty good cards. We had to fold our "no comment" cards.

Ambassador Horan suggested that each be told that five hundred or so Ethiopian Jews remained and that they would be rescued "soon." If the journalist waited until after the exodus, all questions would be answered in an exclusive interview. Milt grinned and joked: "Why not promise a book? In six months, no one will care." Satisfied with the offer, Miller left for Cairo, Powers for Nairobi.

Two weeks passed, and it was time for the Refugee Bureau's annual conference of African region refugee officers scheduled to be held in Nairobi for March 17–19. Should I attend or not? Operation Sheba was to take place on the 21st or 22nd. I checked with Washington. They advised me to go to Nairobi. My contribution to "Sheba" was completed, and my absence from Khartoum in the run-up to the airlift would help "cover" the operation. After I checked in with the American embassy in Nairobi, the information officer told me that Charles Powers had left word to phone him. I had known Powers and his wife since their days in Los Angeles, and we each provided hospitality to the other during our years in East Africa. I called Powers and gladly accepted his invitation for a home-cooked meal at his place.

After dinner, Powers told me that the *Times'* man in Washington had received more information about "Moses" from a back-channel source and that the paper was pressing Powers to write his account. Powers claimed that he knew the Ethiopian Jews who didn't make it to Israel via "Moses" were about to be moved, and that he was flying to Khartoum in a couple of days to keep an eye on Tawawa.

Next morning, I met with Gene Dewey who was in Nairobi to chair the regional conference. I told him of my meeting with Powers, and we discussed how to keep a lid on him, at least until after the 22nd. On March 20th, Dewey and I flew to Khartoum on Kenya Air. Powers and two other journalists were seated in business class on the same airplane.

Early March 21st, Powers came to my office and requested help in hiring a car to Gedaref. Although he did not tell me, I presumed he wanted to drive to Tawawa. As soon as he left the office, I called El-Fatih and told him of Powers's itinerary. The colonel replied, "Deng will detain him in Gedaref."

An hour later, I walked with Mandrides and Musa Saeed out

of the embassy. They were headed for a rendezvous in Gedaref with some CIA communications men staying with James in the safe-house. Before they left, Musa embraced me and said: "I wish you were going with us." I replied: *"ma'as salaama; alla yibaarik fiik"* (Go in peace, and may God bless you). It was the last time I saw this most-trusted paladin.

It was March 22, the morning of the lift. An Air Force brigadier general bedded down in the embassy conference room awoke at 0500 and joined Ambassador Horan, Milt Bearden, me, and several men from Langley in the communications center. As dawn broke, C-130s began to drop from the sky, one about every fifteen minutes. CIA men at the strip and Air Force personnel circling above it sent a stream of reassuring reports. About as often, the brigadier general took calls from General George Vessey, chairman of the Joint Chiefs of Staff back in the Pentagon, wanting "situation reports." Six planes landed. About 480 Ethiopian Jews were flown out. By 0900 the airlift was over.

At dusk, Nicholas Mandrides showed up at my apartment. With him was Chuck Powers, who had his own dramatic tale of adventure. Powers had spent the previous twenty-four hours a guest of Colonel Deng. When he reached Tawawa the previous afternoon, Powers spotted Nicholas's Toyota Land Cruiser and followed it to Gedaref. Failing to get the information on the lift from Mandrides, Powers nevertheless surmised that Nicholas's presence in Tawawa signaled something was afoot. He returned to Tawawa and went to a health clinic which, it was rumored, had been the assembly point for Ethiopian Jews during Operation Moses. Yes, something was up because there weren't any Ethiopian Jews around anymore. Leaving the clinic, Powers was detained and taken to Gedaref's State Security prison.

In the middle of the night, twenty or so State Security soldiers arrived, took up AK-47 assault rifles and sped away in military trucks. At dawn, Powers heard large planes in the distance; one after another landed close-by and quickly took off. Powers was released around 1000 with no explanations. Awake to what had happened, he drove immediately to Tawawa where Americans and Europeans working at medical clinics confirmed that U.S. Air Force c-130s had been seen only a mile or so away. Returning to the Khartoum highway via a rented car and driver, by chance he met Mandrides who offered him a ride to the capital. The journalist took Mandrides's offer, got into his car and instructed his driver to follow them back to Khartoum. When they reached Khartoum, Powers asked Nicholas to take him to my apartment.

I listened to his adventure. He neither asked for nor was given any confirmation of the airlift. After several liquid refreshments and a quick shower, Powers left – ostensibly for his hotel.

Next morning, Nimeiri, El-Tayeb, and the rest of the world awoke to BBC's "morning news roundup" reporting Powers's account of the "Sheba" rescue. He had used the overseas telex at the hotel to send his report out of Sudan.

Life after "Sheba"

About noon on the 23rd, El-Fatih called and asked me to meet with him at security headquarters. He took me directly into the office of Major General Osman Al-Sayed, second-in-command of State Security. Affable and seemingly relaxed, Osman wondered aloud how it happened that Powers had gotten wind of the operation. He mentioned without stressing that the airport arrival cards from the 21st showed that Powers and I had entered Sudan on the same flight from Nairobi. I agreed, but pointed out that two other journalists and three State Department officers also were on the same flight.

I reminded the general that I saw to it that State Security was notified as soon as I learned that Powers was going to Gedaref. Indeed, as soon as he arrived, he was detained as planned. State Security had released him and permitted him to come to Khartoum. And no effort had been made to control the international telex. I pointed out that the publicity generated by Powers's article again showed Sudan's compassion and willingness to assist a great humanitarian cause. Besides, I added, the story would have gotten out eventually – look at "Moses."

Apparently satisfied, General Osman turned to Operation Moses. He praised the close and successful cooperation between the U.S. and Sudan. He was very proud of how his men had performed. What, he inquired, could he do for me to show his appreciation for all that State Security had gained from "Moses"? I replied that after nearly seven years in Sudan, I would be leaving within several weeks for a new assignment. I had never met President Nimeiri and wondered if General Osman could arrange a meeting. Osman smiled and said: "Of course. When he returns from Washington, we'll have *fetur* with him. Do you like Nimeiri?" asked the general. "Not particularly; but I respect him." Osman laughed: "Just like a Sudanese! We don't like him either, but he has big balls."

The breakfast with Nimeiri never happened. Within days of his departure to receive a "golden handshake" from President Reagan, riots spawned by the economic reforms dictated by the International Monetary Fund, plus the pent-up frustrations and grievances arising during a sixteen-year authoritarian rule, brought him down. Nimeiri was accused by the "Moslem Brothers" and other Islamists of treason to the faith by aiding Israel, a charge that some in Washington picked up to blame "Moses" and "Sheba" for his overthrow.

By March 26th, doctors, teachers, government bureaucrats, and students had joined the laborers in the streets. It is axiomatic in analyzing Arab politics that a few radical imams (Muslim clerics) can bring workers and peasants out of the mosques and into the streets; but a government is really in trouble if white collar and professional people hit the bricks. When this happened in Khartoum, Omar El-Tayeb's troops stepped aside and joined the regular army on the sidelines.

One result of the breakdown of control was a stream of banners on the walls around the University of Khartoum. When one banner named Ambassador Horan, Milt Bearden, and me as responsible for the movement of the Ethiopian Jews, Washington ordered me to join Horan and Bearden who were already back in Washington. Mandrides and I packed a week's worth of winter clothing and flew to Paris. When things cool down, we told friends and family, we'll be back to help break in my replacement who would be coming in two weeks. Neither Mandrides nor I realized that we would never see Khartoum again.

Postscript

The post-Nimeiri regime arrested the senior State Security officers who had aided Operation Moses. They were charged with treason and put on trial for their lives. El-Fatih, Musa, Deng, and the others were allowed to turn State's evidence and were pardoned after testifying against Omar. The general was convicted of treason on testimony linking him to Israeli money. He was sentenced to death – a verdict which was, in true Sudanese fashion, commuted to thirty years, then to exile abroad. General El-Tayeb moved into a comfortable retirement at his million-dollar *"tukul"* on Lake Geneva.

Jaafar Nimeiri was condemned in absentia and sentenced to death. He remained in Cairo, and then was allowed to return to Khartoum where he lives quietly.

El-Fatih Erwa, son of a very prominent old family, took up flying the plane he had "won" during "Moses." In 1988, he met me and Mandrides by chance in a Washington restaurant. We sat up until morning reliving our adventures. A year later, El-Fatih spent a week with me on my "Blue Nile" farm in Ohio. By 2000, the one-time security man became Sudan's ambassador to the United Nations.

Musa fared less well. He died of a heart attack in 1988 – of a broken heart, El-Fatih claimed, having been unable to save his job or reputation.

Commissioner Al Ahmadi survived the change of government, but did not receive the high-level UN post he had hoped a grateful U.S. government would help him achieve. He was sent as Sudan's ambassador to Libya.

Hume Horan went on to win the "big prize" for Arabists: the ambassadorship to Saudi Arabia. After a tenure shortened by high-level intrigues, he retired from the Foreign Service. He died in 2004.

Princeton Lyman never received the public recognition he deserved, but was rewarded with the ambassadorship to Nigeria. He followed James Purcell as head of the Refugee Bureau. After retiring from the State Department, Lyman became a senior fellow with the Carnegie Endowment for Peace. When western Sudan exploded in communal strife in 2004, he spoke eloquently against the human rights abuses in Darfur by the Khartoum government.

Jim Purcell left the Refugee Bureau to become head of ICM's successor – the Geneva-based International Organization for Migration. Retired, he remains an active consultant and member of several private organizations' boards of directors.

Gene Dewey served as assistant secretary of state, Bureau of Population, Refugees and Migration from January 2002 to July 2005. His post-"Moses" career, like those of Purcell and Lyman, is mute testimony to the commitment, intelligence, and dedication of the three professionals who oversaw from Washington the rescue of the Ethiopian Jews.

Richard Krieger tried but failed to become director of the Holocaust Museum in Washington. Recently he took up a new cause in Florida: searching for war criminals.

Milt Bearden moved from Khartoum to Peshawar, Pakistan, where he became CIA's "bagman" for Osama bin Laden and the anti-Soviet Afghani insurgents. After September 11, 2001, Bearden appeared frequently on television as an authority on Islamic terrorism.

Nicholas Mandrides came to the U.S. in November 1985 as a "political refugee." He is a bank manager in the Washington area.

Ephraim HaLevy continued to climb the Mossad ladder and reached the top rung in 1998. In 2002 he resigned and in 2003 he was appointed head of the Center for Strategic and Policy Studies at the Hebrew University of Jerusalem. René, James, and the other Israeli operatives slipped back into the shadowy world from which they had briefly emerged.

Charles Powers returned to Washington in April 1985. I met twice with him and urged him not to print the "Moses" chronicle because of the potential damage it might do the former security officers facing treason charges. On July 4 and 5, 1985, the *Los Angeles Times* ran Powers's story. Prior to printing, Dorothy Chandler, owner of the paper, called the White House to make sure no national security interests would be compromised. She was referred to the State Department's Refugee Bureau where she reached Robert Funseth, "senior" deputy assistant secretary. Funseth, for reasons never divulged, cleared the story. Powers won several major awards and a fellowship to Harvard. After the story broke, we had one last supper together. He died in 1994 in Bennington, Vermont.

As a result of the newspaper story, the State Department's Internal Security charged me with "unauthorized disclosure of classified information." My personal lifestyle was put under scrutiny and found wanting. Years later, Ambassador Horan explained: "He (Weaver) became a real Typhoid Mary. People knew it wasn't good for their careers to be seen with him" (Kaplan, p. 228). After an eighteen-month examination, I was diagnosed contaminated beyond salvation. Given the choice of a quick death or a prolonged but ultimately futile struggle, I chose "euthanasia" and left governmental service to become a farmer in Ohio.

Postscript by HML: After going over the text of this chapter and the last one, I asked Jerry Weaver why he thought he became a "Typhoid Mary." He replied:

> The causes of my problems in State had little or nothing to do with gold, Rolexes, or things found after I left Khartoum in my office safe or home that I used to coax some minor and major officials. It had everything to do with my being "unconventional." Had Horan come forward and said that he and I had discussed giving Powers the "Moses" story in order to buy time for "Sheba," the "unauthorized" rap might have gone away. Or had Abrams or someone on the Seventh Floor or in the White House told the investigators to buzz off, my problems might have gone away. But after eighteen months, no one spoke up.

I bear no one any ill will – people do what they have to do. I believe that we are judged by what we do, not what we say. I gladly pay the price for being fortunate enough to have been just the right person at just the right place at just the right moment. Besides, I'd have made a lousy diplomat. The department didn't want me; and I sure as hell had had enough of it.

CHAPTER 19

Leaks, Fund-Raising, and Politics

"Professor Lenhoff," he said, "When you tell a secret to one person," and he held up one finger, "that is all right." He then held up two fingers and said, "But when you tell two people, it is like telling eleven (11)." Then, with a rare smile on his face, he held up three fingers and said, "When you tell three people, it is as if you told one hundred and eleven (111)."
— *Yehuda Dominitz to Howard Lenhoff, 1978*

Jerry Weaver knew only too well how premature publicity could stop the lifesaving rescue efforts he had started in Operation Moses. It could also contribute to the overturning of the Nimeiri government and to the imprisonment of his friends.

News Leaks

The first leaks came from fund-raisers of the United Jewish Appeal (UJA) in the United States and from Arye (Leon) Dulzin, director general of the Jewish Agency of Israel, the recipient organization of funds raised for Israel by the UJA. My first clues that there was promise of a rescue of large numbers of Ethiopian Jews from the Sudan came in early December 1984. At that time Nate Shapiro told me to withhold submitting a full-page advertisement for the AAEJ to the newspaper published by the Los Angeles Jewish Federation. That ad would have asked for $3,000 donations to our Chai Campaign to rescue endangered Ethiopian Jews. In his letter of December 5, 1984, Shapiro wrote the following to all board members of the AAEJ:

In the last two weeks many, many Ethiopian Jews have arrived from Sudan. The process…was described to us by our government in meetings with them.

The UJA is currently undertaking a national fund-raising campaign…. They are talking openly and loosely about the numbers arriving in Israel. The Jewish Agency is doing likewise. We are not of the opinion that this is the time to talk. I feel it's the only time when silence is appropriate.

Irrespective of what other organizations publish, we will publish no facts or figures of the numbers arriving in Israel. We request that silence be maintained by our organization and its members. We must respect our government's wishes on a matter they have been so helpful on.

After receiving that letter, I told editor Manny Chait of the Los Angeles Federation newspaper that we would not be submitting the proposed AAEJ ad. To my surprise, the staff of that same newspaper published a full-page advertisement of their own in December. It essentially disclosed Operation Moses and asked for $6,000 donations to the UJA to save an Ethiopian Jew. Similar ads appeared in Jewish newspapers across the country.

The UJA reasoned that it would be easier to raise funds if donors were told that the money was going towards heroic rescue efforts, rather than towards subsequent absorption costs. Hence, rather than waiting until the rescue was completed, they began an intensive fund-raising campaign before the first airplanes of Operation Moses got off the ground, even knowing full well that premature publicity might endanger the secret rescue.

Another reason, a crass one at that, was given for the November UJA decision to raise funds for Operation Moses, rather than waiting until early January when the rescues would have been completed. The fund-raisers reasoned that it would be easier to raise money before the end of the fiscal year when the donors could still get an immediate income tax deduction for their charitable contributions.

Because of the wide use of the name "Operation Moses," even today few know that the Israelis had originally called it *Gur Aryeh Yehuda*, "Cub of the Lion of Judah." The UJA, making its belated public debut recognizing both the existence and the plight of the Beta Yisrael, decided that a more saleable punchy name was needed. "Operation Moses" fit the bill, they thought – though Moses never got to Israel.

According to UJA reports made available to me by the Orange County Jewish Federation, the goal of the UJA was to raise $67,381,000 for Operation Moses. By June 1985 they had $62,931,654 in pledges and in guarantees. Later that year, the UJA surpassed its goal. The AAEJ was pleased to see such a response by donors in the U.S. Jewish community; once secrecy was no longer an issue, a number of us, including me, cooperated with our local Jewish Federations and helped them in their fund-raising efforts.

Robert Cohn, considered dean of editors of the Jewish press, was president of the American Jewish Press Association (AJPA) during Operation Moses. He was asked in an interview: "Do you feel that the campaign people at Federation and the UJA broke the news in their over-zealousness to raise funds?"

Cohn replied: "I do not think they did so with malice aforethought, but I do feel that the zeal to raise funds and a well-intentioned desire to help these people did contribute to the confusion.... [It] continued to be a problem to the very end.... Throughout the whole effort [to rescue the Ethiopian Jews] different local Federations observed the embargo to a different degree. I recall one Federation advertisement placed in the Los Angeles Jewish Community Bulletin [an organ of the local Federation itself] which published virtually everything we [at the AJPA] were told was improper to publish."

Though pleased with the success of the eventual UJA campaign, the AAEJ believed that UJA participation was long overdue. Had the UJA used its effective public relations abilities ten years earlier to alert U.S. Jewry to the plight of the Ethiopian Jews, then the crisis facing the Beta Yisrael in 1984 might never have materialized.

When Arye Dulzin, director general of the Jewish Agency, had addressed a group at the annual General Assembly meeting in Toronto during the late fall of 1984, he had divulged news of the rescue. He asked the more than five hundred American and Canadian delegates there to swear to secrecy. A few days later a press release quoted Dulzin describing "an ingathering of an historic, ancient community." Immediately news of Operation Moses started to spread.

Operation Moses began on November 21, 1984. Just two days later, November 23, Jewish newspapers broke the story. The first were the *Washington (D.C.) Jewish Week* and the *Jewish Week* of Long Island. The latter newspaper wrote about "the mass rescue of thousands of Ethiopian Jews." The editor stated that he had gotten permission to publish the article from the UJA of New York City, which all too coincidentally, subsidized that newspaper. The article quoted Dulzin as stating that "one of the ancient tribes of Israel is due to return to its homeland."

Major American secular newspapers, such as the *New York Times*, followed suit on December 11, 1984. An even more detailed story was published the next day by the *Boston Globe*. Despite publicity in the U.S. secular press, Operation Moses was not interrupted and continued to bring Ethiopian Jews from the Sudan to Israel daily. As Weaver wrote, "'Moses' dodged a potentially fatal bullet, one that need not, and should not, have been fired."

Nailing the Coffin

Specific announcements by two high-ranking Israeli officials led to the rescue being stopped by the Sudanese government. In the first of these two blunders, Yehuda Dominitz, the man in charge of the Jewish Agency's immigration policy and operations, described the secret rescue from the Sudan to a small West Bank Hebrew monthly, *Nekuda*. Supposedly the story, like the speech by Dulzin, was off the record. But the article was picked up and published on January 3, 1985, on the front page of two of Israel's major newspapers, *Maariv* and *Yediot Aharonot*. The story was then taken up by

Reuters and the Associated Press, and with details of the rescue, it was published worldwide. This is exactly what the United States government and President Nimeiri of the Sudan did not want.

Adding more fuel to the fire was Prime Minister Shimon Peres, who, on the next day, called on his aide, Akiva Lewinsky, to hold a press conference that confirmed the rescue and the roles of the United States government and of Nimeiri. In less than twenty-four hours, the Sudanese government put a stop to any further airlifts, leaving an estimated five hundred Ethiopian Jews stranded in the refugee camps.

Defenders of Dominitz say that he was discreet when he spoke with reporters of *Nekuda*, but the newspaper did not, as required by law, submit the story to the Israeli military censor. Nonetheless, Dominitz knew too well how a secret told is quickly spread. There is a special irony in his actual words to me on secrecy that are italicized in the heading to this chapter. If only Dominitz had heeded the Talmudic lesson which he explained so elaborately, then perhaps Operation Moses might have been completed as planned and Operation Sheba would not have been necessary. He was subsequently relieved of his post with the Jewish Agency. Not long afterwards, Dominitz was appointed the Israel Representative of the New York UJA, a position which he held in Jerusalem at least through 2003.

Some Hindsight on Fund-Raising

Not only did the local Federations and the UJA raise funds, but so did most Jewish organizations in the United States which sponsored programs in Israel. Within a week after Operation Moses started, for example, we learned from Bernard Resnikoff of the American Jewish Committee's Jerusalem office that his organization had raised more money in a one-week period than ever before, and, to boot, those funds were not even solicited! We heard similar stories about other Jewish organizations.

While raising money to help the Ethiopian Jews integrate into Israeli society was commendable, some related behaviors had negative consequences. One episode that sticks in my memory was the brainstorm of the ADL (Anti-Defamation League) leadership. ADL workers bought eight hundred black Cabbage Patch dolls to give to children who came to Israel during Operation Moses.

Regarding such gifts, psychologist Ruth Westheimer and scholar Steve Kaplan of Hebrew University, wrote in their perceptive book *Surviving Salvation* (1992):

> In some instances dramatic gestures of giving seemed designed more to satisfy the donor than to assist the recipient. Thus, not once, but twice, black "cabbage patch" dolls were brought to Ethiopian children, many of whom quickly consigned them to the garbage heap.

In the same paragraph, Westheimer and Kaplan also stated that while giving presents to Ethiopian children "provided excellent photo opportunities," it contributed to the destruction of the Beta Yisrael family structure, a problem that still haunts us today.

Hard-Hitting Editorial

Miriam Goldberg, the gentle and committed editor and publisher of the *Intermountain Jewish News* of Denver, Colorado, published a strong editorial on January 11, 1985. Except for her comments on the absorption of the Ethiopian Jews, the heart of the editorial is reprinted here:

> What does the Jewish Agency take us for, anyway? A bunch of pawns whose thirst for a bloated sense of self-importance may be nurtured at the expense of good sense? The answer is: Yes. And the context is: Ethiopian Jewry.
>
> It's time it all spilled out: The Jewish Agency's concept of Israeli-Diaspora relations is crass, monochromatic, for that matter, monoverbal: Money. One word. That's the whole content of the relationship, which means there is no content to the relationship.

The Jewish Agency decided to send out the word that "secret" meetings were to be held throughout the U.S. for the sake of raising money to finance the rescue of Ethiopian Jewry. Thousands were to be told, "in secret." So that money could be raised now, while "Operation Moses" was underway, notwithstanding the fact that the slightest word of the operation in the press would kill it. And kill is the word. Publicity killed the operation and now threatens, very graphically, very factually, very immediately, to kill remaining Jews in Ethiopia.

For heaven's sake, what does the Jewish Agency take us for, anyway? Would we have not given money a short time later, once the operation was completed, when lives did not depend on secrecy? Would we have turned our backs cold, just because we would not have been ushered into secret revelations of high policy?

And besides, just what is the obsession with fundraising? Was Israel going to go bankrupt because it had 10,000 more Jews without our extra millions? Is the only reflexive association in the mind of the Jewish Agency between problem and solution one single word: Money? Here you have an unprecedented logical problem, unprecedented even for Israel, settler of immigrants from all over the world – a problem touching on the emotion, history, social work, social psychology, religion, language, culture, administration – and all the Jewish Agency can do is to boil everything down to one panacea: Money....

[The next seven omitted paragraphs dealt with Jewish Agency mistakes in absorption.]

This Ethiopian airlift is a majestic opportunity of unprecedented dimension. It is time for large minds to take over, for small minds to step aside. We must all harness our best energies to contributing whatever we can to insuring the successful absorption of the Ethiopian Jews – meaning, adjustment to Israel together with the preservation of their integrity – and to struggling to bring the rest of Ethiopian Jewry to Israel. It's a big struggle. Much bigger than the obsessive, unwise and now, alas, highly dangerous spreading out of Jewish Agency representatives to inform thousands of a secret that, at best, a very select few of operational actors should have known. The Jewish Agency's penchant to boiling down everything to money is something of a sickness incarnate. We've paid the price for this for a long time. It's just that now we can see it more clearly.

About the only changes that I would make to Miriam Goldberg's powerful words would be to equate the Jewish Agency with the UJA, the American organization which raises the money for the Jewish Agency.

Operation Sheba

Not only was Nimeiri's survival endangered when Operation Moses and his role in it were made public, but so were the U.S. government officials who had pressured Nimeiri. The State Department found it even more galling that although this operation was conceived to help save Jewish lives, its secret was revealed by UJA fund-raisers in the U.S. and by Israeli politicians.

Shortly after "Moses" was aborted, attention in Washington and Tel Aviv turned to finishing the rescue. While the AAEJ reacted loudly and lobbied for a quick completion, many other Jewish organizations did not. Nate Shapiro had learned that the influential New York-based National Jewish Community Relations Advisory Council (NJCRAC) made it known to its affiliates that they should not pressure the United States to get involved again in order to rescue the estimated five hundred Ethiopian Jews who were thought to be stranded in the Sudan after Operation Moses was closed down. In an interview with Mitchell Bard, Shapiro said:

There was no American [Jewish] initiative at all. The Israelis told everyone to do nothing. NJCRAC...[issued] a memo saying "do nothing, say nothing, take no action." Don't talk to the

Israelis, don't talk to your congressmen, don't talk to your federation…. In the meantime, people [Ethiopian Jews] were stuck there [in the Sudan].

Such an attitude by the Jewish establishment's NJCRAC steeled the AAEJ to keep up pressure until the last of the Beta Yisrael were out of Ethiopia and the Sudan. This pressure and involvement of the AAEJ proved necessary until the last airplanes of Operation Solomon took off on May 25, 1991 (chapter 21). In the early months of 1985, the AAEJ and its friends came up with a plan for rescuing those left behind when Operation Moses was stopped. Together they sought the necessary political support to get the plan approved by President Reagan.

It started with Phil Blazer, publisher of the newspaper *Israel Today*, and producer of some Jewish-oriented Sunday TV shows for the Los Angeles area (see chapter 11). Senator Alan Cranston of California as well as influential Hollywood friends of Reagan were confidants of Blazer. In early February 1985, Blazer and Nate Shapiro had breakfast with Cranston. The senator was fully supportive, and within a day and a half, he and his staff composed a letter to President Ronald Reagan with the signatures of eighty senators. In the next few days, Senator Alfonse D'Amato of New York obtained signatures of the remaining senators, and the letter was delivered to the president. Their letter, which requested that the president seek Nimeiri's permission to resume the airlift, was given to President Reagan on February 21, 1985. The president called Cranston and told him, "We'll take care of what's going on." Republican Senator Rudy Boschwitz of Minnesota was important in influencing Reagan and Vice President Bush.

On March 5, 1985, Vice President Bush met with Nimeiri. Bush found that Nimeiri did not want a repeat of the earlier fiasco of revelations about secret rescues. Nonetheless, Sudan needed financial help from the U.S., so Nimeiri agreed to a quick, one-shot operation, insisting that the rescue be carried out by the Americans. Within the next week, $15 million of the $200 million in aid for Sudan that had been withheld by the U.S. was ordered released. Soon afterwards the Nimeiri government was toppled.

In retrospect, George Bush and Ronald Reagan never sought credit publicly for their crucial role in Operation Sheba. Perhaps they felt that the Jewish world would learn the truth one way or another and that silence would better serve their relations with their Arab friends. Regardless, the fact remains that hundreds of Jewish lives were saved in Operation Sheba through the direct actions of the Reagan administration.

Lessons and Questions

I came away from the saga of Operation Moses with renewed hope for the future, but also with clarion bells of warning ringing in my ears. These heroic and historic rescues of the Beta Yisrael never would have happened had American Jews not been informed about the plight of the Ethiopian Jews. When I first started in 1974 to lecture at synagogues about the Beta Yisrael, no more than one or two Jews per one hundred attending had ever heard much, if anything, about the Ethiopian Jews and the threats facing them. By 1984, the large majority, perhaps 90 percent or more of affiliated American Jews, were aware of the existence and plight of the Beta Yisrael in Ethiopia and in the Sudan. Many informed and caring American Jews expressed their concerns to their rabbis, to local and national Jewish organizations, and to their congressional representatives. The required pressure thus was mounted for the rescue of our brethren in Africa. That widespread concern contributed to getting members of Congress involved.

World Jewry was fortunate that Henry Rosenberg's "flare" then brought Jerry Weaver and his friends, with the cooperation of Ephraim HaLevy and the Mossad, into a position to make Operation Moses happen. It warmed the heart to witness Israelis, especially the young servicemen and women, participating in helping these new immigrants start a new life as Jews in a free country of Jews. The rescue of the Beta Yisrael also brought a great uplift to the spirits of Israelis who longed to see again the pioneering *ruach* (spirit) that helped make Israel great.

As magnificent as were Operations Moses and Sheba, a careful examination of the facts leaves a number of troubling questions. The question of why in 1984 the Beta Yisrael village elders chose the worst possible time to trek to the Sudan was addressed in chapter 16. More troublesome: Why as late as the end of 1982 hadn't the American embassy in Khartoum been informed by the U.S. State Department about the presence of Ethiopian Jews transiting Sudan?

Richard Krieger was a vocal advocate for the rescue. Princeton Lyman, who had been AID director in Ethiopia before returning to Washington in the early 1980s, was aware of the endangered Ethiopian Jews. Many members of Congress had been expressing interest in the Ethiopian Jews since the late 1970s, and in October 1981 some met with James Purcell, then acting director of the U.S. Bureau of Refugee Affairs, to discuss "the matter of Jews leaving Ethiopia." That U.S. Ambassador to the Sudan C. William Kontos and Refugee Coordinator Jerry Weaver were not informed of U.S. government interest in the rescue of the Ethiopian Jews remains a disturbing mystery. Why did it take the fall 1982 visit of Henry Rosenberg to the U.S. Embassy in Khartoum to get Kontos and Weaver informed? What if Rosenberg never had gone to the embassy?

We can also ask: Why didn't Israel use the ICM route to extract large numbers of Ethiopian Jews during 1980 and 1982? Israel was a member of the ICM. One of its citizens, "Ruth," was in a key position of ICM in the Sudan. Israel could have asked the United States to allow the Beta Yisrael refugees to leave the Sudan as part of the U.S. quota of 2,500, as Weaver later arranged for 1,440 Beta Yisrael in 1983 following the Rosenberg visit.

After the dramatic airlifts from the Sudan, the AAEJ did not have time to seek answers to these questions. We needed to deal with a changed set of circumstances.

AAEJ Response to the Cessation of Rescues

It soon appeared that Israel and world Jewry felt that the job was done; rescue of the Beta Yisrael from Africa by the Jewish Agency ceased. The AAEJ had its work cut out for us yet again. During the years 1985 through 1990 the AAEJ was once more to organize its own clandestine rescues of Beta Yisrael through what I call Operation *Pidyon Shevuyim* ("Ransoming of Captives"), this time directly from Ethiopia. We needed to increase awareness in the U.S. of the dangers surrounding tens of thousands of Beta Yisrael remaining in Africa, to raise funds to assist them there, and to create new ways to help them leave Ethiopia for Israel.

Now two women of valor take the stage.

PART VI

FROM SHEBA TO OPERATION
SOLOMON, 1985–1991

CHAPTER 20

Operation Pidyon Shevuyim

Defar ena tise mawcha ayatam.
"A determined person and smoke will find a way out."
— *Ethiopian proverb provided by LaDena Schnapper*

The dramatic successes of "Moses" and "Sheba" had led to a massive outpouring of donations from generous and caring American Jews who wanted to help the Beta Yisrael. General interest in rescuing the twenty thousand or more who still remained inside Ethiopia, however, seemed nonexistent. It was as if American Jewry and the major Jewish organizations believed that the majority of the Ethiopian Jews had been rescued and were now in Israel.

To boot, the logistics for further rescue were difficult and complex. The escape route through the Sudan was closed after Nimieri's overthrow, and Ethiopia was still strongly in the Soviet camp. The AAEJ needed to be creative. We found our answer in LaDena Schnapper.

LaDena Schnapper and the AAEJ Infrastructure

In the 1960s LaDena Schnapper had served as a Peace Corps Volunteer in Ethiopia. Although she had no contact with the Ethiopian Jewish community during that time, she was aware of them and their plight from having read a brief paragraph about "Falashas" in the Peace Corps training literature. In the early 1970s she also read an article by Graenum Berger about "saving this last remnant" of black Jews from Ethiopia. After a second tour with the Peace Corps, this time in the Pacific, she became involved with the AAEJ as a member of our volunteer speakers bureau. Unlike other speakers, LaDena could talk from firsthand experience about life in Ethiopia, spoke passable Amharic and, on occasion, would bring a non-Jewish Ethiopian friend to add authenticity to her lecture. The more she spoke and raised awareness as well as money, the more she found herself committed to the AAEJ's mission. LaDena, a convert to Judaism, seemed ideally suited to become a key player on the AAEJ team.

Soon after Nate Shapiro became president of the AAEJ and opened an office in Chicago, this young, active businessman realized that he would need a full-time assistant to manage the flood of correspondence, donations, requests for speakers and offers to help. I recommended that he hire LaDena because of her commitment, broad knowledge of the issues, and proven and tireless hands-on experience as a member of the Peace Corps, and because she was a resident of Chicago. In 1982 he did so.

LaDena understood intuitively the meaning and importance of my mantra, "infrastructure." She visited my home office in Costa Mesa, California a few weeks after Nate hired her. I was surprised at the way we both seemed to sense what the other was going to say. Together we went through many details of the model I was trying to build for the AAEJ.

Building and maintaining an infrastructure, I emphasized as we spoke, did not apply only to AAEJ activities in the U.S., but also to those in Israel. Later that fall, she and I visited Israel together. During the long flight, we discussed Israeli contacts, including leaders of the several Beta Yisrael groups, friends, antagonists, officials of the government and the Jewish Agency, scholars, activists, social workers, and rabbis. Once in Israel, we met with our "guide," volunteer Murray Greenfield, often assisted by Rahamim Elazar. They became new friends that LaDena could depend upon whenever she would need help in Israel. Murray and Rahamim introduced LaDena to the Ethiopian Jewish community there and to many key contacts. They took us to absorption centers, homes of veteran and new immigrants, government offices, schools, and religious centers. I can still see LaDena, with her warmth, knowledge, and relative fluency in Amharic, charming the *kessim* (priests) who were studying in Jerusalem.

The next three years saw LaDena not only retain the programs we had started in California, but improve on them. The membership of the AAEJ gradually increased from twelve to thirty-five thousand, and the budget from a quarter million to a million and a half a year. By 1985 she began to hone in on how she could help in saving the Beta Yisrael families still languishing in Ethiopia. How could she direct the energies and resources of the AAEJ to fulfill the great *mitzvah* of *pidyon shevuyim* (the ransoming of captives)?

LaDena saw to the heart of the matter. It was not money. The AAEJ was not extravagant, had a low overhead and a solid financial base. When more money was needed, Nate and his friends would find it.

LaDena focused on two essential needs: to devise methods to obtain exit and entry visas for the Jews of Ethiopia wishing to go to Israel, and to devise unconventional but legal ways to use those visas clandestinely to take the Beta Yisrael out of Ethiopia and then to Israel.

Creative Rescues

To get her feet wet in unconventional legal rescues, LaDena tried a ploy already in the AAEJ portfolio, the manufacture of bogus invitations for Beta Yisrael students to attend foreign universities (chapter 8). Supposedly en route to those universities, the students would fly from Addis Ababa to Europe, and from there, rather than going to the university which supposedly had accepted them, they would be taken to Israel instead.

LaDena used this method frequently. The major drawback, however, was that after a lot of paperwork, each effort would take to Israel only one person at a time.

After learning from her Ethiopian Christian friends in Chicago that groups of their friends were leaving Addis Ababa through legitimate governmental channels, LaDena thought of trying to rescue Beta Yisrael the same way. To do so she would need a reliable contact in Ethiopia. She sought help from a variety of sources including former Peace Corps colleagues and her Chicago friends, all to no avail.

Through a chain of players in the Beta Yisrael rescue drama she finally found that critical contact. This was the chain: A recommendation came via a phone call from Semu Desta, an Ethiopian Jew living with his wife and daughter in Los Angeles. He had been the best friend of Bill Halpern, who had been killed in an automobile accident in Kenya during a personal attempt to get Semu out of Ethiopia. Later, Barry Weise working for the NJCRAC in NY and Henry Rosenberg for the AAEJ were instrumental in getting Semu to the United States. But the chain originally started with Baruch Tegegne, an older cousin of Semu. Baruch, who first met Bill Halpern at the home of Yona Bogale in Addis, introduced Halpern to Semu. While in Gondar, Baruch also had introduced Semu to one of his closest, most-trusted Christian friends there, Berhanu Yiradu.

Berhanu Yiradu, an Ethiopian Jerry Weaver

Semu told LaDena that she must contact Berhanu, Baruch's trustworthy Christian friend in Gondar who understood how the system worked in Marxist Ethiopia. LaDena finally reached Berhanu by phone after nearly forty unsuccessful attempts. As they chatted, she in her limited Amharic, LaDena was amazed at how they "resonated." When Berhanu agreed to discuss helping some Beta Yisrael get to Addis Ababa in order to leave the country, she told him that she would mail the details and call again.

LaDena instinctively felt that Semu was right, that Berhanu, a man she had never met and who was ten thousand miles away, was "a man to be trusted." But could he help move hundreds of Beta Yisrael from the Gondar countryside down to Addis from where they might be able to fly directly to Israel?

Yes, he could. Schnapper describes this extraordinary man as the "essential link" in this *aliyah*. He was shrewd, wise, honest, and he cared about results. He had many contacts and knew how to get things done in Ethiopia. An unassuming man, he knew his own limits. He knew how to negotiate, how to persuade and convince. He understood the culture and people of Ethiopia. For six years, working by telephone and using code words, Berhanu and LaDena established an infrastructure that facilitated the rescue of some one thousand Ethiopian Jews during the next five years after Operations Moses and Sheba. They did this at a time when neither Israel nor major American Jewish organizations were willing to make the effort.

Rather than begin with the more difficult task of moving entire families from Gondar to Addis, LaDena, sometimes with the help of Berhanu, experimented with seemingly more simple tasks. Before approaching Ethiopian authorities for exit visas, for example, she needed to have reasons to make such a request. One model was similar to that suggested by Barry Weise and used by the AAEJ in 1976 with the University of California (chapter 8), but often more ambitious and complex. LaDena had already used it successfully. Before Berhanu or one of his agents approached the Ethiopian authorities for exit visas, LaDena would mail him forged U.S. student immigration papers, the ubiquitous I-20 forms, and fake acceptances from U.S. colleges and universities.

LaDena used a host of other excuses to get Beta Yisrael out of Ethiopia, all phony. In some cases she got work papers from Chicago businessmen saying so-and-so had a job awaiting him or her in America. Or she arranged for invitations to attend a family wedding outside of Ethiopia. Another time, she collaborated with a Chicago policeman, Steve Brownstein, in a scheme that saw a Finnish orphanage in Ethiopia bring fourteen Beta Yisrael "orphans" to Israel.

LaDena discovered that the more official-looking the documents she obtained, replete with numerous official seals, the easier it was to win an exit visa. She soon learned how to secure notary seals from local, state, and national offices that were generously affixed to legitimate documents. "The beautiful red ribbons of the U.S. State Department always impressed Ethiopian officials," she said.

Fancy paper might sway a bureaucrat, but nothing was easy in this process! To get from village to visa required thirty different steps, each one costing time and money. To travel from a remote northern Ethiopian village to Addis Ababa five hundred miles away was exceedingly challenging. Obtaining clearances from farmer associations, banks, youth associations, doctors, and local political officers required patience and cunning.

For most of the Beta Yisrael, the trip down to Addis was the first time they had left their village and ridden in a mechanized vehicle. After three days' travel and often more if the bus broke down, Berhanu needed to arrange for lodging, negotiate with bureaucrats in government offices, buy airline tickets, and coordinate with the Israelis. He also transmitted money to each individual or family to sustain them for as long as one year while they waited to leave. These grants averaged U.S. $1,000–$2,000 in local currency. Since the government of Ethiopia had strict controls on hard currency, local middlemen had to make black market conversions. And of course, there was always the expected *gubo* (bribe) passed under the table.

These 1985–1989 operations rested so completely on one man that a nagging question persisted: How were we to know that he was sending out only Beta Yisrael, not gentile friends or members of his family? LaDena admitted that sometimes it was hard to verify that the families were Beta Yisrael. Thus, she created a set of procedures to check would-be immigrants with the community in Israel and then through Haim Halachmi or through Micha Feldman, an employee of the Jewish Agency assigned to issues regarding the Ethiopian Jews.

Once a family was approved, she would contact them via letter or phone. That, too, was not always easy; but as more Beta Yisrael left Ethiopia for Israel, word spread through the Gondar community. Soon the Chicago office began receiving more and more letters from Beta Yisrael in Ethiopia, as well as from their Israeli relatives, begging for assistance. Before she sent help, she asked each family to describe the family background and finances and to identify relatives in Israel. It was tedious, but it helped keep out interlopers.

LaDena asked Berhanu to contact the families and invite them to start the process, but also to explain to them the obstacles and risks. That two thousand-year-old dream of "returning to *Yerusha-layim*" was so strong that most of the families were willing to leave behind their home, albeit a mud hut, belongings, cattle, relatives (often the elderly who were too frail to travel), friends, and memories rooted in centuries of life in Ethiopia. They left the Gondar, Gojam, Wollo, and Tigre regions, and, with the money Berhanu provided from the AAEJ, they traveled to Addis Ababa. Each case was unique with different needs. Sometimes LaDena and Berhanu processed a single man or woman; other times, families with eight children. Clearances, travel, lodging, passports – these steps were complicated and took time.

After exit visas had been secured, Israeli entry permits had to be obtained. Even though Israel approved of LaDena's plans, it took time to get those permits, because Israel did not have an embassy in Ethiopia at that time. Fortunately, Israel had the Swedish embassy in Addis to handle all consular affairs, which included issuing Israeli entry visas to the Beta Yisrael.

Once the evacuees received an Ethiopian passport and exit visa, LaDena, through a U.S. travel agent, would make reservations on flights bound ultimately for the United States via Greece and Italy. She wired the tickets to Berhanu who would then ensure that the families got to the airport and boarded the planes.

Challenges and Setbacks
The process was not perfect. Things could go wrong. As the workload increased, so did the stress. As LaDena describes it:

> Before each departure, I would be on edge. Hundreds of hours of work, persistent patience, and voluminous trust were required. Every case was beset with obstacles. In my letters to the families we were helping, I would underline the phrase, "*Just remember,*

something ALWAYS could go wrong." The entire process was hazardous. It usually took a year or longer for us to take one individual or a family out of Ethiopia.

The only time I breathed easier, though only momentarily, was when I got word that they had landed in Athens or Rome. From then on it was much smoother sailing. We had our agents there to pick them up at the airport, put them in hotels, and get visas from the Israeli embassy. We placed them on the next available El Al flight for the last leg of their incredible journey to reach Israel. When they arrived, we usually had arranged beforehand for relatives and former neighbors to greet them. Only then was I relieved. But there were still so many more families in our pipelines that we had to assist.

It was a lot of responsibility, and I always feared that something could go wrong and I might have endangered someone's life. I always expected a problem. When the phone rang in the wee hours of the morning, I knew there was another glitch. To this day, I feel traumatized if I receive a telephone call in the middle of the night. Back then when I was most active with the process, I literally received three to four calls a night asking for papers, money, and help.

Because my Amharic left much to be desired, and many of the families that called me had not used a phone before, the Ethiopian telephone operators were most gracious and assisted in translating with phone calls. Yes, they listened in! Whether they revealed all the contacts and plans, I don't know. I do know though there were many times after I hung up, an operator would call me back begging me to help her children. In exchange for their assistance, I helped where I could. Today I know of five youngsters, children of those Ethiopian telephone operators, who are now legally living in the United States.

Meanwhile Berhanu was facing his own challenges. At first he worked alone, but as the numbers grew, he needed to build a support organization. Eventually Berhanu brought together twelve

Ethiopian Jews, paid by the AAEJ, to help him. Known as "the Committee," they became the facilitators who advised, directed, bribed, arranged, and eased the process for the would-be immigrants. Later, in 1989–1990, they played a critical role in arranging the mass exodus of the Jews from Gondar to Addis in preparation for Operation Solomon.

The Committee worked as quietly and clandestinely as possible to avoid official interference, but it was clear that the Ethiopian government knew what they were doing. Given the number of Beta Yisrael being moved, it is not surprising that serious security problems arose. One came about when Ethiopian authorities arrested several Jews, including Waizero Hirut Tekle, a female member of the Committee. It took two years to secure her release. Will Recant, the AAEJ executive director in Washington, lobbied on Capitol Hill for her and the other prisoners. Eventually his campaign resulted in strong diplomatic pressure from the State Department being brought to bear on Addis. As this came after the Soviets had abandoned Colonel Mengistu, forcing him to seek U.S. humanitarian assistance to aid millions of drought and famine victims, Recant's pressure paid off. Hirut was released, but prison took a terrible toll on her. Hirut's heroic and moving story is told in the excellent film *For Zion's Sake*, produced and directed by her son Fasil, who today is a film and TV producer in Israel.

Help from Others
In addition to working with Berhanu and the Committee, Schnapper saw to it that AAEJ funds went to other rescue activities. Most of the ideas came from those with firsthand knowledge, usually of additional escape routes. Frequently, Ethiopian Jews in Israel contacted her with creative ideas for rescue. They asked for money to return to Ethiopia and get their families out. For example, Assafa Mengesha used a Kenya route successfully. Girma Bayouh was the first to try the Christian Easter pilgrimage route, using it to get his family to Israel. Unquestionably the information from Rahamim Elazar, Meharie Robel, and Rahamim Yitzhak in Israel, Aberra

Meharie and Worku Abuhay in Canada, and David Seyum in Kenya resulted in many successful small-scale rescues.

Some of these clandestine movements brought other Jewish organizations into collaborative ventures. Notable among dozens of such organizations were the North American Conference on Ethiopian Jewry, Save All Ethiopian Jews (SAEJ), and the Jewish Immigrant Aid Society of Canada. The SAEJ group was led by Elie Halpern, brother of Bill, and Sid Weiner, a longtime Seattle activist. Cooperation, communication, and collaboration on cases were the norm behind the rescue scenes.

Helping Families

In addition to moving human beings out of Ethiopia, the AAEJ moved dollars in. Grants were made to thousands of Ethiopian Jews. Sometimes funds went to families who, because they had applied for resettlement, lost their jobs or were driven from their villages. Other recipients were identified by relatives already in Israel as destitute, on the brink of starvation. Still others were single young men or women living in Addis who had no means of support.

LaDena's method for getting money to them was as simple as it was effective. Through the U.S. and Ethiopian postal systems, cashier checks for up to $1,000, with the "return receipt requested" card attached, were sent from Chicago into such isolated villages in rural Ethiopia as Dabat, Dabark, Gondar, Goragora, Tedda, and Bahar Dar. These cards came back signed, followed by a letter stating the check was received and cashed. Over 95 percent of this mail reached the people through the complex but efficient Ethiopian postal system without loss or theft.

Once word of the monetary distribution circulated in Ethiopia and Israel, several individuals initiated similar programs. And they had far-reaching effects. For example, Tesfaye Aderju, a young Ethiopian Jew who reached Israel via Sudan, began to distribute funds to assist Beta Yisrael who lived in ten remote villages in the Woggera area. Through his imaginative plan and with the funds the AAEJ provided, most of the community abandoned their villages and went to Addis Ababa where they eventually were able to leave Ethiopia for Israel.

In total, under the auspices of the AAEJ and the other organizations and individuals cooperating with LaDena, about a thousand Beta Yisrael were taken out of Ethiopia and reached Israel in the four years following Operation Moses. During that time, Israel and major Jewish organizations had no rescue program operating in Ethiopia. To Israel's credit, however, under dangerous conditions following the overthrow of President Nimeiri in 1985, the Israeli government rescued 640 Ethiopian Jews from the Sudan during 1986, 1987, and 1988.

I asked LaDena what she thought of the AAEJ's successes. LaDena, humble and self-effacing, gave a classic reply:

> Well maybe it was *bashert* ("destined to be"), but I still marvel at our success! Imagine Ethiopians trusting this female *ferengi* (foreigner) whom they've never met and who speaks broken Amharic! Perhaps that I kept on sending money pushed my credibility rating up high! I am still in awe that these illiterate Beta Yisrael farmers dared to trust me and my newly found Christian friend, Berhanu.

CHAPTER 21

Last Flights to Jerusalem

Entering the huge, cavernous Hercules cargo plane was like
entering the belly of a woman who after five hours would give
birth on the sacred soil of Israel.
   – *LaDena Schnapper, on boarding the next-to-
   last airplane of Operation Solomon, May 25, 1991*

"*A* new dawn began when Israel opened up an embassy in Addis
Ababa in November 1989," said LaDena Schnapper. It was the single
most important event preparing the way for the rescue of most of
the Beta Yisrael remaining in Ethiopia. To LaDena, the presence of
the embassy meant that she could greatly reduce the workload and
time previously needed because so many offices that had to approve
immigrants, issue entry visas, and book seats on El Al airlines were
in one place. Berhanu and the Committee could now do in a few
hours what it had taken LaDena, operating via telephone and mail
from Chicago, days, weeks, even months to accomplish.

Soon after the embassy opened, an event triggered by the Soviet withdrawal from Ethiopia at the end of the Cold War, between
fifty and a hundred Beta Yisrael left monthly for Israel. This number
soon rose to two to three hundred. The numbers increased even
more in 1990 when 4,153 Ethiopian Jews arrived in Israel.

The Amazing One-Day Mass Rescue: Setting the Stage

A major player in the prologue to Operation Solomon was to be
Susan Pollack. In the winter of 1981 she had attended one of my
lectures, this one at the Hebrew Union College. As had happened
with so many young people before, the plight of the Ethiopian Jews

stirred her emotions and engendered a rock-hard commitment to help. For a while she worked with the Canadian activists and later joined the staff of the AAEJ. In mid-1990 she went to Addis Ababa with some much-needed medical supplies and soon was working with Berhanu and his Committee.

By March 1990, there were a little over three thousand Beta Yisrael in Addis Ababa. More kept arriving, some urged to go there by relatives in Israel, and others making the journey with the help of Berhanu. An agreement between Israel and Ethiopia permitted this group to leave Ethiopia for Israel. Micha Feldman of the Jewish Agency was in Ethiopia to oversee their flights to Israel at the set rate of two to three hundred per week. Although an encouraging 4,051 Ethiopian Jews did reach Israel that year, for the Beta Yisrael remaining in the hinterlands, the wait was intolerable.

Susan Pollack had a better idea: If all Beta Yisrael in Gondar province came to Addis, the sheer numbers in Addis would force Israel to bring them home. In 1949, Operation "Magic Carpet" had brought over forty thousand Jews from Yemen. So why not the Beta Yisrael now? She spoke with Berhanu and the Committee who agreed: all that was needed was money to rent buses and trucks to bring the people to Addis. Once in Addis, they would need shelter and food while waiting to be taken to Israel. Susan called LaDena with the idea, and LaDena relayed the message to Nate Shapiro. He agreed in principle and sent Will Recant to Addis to review the plan and assess its likelihood of success.

During Passover 1990, Will Recant and Susan Pollack met in Addis. They could not fix the number that might come. Obviously, Pollack's plan was very risky; insurgents opposed to dictator Mengistu Haile Mariam were making their way towards the capital. If security deteriorated, soldiers or insurgents might turn their guns on the Beta Yisrael. And what if Israeli authorities refused to issue thousands and thousands of visas? Yes, it was risky; but it appeared viable: LaDena had developed a strong infrastructure in Ethiopia with the leadership of Berhanu and the assistance of the Committee. They were ready. Recant recommended approval. With such a strong case, the AAEJ executive committee concurred. Shapiro gave the go-ahead.

Berhanu and his committee members headed for Gondar, their pockets filled with AAEJ cash to buy transportation, bribe local officials and military at checkpoints along the road, and purchase necessities.

Meanwhile Susan rented six buildings about half a mile from the Israeli embassy. This location passed into folklore as "Susan's Compound." The first group of seven hundred Beta Yisrael arrived at the compound during one night in May 1990. To their minds, they were fulfilling their dream of immigrating to Jerusalem. All told, twelve thousand Beta Yisrael were brought in by the Committee and another six thousand came by themselves; three thousand already had been in Addis. The "crisis" Pollack had hoped to create materialized.

At first the expected crisis was skillfully handled. Some of the Beta Yisrael were sick; others arrived severely malnourished. As with every new influx of refugees, the old, very young, and infirm had to be treated quickly. The lessons of Um Raquba, the recent great East African famine, and other mass rescues had been well and truly learned. The AAEJ hired doctors and nurses and bought medicine and food for the residents. This initial lifesaving effort was augmented in July 1990; the Joint Distribution Committee (JDC), an American organization that helps Jews and others in distress overseas, closed its clinic in Gondar and reopened it in Addis Ababa so that it could aid the residents of the compound.

The three thousand children in the compound required special services. The AAEJ opened a school. There they received much-needed primary health care and nutritious meals. Each child received daily a minimum of an egg, orange, potato, and bread. In September 1990, the JDC took over the school and meal program.

For the adults in the compound, special programs also helped. Shapiro dispatched Glen Stein and Joyce Miller to Addis to help Susan. Stein set up a women's handicraft enterprise for about a thousand women who wove colorful straw baskets. The AAEJ sold them to its members all over the United States. Americans who purchased the baskets had a tangible object to remind them that they were helping the Beta Yisrael in Ethiopia. This project also helped foster a feeling of self-esteem in the Beta Yisrael weavers, knowing that they were contributing to their families' survival. Each family also received a stipend from a fund administered by Micha Feldman of the Jewish Agency.

It was a major victory for the AAEJ that the immense resources of the Jewish Agency along with those of the JDC were being allocated to cover most of the major expenses and care of the Beta Yisrael in "Susan's Compound." First, it helped relieve the financial strain on the relatively small budget of the AAEJ. Second, and probably more important, it pointed out that there was growing official acceptance by the Jewish establishment of the AAEJ's "little amateur organization."

During a visit to Israel late in the summer, Will Recant and Susan Pollack were warmly welcomed by JDC and Jewish Agency officials and were told: "You have earned a page in history; job well done. Now we will take over." Will and Susan thanked their hosts for the kind words, but told them that AAEJ would stay in Addis until all twenty-one thousand Beta Yisrael got to Israel. Exhausted by the physical and emotional demands of their work, Will and Susan returned to the United States in October 1990. They were replaced by LaDena Schnapper – returning to Ethiopia after an absence of thirty years.

Officially, Schnapper and the other AAEJ staffers were now playing a "monitoring" role; the JDC, the Jewish Agency, and Israeli embassy personnel were in charge of the compound. The influx into the compound of twenty thousand Beta Yisrael and the long delays most faced leaving for Israel, however, had now created additional massive unmet needs. So many problems: money, family reunification, rejection of their claim of Jewishness. LaDena found that much of the confusion and delay stemmed from poor cross-cultural communications. She found herself increasingly on the phone to Ethiopian Jews in Israel to locate family or friends who could vouch that a candidate for immigration to Israel was a Jew.

Many cases brought her into conflict with an Israeli embassy staff who had little or no previous experience with the Beta Yisrael. Her persistence paid off, and hundreds of Ethiopians initially denied entry visas were finally allowed to exit. LaDena soon became an invaluable resource for the JDC and embassy personnel.

Mengistu Politics

Those AAEJ activities were not occurring in a political vacuum. Simultaneously, starting in July 1990 while Susan was still in Ethiopia, some troublesome moments arose between the governments involved. Mengistu slowed down the *aliyah* by refusing to expedite the issuance of exit visas. In response, according to Will Recant, the Israeli government asked Washington to pressure Mengistu to allow more Beta Yisrael to emigrate. In October 1990, Assistant Secretary of State Henry Cohen went to Ethiopia to meet with Kassa Kebede, Ethiopia's secretary of foreign affairs, and Israel's key person there, Uri Lubrani, a former ambassador to Ethiopia. The three agreed on a family reunification plan allowing five hundred Ethiopian Jews to leave for Israel each month.

Key to these negotiations were Kebede's links to Israel and to the AAEJ. Kebede had studied at the Hebrew University in Jerusalem and became friends with AAEJ board member Gil Kulick when Kulick served at the American embassy in Addis. He also had been a friend of Baruch Tegegne.

Following that October meeting, during the first five months of 1991, the number of Ethiopian Jews leaving for Israel increased sharply. Unknown to the rest of the world, 5,188 Ethiopian Jews were taken to Israel in those months *before* Operation Solomon. This was the largest rescue of Ethiopian Jews in any short period since Operation Moses in 1984.

The increased rate of emigration of Beta Yisrael starting in January 1991, however, coincided with a severe worsening of Ethiopia's military situation vis-à-vis the insurgent armies. Addis officials requested U.S. assistance, but were told they would get it only if Ethiopia would allow more of its Jews to leave for Israel. Such was the message delivered through Kassa Kebede to Prime Minister Mengistu. In the meantime, Lubrani and the AAEJ asked the U.S. to send an envoy to Ethiopia immediately to negotiate a large-scale exodus of the Beta Yisrael from Addis. Will Recant described the whirlwind of political activities in Washington during the month preceding Operation Solomon:

- A representative of the Presidents' Conference of Major Jewish Organizations asked Senator Boschwitz to see President Bush. Boschwitz conferred with Nate Shapiro and Will Recant before meeting with the president.
- The senator went to Ethiopia and asked Mengistu for the release of all the Ethiopian Jews.
- Peter Jackson of the AAEJ executive committee went to Ethiopia to replace Glen Stein and to serve as AAEJ liaison.
- In large part due to Boschwitz's intervention, a peace conference between Ethiopia and the rebel leadership was set for May 27.
- President Bush put more pressure on Mengistu, saying there would be no peace conference until all the Jews in Addis Ababa were out of Ethiopia.
- The insurgents assured the U.S. that they would not hurt the Ethiopian Jews in Addis, nor would they interfere with their exodus.
- Israel sent Uri Lubrani back to Addis to conclude arrangements for the release of the Beta Yisrael in a one-shot deal. He spent two weeks there negotiating. Lubrani left Ethiopia for Washington and asked the AAEJ to pressure the U.S. government to help get the airlift started.
- The AAEJ had entrée to Bob Frazer of the National Security Council, to Henry Cohen of the State Department, and to Kassa Kebede in Addis.

- On Wednesday, May 22, the AAEJ helped get a letter from President Bush to the new president of Ethiopia, Tesfaye Kidane, stating that the U.S. would facilitate the peace conference in London *only* if the Jews were freed immediately.
- Meanwhile, the rebels assured the U.S. and Israel that they would not interfere with an airlift and would leave the airfields open. Within hours after receipt of Bush's letter, the exit agreement was sealed.
- On Friday, May 24, 1991, Operation Solomon started, and by Saturday evening the mission was completed.

LaDena Schnapper remembers these historic days preceding Operation Solomon:

The week of May 19th arrived. Mengistu Haile Mariam, the Dergue Communist dictator, left the country on Tuesday the 21st with a purported $26 million given by American Jews. Tension was high. Top government officials changed; a tighter curfew was enforced. What was to be the country's fate? Speculation abounded with every Ethiopian, more so with those involved with Ethiopian Jewry. Would the Beta Yisrael be safe if guerrillas took over the city? Those of us on the ground in Addis did not know of the behind-the-scenes agreements with the TPLF. Would the Ethiopian Jews become the scapegoat and be harmed? Rebel forces had reached Bahar Dar in Western Ethiopia about 150 kilometers (93 miles) from Addis and were rapidly approaching. The American embassy advised us to leave the country. We stayed.

On Thursday, May 23, Berhanu, sensitive to the growing tension, advised we leave work early. Tzsaki Ostrafsky, a visiting Israeli photographer, and I decided to cool off at the Hilton's swimming pool. There we met Avi Mizrachi of the Israeli embassy who advised us to be at the embassy at 5 P.M. that afternoon. When entering the compound, I knew the time had come for the rest of the drama to unfold. I encountered tall, handsome, swarthy, very capable-looking Israelis who had not been there in the morning. Later I learned that Prime Minister Shamir had ordered two hundred of Israel's "elite," dressed as civilians, to Addis to provide security for the operation.

We were briefed for two hours by Avi Mizrachi and Micha Feldman. I was told that tomorrow everyone, yes everyone, would leave with only the clothes on their back. Hercules transports and El Al cargo carriers would fly out of the Addis airport, all with the permission of the new Ethiopian government. The Ethiopian Jews were to learn by word of mouth tonight that tomorrow they would be leaving for Israel.

The process was simple. The refugees would go through a series of checkpoints set up on the embassy grounds. At the final station, they would receive either a yellow or blue decal to be placed on their clothing or body indicating they could board the busses and leave for the airport. We were shown the ropes which were to keep people in lines and stations to check each person's ID card to make certain that their name matched those on the Jewish Agency list of Ethiopians known to be Jews. We were given our assignments and told to go home, get a good night's sleep and be at the embassy at 5 A.M. to help with the processing.

On my way to the Hilton Hotel, I stopped at an Ethiopian Jewish family's home to tell them about the plans; but I neglected to check my watch and stayed past the curfew. As I approached the Hilton, I was stopped by two policemen who pointed their weapons at me. I quickly set my watch back and in Amharic pointed to the fact that I had a few minutes left before the 9 P.M. curfew. The police were not convinced. I started talking Amharic, asked their names, bolstered their male egos, slipped a fifty-*Birr* note inside my license and handed it to them. Smiling, they waved me past.

Operation Solomon

For Schnapper, and thousands of other Jews, sleep was impossible that Thursday night. At 5 A.M., May 24, she drove to the Israeli embassy and began thirty-six straight hours of work. The neat, orderly system of ropes and stations degenerated into chaos when fourteen thousand Jews arrived at once, along with ten thousand of their Christian neighbors. Pandemonium reigned. Food was not available. People arrived with bags of belonging – pictures, clothes, jewelry, and money – only to give it all up. All was put into a secured room. A few put on extra Ethiopian traditional clothes, stuffing their jewelry and a few prized photos into their pockets. Money was given to "checkers" and recorded. The people came with little; they left with nothing except profound faith born centuries ago and deepened by the dream of "one day in *Yerushalayim.*" Schnapper tried to imagine herself taking a rocket to the moon only because someone told her that she would be better off there. She wasn't sure she could have done that.

The screaming, shoving, and pushing continued throughout the day until a chaotic order emerged and people started leaving on the big red and yellow Ethiopian buses. At 7:30 Shabbat morning there were no more lines: all Beta Yisrael had left for the airport. Schnapper and other AAEJ personnel were ordered out. She felt conflicted – what about the safety of Berhanu and the others who had helped? But she obeyed and boarded the bus.

Thirty-four airplanes, including Hercules C-130 cargo planes and El Al jumbo jets, flew into the embattled Addis Ababa airport. The El Al planes were stripped of their seats to make room for more passengers, and the Israeli insignias were masked. Further, Prime Minister Shamir instructed El Al to ignore its regular policy of not flying on Shabbat. One El Al airplane set a world record by carrying 1,087 passengers. That number was possible because none of the Beta Yisrael passengers brought along any luggage. At one time, a remarkable twenty-five airplanes were in flight simultaneously; some of the planes were on the ground about half an hour before they took off, filled to capacity with Beta Yisrael immigrants. Not a single person died during the operation, and ten babies were born.

LaDena remembers the flight: "Entering the huge, cavernous Hercules cargo plane was like entering the belly of a woman who after five hours would give birth on the sacred soil of Israel. The passengers' discipline was remarkable. No toilets; no food; no seats; only trust that this 'bird' was taking them 'home.' Over two hundred hushed, crammed, exhausted, anticipating people, Israeli Ethiopian Jewish operatives, the pilots, Glen, Joyce and I flew this historic flight. We were the second-to-last plane to leave."

An average of one thousand Ethiopians landed each hour at Ben Gurion airport. With the experience of "Moses" and "Sheba" behind them, the Jewish Agency whisked the latest immigrants away to makeshift absorption centers. Operation Solomon had succeeded in lifting a whole community, 14,193 Ethiopian Jews, from Africa to Israel in a single day. Overcome by emotion, Schnapper called her family; then, true to AAEJ discipline, she phoned Nate Shapiro. Only after doing her duty did she collapse in tears, overcome by the sense of relief and joy that her mission, and that of the AAEJ, was done. Later she said: "I likened myself to a midwife who had labored for twelve years to finally witness this wondrous miracle. I smiled. Yes, indeed the Amharic proverb, *Tegest marara naw; ferayhew tefage* was true. 'Patience is bitter; its fruit, sweet.'"

For me, the bombshell burst on Sunday morning, May 26, 1991 when Will Recant called and said:

> Howard, I want you to be the first to know. The Israelis pulled it off. They took over fourteen thousand Falashas from Addis to Israel in the past day. The last two airplanes of immigrants have just left the ground. LaDena is with them. You can relax now. We've won!

Postscript

Well, not quite. LaDena Schnapper returned to Ethiopia again two weeks after Operation Solomon. There are always a few who miss the bus. Some in Israel claimed at least six thousand Beta Yisrael were left behind. LaDena moved into a private home and hosted many Israeli Ethiopian Jews who returned to Ethiopia to help those still hoping to leave. The Israeli embassy was intact and was busy processing those who hadn't gotten on board during Operation Solomon. The JDC, AAEJ, and NACOEJ workers continued to cooperate to identify Jews for the exodus. "Susan's Compound" was taken over by the Israelis; the NACOEJ compound became the center of activities with a school, employment program, and Hebrew classes. Berhanu was asked by the Israelis to work with the JDC and the embassy. LaDena continued as facilitator with the Israeli embassy and established the Jewish identity of at least two hundred Beta Yisrael, allowing them to be eligible for their exodus to Israel.

Some Beta Yisrael who had gone to Sudan after "Sheba," hoping to escape to Israel, now returned to Ethiopia – too late for Solomon. And there was the Quara community, some five thousand souls, left behind during Operation Solomon, who now wanted to leave.

Officials from the Israeli embassy journeyed to Quara and met with community elders. After the processing was completed, the AAEJ paid to transport them to Addis Ababa. With the help of American Christians, three thousand Beta Yisrael from Quara were taken to Israel in 1998.

Schnapper left Ethiopia for the United States via Israel in September 1992. While in Israel, she visited a community she had helped bring there just one year before. They were now speaking Hebrew, serving in the army, moving into apartments, and struggling with the problems that face new immigrants. Many of them repeated back to her a proverb she had told them during the seemingly endless wait: *"Kes be kes inkulal be igur yeheda"* (Slowly, slowly – even an egg will walk). She returned to the United States for final debriefing in Washington and Chicago. In 1993 the AAEJ voted to close its doors, satisfied that it had played a vital role in saving the Ethiopian Jewish community. LaDena moved to the northern Michigan peninsula to care for her aging mother.

A Beginning, Not an End

The heroic mega-rescues of the Ethiopian Jews via Operation Moses and Operation Solomon have been credited with rekindling the pioneering spirit in Israel. As they knelt and kissed the earth at Lod Airport, the Beta Yisrael were warmly welcomed. After Operation Moses, the *New York Times* wrote: "For the first time in history, thousands of black people are being brought into a country not in chains but as citizens." The AAEJ rejoiced too, pleased with its particular role as gadfly in achieving the rescues. The end of the dramatic rescues, however, marked the beginning of a new, challenging Israeli chapter in the saga of the Ethiopian Jews.

Long-time activists were looking forward to the weaving of the Beta Yisrael into the multicultural social fabric of Israel. Professor Tartakower had cautioned in the early 1970s that success would require more than bread and homes and a decent standard of living. Certainly bread and homes, but equally important would be preserving their own cultural strengths as valuable assets in the life of Israel.

Tartakower's vision has not materialized. In 1974, when the AAEJ was born, virtually all of the 168 Ethiopian Jews living in Israel were gainfully employed: police, nurses, factory workers, farmers, university students. Today (as of the spring of 2006), there are twenty Ethiopian lawyers, over a dozen rabbis and many professionals, technicians, and university graduates. But too large a percentage of the Ethiopian Jews in Israel live below the poverty line and suffer disproportionate unemployment. Too high a percentage of Ethiopian students in grades one through nine cannot read or write at the appropriate grade level, and the numbers who pass the matriculation exams are less than half the national aver-age. Not surprisingly, juvenile delinquency and antisocial behavior are on the increase in the Ethiopian population. Are the Ethiopian Jews on the road to becoming an underclass, complete with the deculturation and social pathologies that Rabbi Yitz Greenberg, among others, feared?

Academics, social workers, and Ethiopian Jews recognize the problems and shortfalls of the prevailing absorption processes. Many Israeli advocates possess the requisite experience, intelli-gence, and dedication to implement needed improvements. Hun-dreds of millions of dollars and countless hours have been spent on the absorption process – with more failure than success, how-ever. What then is missing? The story of the AAEJ shows that moral outrage, conviction, devotion, and even money are necessary but not sufficient to bring about major change. We learned that gov-ernment policy can be altered, but that it takes a sustained and coordinated effort by activists.

We American Jews have seen the State of Israel beset by so many crises, problems, and obligations, that it has been impossible for the Israelis alone to take on the challenge of effectively absorb-ing the Beta Yisrael. The problem has only been compounded by the shattering effects of the First Intifada, which started exactly three years after Operation Moses, then the suicide bombings, which began two years after Operation Solomon, and the Second Intifada starting in 2000. And, as of the summer of 2006, we can append to this list the terrorism, missile attacks, and kidnappings by the Hezbollah in the north and Hamas in the south.

We might reflect as well on our own U.S. history. Lincoln signed the Emancipation Proclamation freeing the slaves in the southern states 140 years ago. The Thirteenth Amendment which outlawed slavery throughout the U.S. is 135 years old. The Warren Court, fifty years ago, ruled that racial segregation in public schools was unconstitutional. Over forty years have passed since President Lyndon Johnson pushed through the Civil Rights Act of 1964. Are African Americans now no longer an underclass in the U.S.? Hurricane Katrina in 2005 has put a spotlight on our own unresolved social pathology.

Ample evidence signifies that conditions now are right to remedy the absorption of the Beta Yisrael. The UJA has committed itself during 2005–2006 to raise $60 million for projects involving Ethiopian Jews. The Joint Distribution Committee (JDC), which receives 25 percent of UJA funds, has established programs to assist Beta Yisrael absorption. Some Israelis close to the levers of power want to make constructive changes. And, most of all, today an increasing number of professionally trained Ethiopians in Israel are prepared to participate.

A personal experience from our family's recent move to Mississippi may be relevant. We were stunned to find that in four Delta counties near our home, hundreds of African American children each year could not attend school because their impoverished families could not afford to pay for school clothing and supplies. When we volunteered to help an outstanding African American organization raise funds to get many of those children to school, we were pleased to learn that not only did we help the children, but also the social workers with whom we worked were enabled to reach the children's families and work with them to obtain other essential services.

The 2005 literature of the JDC states: "forty-five percent [of Ethiopian families] cannot afford basic school supplies for their children." We are struck that Ethiopian children in Israel face the same problem as our African American children in the Mississippi Delta. It would seem especially vital to focus heavily in Israel on getting the Beta Yisrael youngsters to school. Thanks to JDC intervention programs such as *Ofek Bagrut*, the number of Ethiopian-Israeli high school students who succeed in their national matriculation exams has risen from 9 percent ten years ago to over 41 percent today.

To influence absorption policy, a grassroots organization needs to come forward. One possible approach the group might rally around would be to call for the creation of a special body to advise, direct, and monitor the absorption process. The late Hanan Aynor had this in mind when he called for a new high-level "Ethiopian Jews Authority" to draw the best minds in Israel and the Diaspora to redesign and supervise the complete absorption cycle.

A generation ago, a few concerned and committed Jews heard the words of Faitlovitch, Ben Asher, Bentwich, Bar Yuda, Tarta-kower, and Berger. The Beta Yisrael now live as free Jews in Israel primarily because grassroots American Jews catalyzed the governments of Israel and the United States into noble action. A new generation of activists is needed to respond to a new set of issues. Perhaps once again grassroots American Jews will take the counsel of scholar Rabbi Adin Steinsaltz of Israel that leadership to meet this challenge must come from outside of Israel.

My odyssey with the Ethiopian Jews began in the spring of 1974 when we first met Rahamim Elazar, a high school student who had left his family to live in Israel. It did not take long to recognize that his achievements in academics and the successful absorption of his veteran Beta Yisrael friends in Israel were impressive. They could be a model for later Beta Yisrael immigrants. The rescue of the Beta Yisrael community from Africa – if followed by their successful absorption in Israel – would be such a fitting story of what Israel, the tiny and only democracy in the Middle East, truly stands for.

APPENDIX A

Important Dates in Falasha History

Adapted from Hirt-Manheimer, Aron, *Keeping Posted* vol. 26, no 5, February 1981, with permission of Aron Hirt-Manheimer, Union of Reform Judaism.

NINTH CENTURY C.E. Earliest reference to Falashas appears in the diary of Eldad ha-Dani, a merchant and traveler claiming to have been a citizen of an autonomous Jewish state in eastern Africa, inhabited by the tribes of Dan, Naphtali, Gad, and Asher.

TENTH CENTURY C.E. The Beta Yisrael Queen Yehudit vanquishes the Christians, destroying churches and massacring the royal Abyssinian family. The Beta Yisrael have never been forgiven for her anti-Christian campaign. Among Christians, Yehudit is still regarded as a despised demon. She is called "Yehudit Bud'it," meaning *buda*, the evil eye, a curse that is used interchangeably with the word *falasha*, which means exile and stranger.

TWELFTH CENTURY C.E. The famous Spanish Jewish traveler Benjamin of Tudela describes fortresses of Jews in south Arabia and northeast Africa. He writes: "There are Jews who are not subject to the rule of others, and they have towns and fortresses on the tops of mountains."

SIXTEENTH CENTURY C.E. Rabbi David ibn Zimrah, known as Radbaz, issues a legal responsum in Cairo declaring that "those who came from the Land of Cush (Ethiopia) are without doubt of the tribe of Dan..." This is a landmark decision for the Beta Yisrael.

1541 Portuguese Jesuits begin missionary work among Falashas. They are the first Europeans to come into contact with Falashas. In the seventeenth century, they are expelled by local priests for political meddling.

1632 Christians conquer Falasha kingdom after a four-hundred-year period of warfare. The vanquished Falashas are sold as slaves, forced into baptism, and denied the right to own land, a status they hold until 1974 when Emperor Haile Selassie ("The Holy Trinity") is overthrown.

1804 Scottish explorer James Bruce awakens the western world to the existence of the Falashas, their customs, and beliefs in his *Travels to Discover the Source of the Nile* (1804). He estimates the Falasha population at 100,000.

1826 Swiss clergyman Samuel Gobat becomes the first Protestant to spread Christianity among the Falashas.

1830s Protestant missionaries from England, among them Jewish apostates, begin a determined effort to convert the remaining Beta Yisrael to Christianity.

1855 The first Falasha to travel abroad, Daniel ben Ananya, arrives in Jerusalem.

1862 Prompted by a false messiah, Falashas set out for Israel en masse. But the miracles of the Bible fail to deliver them to the Promised Land. They are, instead, humiliated and decimated by hunger and disease.

1864 Rabbi Azriel Hildesheimer of Germany, the founder of Agudat Israel, citing the Radbaz's decision, issues a call for action to counteract missionary activities aimed at converting the Jewish tribe of Ethiopia.

1867 Alarmed by reports of large-scale conversion among Falashas, noted Orientalist and Semitic scholar Joseph Halevy is sent on a fact-finding mission to Ethiopia by the French *Alliance Israélite Universelle*. He takes two Falasha boys to Palestine for instruction in Hebrew and modern Judaism.

1904 Jacques Faitlovitch, a Polish-born Orthodox Jew and student of Professor Halevy, makes his first trip to Ethiopia in search of the Beta Yisrael. After spending a year with the Falashas, he is convinced that they are Jews and spends the rest of his life – 51 years – winning worldwide Jewish support for the Falashas; providing them with material and medical relief; building Jewish schools in Ethiopia; arranging for the training abroad of future Falasha teachers and leaders; and bringing the Beta Yisrael closer to traditional Jewish practices, unfamiliar to them because of their long isolation. Jacques Faitlovitch saves the Falashas for Judaism.

1908 The chief rabbis of 44 countries proclaim the legitimacy of the Falashas as authentic Jews.

The *Alliance Israélite Universelle* sends Rabbi Haim Nahum to confirm findings of Faitlovitch. He reports that the Falashas are not of Jewish lineage and should not be taught modern Judaism.

1921 Abraham Isaac Kook, the first Ashkenazic chief rabbi of modern Eretz Yisrael, issues a public manifesto calling on world Jewry "to save our Falasha brethren from extinction and contamination…and rescue 50,000 holy souls of the House of Israel from oblivion."

1935–1941 Italian fascist army occupies Ethiopia and meets fierce resistance from Falasha fighters.

1948 Isaac Herzog, Israel's first Ashkenazic chief rabbi, expresses concern for the Jews of Ethiopia.

1955 Israel and Ethiopia establish diplomatic relations, and interest in Falasha *aliyah* is renewed.

Twenty-five Falasha students are sent to an American Mizrachi Women-sponsored school at Kfar Batya, Israel.

1968 The Jerusalem Rabbinical Council refuses to register for marriage an Israeli Falasha. The Israeli Supreme court upholds the council's decision, arguing that such matters are the domain of the rabbis.

Only ten Falashas live in Israel.

1973 Ovadia Yosef, Israel's Sephardic chief rabbi, declares Falashas as "Jews whom it is our duty to redeem from assimilation, to hasten their immigration to Israel, to educate them in the spirit of the holy Torah, and to make them partners in the building of our sacred land..." [About 170 Ethiopian Jews lived in Israel at this time. – HML]

Ethiopia breaks diplomatic relations with Israel during the Yom Kippur War, but informal contact continues.

1974 The American Association for Ethiopian Jews (AAEJ) is formed. It is a merger of the American Pro-Falasha Committee (established by Jacques Faitlovitch) and the Friends of the Beta-Israel (Falasha) Community in Ethiopia. Graenum Berger, its first president, more than anyone else, brings the plight of the Falashas to the attention of North America's Jews.

Haile Selassie, who ruled since 1916, is deposed in revolution. A nationalist-Marxist regime is set up with Mengistu Haile Mariam as its leader. In the aftermath of the revolution, an estimated 2,500 Falashas are reportedly killed in the crossfire of warring factions and an additional 7,000 are made homeless.

APPENDIX B

Ethiopian Jews Rescued by the AAEJ

1972	5	From Ethiopia to Israel by Meyer Levin
1974	2	From Ethiopia to Israel by Bernie Alpert
1975	1	From Ethiopia to Israel by Howard Lenhoff
1975	1	From Ethiopia to Israel by Henry Rosenberg
1979	32	From Sudan to Israel by AAEJ team of William Halpern and Baruch Tegegne with Israeli team led by Aklum Feredeh
1980	22	From Sudan by AAEJ team led by Baruch Tegegne
1981	20	AAEJ efforts from Sudan and Ethiopia (reported by Graenum Berger)
1982	18	From Sudan by Rosenberg team
1983	124	"
1984	52	From Ethiopia by routes designed and managed by LaDena Schnapper of AAEJ
1985	106	"
1986	182	"*
1987	95	"*
1988	165	"*
1989	373	"*
TOTAL	1,239	

*Some of these rescues were done with the cooperation of HIAS (Hebrew Immigrant Aid Association), NACOEJ (North American Conference on Ethiopian Jewry), and SAEJ (Save All Ethiopian Jews). All those rescued went to Israel except 3 who went to the U.S. and 30 who went to Canada. Many of those who went to North America came through programs in cooperation with HIAS.

INDEX

Numbers in italic indicate site on map
Note: Because the term Beta Yisrael (and its equivalents: Falashas; Ethiopian Jews) appears frequently, it is not included as a main entry in the index.

The American Association for Ethiopian Jews (AAEJ), Ethiopia, Sudan and Israel, each of which also appears frequently, are listed as main entries only for specific details.

Since the book is written in the first person, not all citations of Howard Lenhoff appear under a main entry.

More Gefen Books
on Ethiopian Jews

THE MOON IS BREAD, 1999
Naomi Samuel
Samuel tells the incredible story of her husband's exodus from
Ethiopia.
ISBN: 965-229-212-5

THE DREAM BEHIND BARS, 2001
Baruch Meiri & Rachamim Elazar
The Story of the Prisoners of Zion from Ethiopia
(English) ISBN: 965-229-221-4
(Hebrew) ISBN: 965-229-192-7

FROM FALASHA TO FREEDOM, 1996
Shmuel Yilma
An Ethiopian Jew's Journey to Jerusalem
ISBN: 965-229-169-2

TRANSFORMATIONS: FROM ETHIOPIA TO ISRAEL, 2006
Ricki Rosen (Photography)
ISBN: 965-229-377-6

MOSAD EXODUS, 2007
Gad Shimron
ISBN: 978-965-229-403-6

THE LIFE OF BARUCH, 2007
Baruch Tegegne as told to Phyllis Pinchuk
ISBN: 978-965-229-404-3

www.Israelbooks.com